CONTENTS

THE PROCESS
OF SCREENWRITING

CLIVE FRAYNE

This book is dedicated to every dyslexic writer who writes despite the struggle. The writer who has anxiety over every typo and weird use of grammar. Dyslexia has given you a unique take on language. No one will ever write the way you do.

This book is dedicated to every working-class writer who writes despite feeling like an imposter. You have experienced things that most writers will never understand. Your past is your strength.

This book is dedicated to every outsider. Your perspective on the world is uniquely yours.

CHAPTER I
7 Steps

This is a book about the process of planning and writing a film or TV script. You have an idea. You write your script. It's not perfect. So, you analyse the problems. Then you rewrite. For many screenwriters this is the process you go through to write a finished script. Some writers believe any script problem can be solved with enough rewrites. This may be true. But I hate rewriting. So, I figured out a way to get to a finished script with fewer rewrites. A way to write better first drafts. A process based on combining a writer's instincts with focused planning.

This book is based on my process. The process I use to write scripts. It's really flexible because it's not a set of rules or a formula. It's seven steps. Each step can be approached in ways which play to your individual strengths as a writer. It doesn't matter whether you write using your instincts or as a focused planner. It works for simple, structured genre films and experimental, multi-protagonist arthouse dramas.

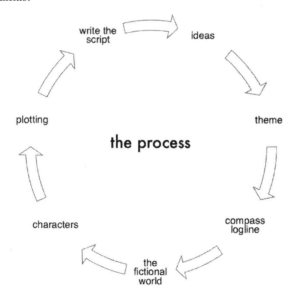

By the end of the book this diagram will make perfect sense. It will also help you develop better ideas, to write more dynamic drama and to craft great cinematic stories.

6

CHAPTER 2
The Process

This book teaches a method called process-driven screenwriting. The process is a series of planning steps a writer takes before writing their script. The process works for any kind of movie. It works for Hollywood Blockbusters or experimental art-house films. As long as our intention is to create drama, the process will help us write better scripts. It works because it addresses problems common to most screenplays. This book doesn't offer a formula or plot-template. Instead, it helps screenwriters find a writing technique that works for them. At the heart of this book is a simple idea.

Dogma is the enemy of creativity

A lot of the advice about how to write film scripts only tells us how to formulate plots. I've always been suspicious of any claim about simple formulas for movie scripts. Trust me, if there was a simple formula for successful movies the film industry would never make a bad film. If there was a simple formula to guarantee great scripts the industry would have replaced us with computers years ago. The industry continues to make dreadful films. We still haven't been replaced by computers. It's safe to assume there is more to writing a movie script than following a plot template.

Screenwriters don't need templates. We need to understand how drama is created and how stories are formed. This book contains a set of practical tools. Tools designed to help writers create drama and to craft great cinematic stories. This is also a book that explores the ideas behind drama, story and what it means to write cinema. Although the tools in this book are simple, the conversation about how we write screenplays isn't. I have not separated the conversation about writing from the discussion about the tools. That's because the two things are connected. We need tools like this because writing cinematic drama is complicated.

It's not possible to separate the process from the challenges of screenwriting. I have been teaching screenwriting for many years. I teach writing because teaching is how I learn. This book reflects my teaching style. In it, we will come back to the same ideas several times. Each time we will look at the idea in greater depth or from a different angle. I only teach tools and techniques I use myself. That is why, as we progress through the book, most of the examples used are original material. When I explain a technique, I demonstrate how I use it. Very few of the examples in this book were prepared ahead of time. When we look at techniques for generating ideas, the ideas in the book are ones I came up with as I was writing. When I present excerpts of scripts as examples of technique, they are all first drafts and presented as they were written. Each example was written at the point it appears in the book.

So, let's get started. Let's take our first look at the process. The process itself is very simple. Anyone can learn the basic steps in a short period of time. However, as with any tools, it takes time and practice to master their use. These tools can be used to create simple stories or to craft complex narratives. So, what are these tools? What are the steps?

Raw idea - our initial inspiration or idea

Theme - decide what facet of human experience we're exploring

Compass logline - decide who the film is about, when and where it is set

Chase our fascination to create the world of story - creating a fictional world

Character development - populate the world with characters

Create a plot - decide what happens and the order in which the audience finds things out

Write the script - write cinematic drama in a form that is acceptable to the production team

Every screenwriter has to deal with these issues, one way or another. This is because each of these steps is essential to creating drama and a cinematic narrative. In process-driven screenwriting we create the foundations of cinematic-drama by planning. We do a lot of the heavy lifting before we start writing the script. This isn't the only way to do it. The other way is to plan some elements and to sort out the rest on-the-page.

In reality, everyone is a process-driven screenwriter whether they know it or not. Every writer has a process, even if that process is to stare at a blank page until they have an idea. That seat-of-the-pants, all intuition and no planning way of writing, I call messy writing. I like messy writing. I also like planning. The process of writing drama is always somewhere on a scale that ranges from messy to focused. The concepts of messy and focused writing are important ideas, so let's take a moment to understand them.

—

messy and focused writing

The messy end of the spectrum is when we write with almost no preparation. This is the most instinctive, visceral form of writing. The great thing about messy writing is it forces writers to trust and nurture our instincts. What are our default characters? What kinds of stories do we choose to tell? How do we create drama on the page? When we don't have a plan, we are forced to make-it-up-as-we-go. The experience of pulling ideas out of thin air can be terrifying. We stare into the void and reach for whatever feels natural. Some writers find messy writing overpowering and it can cause writer's block. Other writers find something in the void they would never find by planning. Messy writing can lead to true inspiration and a connection to our deepest inner-writer. However, messy writing also tends to reveal how cliched and banal our first thoughts are.

Messy writing can be natural and experimental. On the other hand, messy writing can also be horribly predictable and cliched. At the other end of the spectrum is focused writing. Focused writing happens when we do so much preparation, we know what needs to be written before we start the script. We don't have to pull ideas out of the air as we write, we've got our ideas nailed down. The negative side of focused writing is it is a less instinctive way to write. With messy writing we are open to all the ideas available. With focused writing we concentrate on the creative decisions we have already made. It may appear that a messy approach is more creative than focused writing but that's not the case. With messy writing the creative choices happen on the page. With focused writing we make creative choices during the preparation.

Raw idea - our initial inspiration or idea

Theme - decide what facet of human experience we're exploring

Compass logline - decide who the film is about, when and where it is set

Chase our fascination to create the world of story - creating a fictional world

Character development - populate the world with characters

Create a plot - decide what happens and the order in which the audience finds things out

Write the script - write cinematic drama in a form that is acceptable to the production team

These steps take us from messy writing to focused. They're not rules. It's a process. We are always free to choose when to skip forward to step seven (write the script).

Let's have a look at the way different writers use process. We'll start with an instinctive, messy approach.

instinctive writers

Helen is a deeply instinctive screenwriter. She has a raw idea for a script which she really wants to write. Because she is naturally drawn to create-on-the-page, she goes straight from step one (raw idea), to writing her script. After six weeks she has gutted out a first draft. However, because she discovers her characters as she writes, they are one-dimensional for the first half of the script. Her plot is a bit weak in places. But, despite this, she manages to find a few interesting ideas to develop. People who read her first draft aren't completely sure what her film is about. It's got nice moments, but no real focus. So, Helen goes back to the process and decides on a theme. But again, because she is an instinctive writer, she wants to get back to creating on-the-page as soon as possible. Helen then goes through several drafts. Each draft brings her story slowly into focus. Between each draft she takes one or two steps from the process to help her concentrate on that aspect of the script. The instinctive, multi-draft, approach is the method most used by early-career screenwriters. A lot of writers feel obliged to work solely from their instincts. This is an approach that really works for some people. However, it's not the only way to do this. Let's look at a typical structural approach.

structural writers

Peter is a dogmatic, structural screenwriter. He has a raw idea and immediately crafts it into a high-concept logline. As a structural writer, Peter goes straight to step six (write a plot). He crafts his plot to the structural theory he believes in. So far, his approach is very focused. However, he then goes to step seven (write the script.) He approaches theme, character development and creation of the world of story as things to be achieved via messy writing. Peter likes to create characters on-the-page and also trusts his theme will emerge as he writes. At the end of draft one, Peter sends his script out to a script editor. The script editor tells him the characters and theme aren't as focused as they could be. Peter may go back to some of the steps in the process, or he may write new drafts until the script comes together. Structural writers, like Peter, tend to see plot and concept as the foundation for their story. However, despite their focus when it comes to the plot, structural writers still prefer messy approaches to create drama.

process-driven writers

I am a process-driven screenwriter. I start from a raw idea and use all of the planning steps before writing my script. However, I don't always use them in the same order. I often build messy writing into my process. I write some experimental scenes as part of the character development stage. The decision about whether or how to do step six (create a plot) varies from project to project. Some stories are structured in a traditional manner. Some plots I create on the page. However, it's unlikely that I'll write a first full draft before I have looked at each step in the process. As a result, my first drafts tend to be more focused than you'd expect. I rarely do more than two drafts on a speculative project. When I take gun-for-hire projects, (scripts where a producer pays me to write or rewrite their concept), my process makes writing fast and efficient.

I started as an instinctive writer. In my early-career I became a structural writer. Then I developed the process-driven approach. These days I always use the process. However, as a result of writing this book, I want to explore more experimental screenwriting. The techniques used to write mainstream projects can also be used to explore what is possible in cinematic storytelling.

What I am offering in this book are a set of tools designed to help writers to improve their writing process. This book also teaches what it means to produce drama, create a story and write a movie script.

Our need to master different writing skills is what makes screenwriting challenging. A novelist only needs to write a story. A playwright only needs to create drama. Screenwriting requires the writer to create drama, a story and cinema. In fact, it's more complicated than that. Drama, story and cinema are just the core requirements of screenwriting. There is always something new to learn about cinema, writing and the industry. Whether you are an instinctive, messy, on-the-page writer, a dogmatic structuralist, or someone who needs to plan everything before you write, this book will help.

Chapter 3
How I Plan

This is an example of the spreadsheet method.

idea		
theme		
compass logline		
name		
who are they?		
skills		
flaws		
insecurities		
strengths		
motivation		
needs and desires		
odd behaviour		
appearance		
dilemmas		
secrets		
theme		
sub-theme		
backstory		
seed scenes		
Act One		
Act Two		
Mid-Point		
Act Three		

This is a technique that puts all the planning for a movie script into one spreadsheet. The spreadsheet method is one way of using the process. This isn't the only way. This is just the way I do it. By the end of the book this will make sense. I'm sharing it now, so we get a sense of the road ahead. Although this may look like a worksheet, it isn't. It's a way for writers to play with ideas, characters and plots. It's a way to understand and analyse our story before it's written.

CHAPTER 4
From Idea to Script

Writing a screenplay is a monumentally difficult thing to do. The chances of writing a good film script are slim, even if we have years of experience. It is almost impossible to write a great script by sitting in front of a blank page. Especially if we have nothing more than a vague idea to guide us. Yet, despite this, the vast majority of early-years screenwriters try to do just that. There has to be a better way for us to get from our raw idea to a script. There is. We can develop our ideas before we write. And by develop, I mean play. The process is about playing with ideas.

In this chapter, I want to introduce some of the ideas in the process. These are ideas we'll come back to several times in the book. Each time, we'll dig a little deeper into the ideas and the techniques. The process has seven steps and later in the book we'll get into them in detail. But we can also think about it as four phases. The ideas phase, where we play with ideas. The research phase, where we gather useful information. The planning phase, when we create characters and a plot. And, finally, the writing phase, when we write the script.

the journey from idea to concept

Everyone has an idea for a film. That's not surprising. As a culture, we consume stories avidly. Watching films and TV drama is one of the most popular forms of recreation and entertainment. So, it's hardly surprising that almost everyone has at least one idea for a movie. They may not always be good ideas, but everyone has one. Let's imagine we have an idea. Let's be generous, we'll assume it's a good one. Our first problem is this, an idea for a movie is not the same as having a movie concept. People struggle with this because, after all, the word idea and the word concept are synonyms. Unfortunately, it's not that simple. The easiest way to explain it is with an example. Let's start with this idea.

What would happen if a massive, killer shark attacks people?

This is definitely a starting point. It's an idea. However, it's not a film concept, yet. To turn this idea into a concept we need to do more work. When a killer shark attacks people at a beach resort the newly appointed sheriff discovers he has to battle more than just the shark, to protect his community. This second description is a film concept. The difference between these two statements is the key to developing a screenplay. We could write a script using just the raw idea, what if a killer shark attacked people. We could open a new

---

document, stare at the blank page and write a script. We could write a list of dramatic ways people could be attacked by a shark. Each of these ideas might create an interesting cinematic sequence. However, if we write a script without developing the idea further, we are going to run into problems. When someone pitches me an idea for a film, I have a few questions for them:

Who is this film about?
Where does it take place?
When does it take place?
What is the story really about?

It is the answers to these questions which really start to tell us what kind of script we're going to write. The killer shark idea comes from the film Jaws. So, let's answer the questions that will transform it from being a raw idea into that concept.

Who is the film about? - It's about a newly appointed Sheriff. He sees policing a family beach resort as retirement from the dangers of big-city law enforcement

Where does it take place? - Amity Island, a fictional, American, family beach resort

When does it take place? - The present

What is the story really about? - It's an exploration of the cost of doing the right thing. It's also about the pressures of society to deny inconvenient truths.

When we answer those four questions, the idea

What if a killer shark attacks people?

is transformed into the concept,

When a killer shark repeatedly attacks people at a beach resort the newly appointed sheriff discovers he has to battle more than just the shark in order to protect the people in his community.

Let's give different answers, but we'll use the same idea. Different answers will alter the concept and the film created.

raw idea = what if a killer shark attacks people?

Who is this film about? - Charles Darwin, the naturalist and evolutionary theorist.

Where does this film take place? - The Galapagos Islands

When does it take place? - 1831, during Darwin's voyage on the Beagle.

What is the story really about? - It is the story of Darwin surviving a prolonged shark attack whilst he was part of the crew of the Beagle. He wants to understand why he survived and others didn't. So, he creates the concept of "survival of the fittest."

The same root idea can create the concept for a very different movie. Far too many screenwriters commit to the first concept that occurs to them. They miss the opportunity to develop other, potentially more interesting ideas. It took me less than a minute to take the core idea for Jaws and rework it into a historical drama about survivor's guilt. I'm not saying it's an idea worth writing. I'm just saying we don't understand an ideas potential until we play with it. The process of turning an idea into a concept is a creative process. As writers, we need to play with ideas. We can make huge, radical changes to projects in a very low impact way.

A concept is more than an idea, it's an idea that has a sense of who and what the story is about; and, when and where the story is set.

from concept to fictional world.

The fictional world is an important idea in screenwriting. It's a simple concept. Every story, every film takes place at a specific time and in a specific place. Deciding when and where the story takes places is a huge part of the creative process. The next step is to understand the world we are writing about. Once we know when and where our story is set, we need to research that world. There's a cliché in writing that goes, write what you know. It's sounds like sensible advice. The more we know about a particular world, or way of life, the easier it will be for us to create it on the page. If we have spent our entire life in the world of motor racing, we will understand how people behave in that world. We'll know how they speak and what kinds of tensions arise. Someone from outside that world, would have to do more research to take on the same project. I've never been a fan of the write what you know approach. I much prefer the axiom, write what you care about. In my experience, when we care about something, we make the effort to understand it. More importantly, we'll have something worthwhile to say about it.

There are some things a writer needs to know before we start writing. We need to visualise the world we're creating. It's easier to visualise a scene if we've been exposed to a lot of source material. I tend to use a combination of photographs and video for places I've never been to. When I can, I prefer to write about places I've visited.

Let's set a story in a city which once thrived due to heavy industry, but which is now an industrial wasteland. Streets once full of affluent, working families have become ghost towns. It is a city surrounded by rotting factories and abandoned, rusty machines. I grew up in this kind of city. So, I'm naturally drawn to tell stories in this kind of world. My intention when imagining a fictional world is to create a world unique to this story. I will need to do research to understand and visualise it. I collect YouTube clips and watch documentaries. I hoard hundreds of photographs, read books and magazine articles. The visualisation is more than just a physical landscape. It is about the relationship between the landscape and the people who live there.

Stories can't exist in a world of generalities. A story is always about specific people, in a specific place, at a specific time. If we transpose a story into new places and times it alters the story. A perfect example of this is the adaptation of *Kurosawa's Seven Samurai* into the *The Magnificent Seven*. Kurosawa's original story is about the end of the age of honour in feudal Japan. The most significant moment in the film is the death of Kyuzo. A man who has devoted his life to the art of the sword. He is shot. Killed by an untrained man with a gun. This moment encapsulates a key moment in Japanese history. It is the moment a life-times dedication to a martial art is made irrelevant by superior technology. It isn't just the end of a man's life. It symbolises the end of an era. When the movie is transposed into the American West no such cultural tension exists. The Magnificent Seven is a great film. One of the best westerns ever made. The events in the film are very close to the original movie. But, the shift in time and location completely alters what the story is about. A story that was about the end of the Samurai becomes a story about American heroism in the face of overwhelming odds.

The landscape is more than a pretty place to add cinematic value to the film. The landscape, the period and the culture determine the kinds of stories we can tell. This means our research needs to tell us everything we need to know about that world. What does it look like? What kinds of people live there? What are their lives like? What do they care about? What are the challenges they face? How are they different from the way we live?

———

characters, from cliché to fascinating

Even though I put these steps in a logical order, the creative process isn't linear. The thing that inspires us may be an idea for a plot. I know writers whose initial idea is a scene they can see so clearly in their heads, it haunts them. If that's the case, we should make notes on everything that occurs to us, as it occurs to us. Once that's done, we can forget about it and go back to the process. Notebooks are a screenwriter's best friend. I carry one with me everywhere I go.

Once we start using the process, we may notice the steps start to bleed into each other. Once I start researching the world of my story, characters start to offer themselves up. Take, for instance, the example we looked at in step two. We imagined an industrial city transformed into a wasteland by de-industrialisation and poverty. I can already imagine the kinds of characters I would put into that world.

Creating great characters is the best way to create great stories. Not everyone agrees with this. I've had to listen to a lot of writers make a case for plot-driven movies over the years. However, the whole plot-driven vs character-driven story argument is based on flawed thinking. Let's create a definition of what a story is:

> *A story is what happens when a specific group of characters are forced to overcome a series of challenging circumstances.*

When we talk about plot, what we mean is a challenging set of circumstances. A plot is more than just a list of things that happen. It is really a list of problems for the character to solve. This is important. Plot and character are linked, profoundly. It is impossible to separate them without altering the story. Let me prove this to you. Imagine we create a plot where our primary character is asked to deliver a suitcase. It contains something which is vitally important to both them and the world. Now we're going to try an experiment. We're going to put three different characters into that plot point:

> Tony Stark (Iron Man) is asked by his nephew to deliver a suitcase containing his father's super-soldier research to a mysterious stranger. However, during the flight, an unknown attacker steals the suitcase.

> Miss Marple, amateur detective, is asked by her nephew, to deliver a suitcase to a mysterious stranger. This stranger has just moved into a remote farmhouse outside the village. However, before she can do that her nephew is murdered.

Dr Who, a time traveller, is asked by River Song to deliver a suitcase she has hidden in the Tardis. She sends him to meet a mysterious stranger. However, when they arrive the suitcase is stolen by an unknown alien.

Each of these stories will be different. This happens even though the plot device is the same for each one. The story changes because the character's react in unique ways. Or, in other words, all stories are character driven. I want to give you my definition of story again. Perhaps it will be clearer now.

A story is what happens when a specific group of characters (character) are forced to overcome a series of challenging circumstances (plot)

Even the best plot cannot make a great story if it is populated by cliched characters. My thinking about character development comes from my experience of working with actors. The success or failure of your film may well depend on the quality of the acting talent you attach to the movie. One way to get great actors is to have a huge budget to spend. That route isn't open to everyone. However, the other way to attach the actors you want is to write roles they really want to play. Most actors want to play characters who embody interesting things about being human. An actor will approach a new script with a lot of questions about the character you are asking them to play. The answers you give to those questions have to be part and parcel of the story. Or, in other words, a story is an exploration of an aspect or multiple aspects of what it means to be a human being.

characters to plot

We have reached the sixth step in the process. Despite this, we are still not ready to write the script. At this stage, we know our film's concept, what kind of world it takes place in and the people who populate it. Let's go back to the definition of story to understand the next step.

A story is what happens when a specific group of characters are forced to overcome a series of challenging circumstances (plot).

In the last section, we discovered why you can't create a plot before understanding who your characters are. A character's unique reaction to a plot point drives the story. What they do determines what happens next.

Now we've created our characters, we can start work on the plot. In its most basic form, a plot is just a series of challenging events. Some people have an instinctive sense of story, they know the order in which things need to happen. One way we could figure out the story would be to write it as prose. Let me give you an example of how this might work.

> *Sherlock Holmes and Dr John Watson go to America to promote a collection of John Watson's stories. Dr Watson notices that his friend is ill at ease and distracted. This changes when they are asked to investigate the mysterious death of author Edgar Allan Poe. For the first time in years, Holmes seems to resemble his old self. This all changes when Dr Watson spots errors and anomalies in Sherlock's investigation. It is almost as if he is deliberately leading the police away from the truth rather than towards it. When Watson confronts Holmes, Sherlock reacts violently, destroying their friendship in the process. Hurt and confused, Watson digs deeper. He needs to discover why his friend is behaving so strangely. His investigation uncovers a shocking amount of drug addiction and debauchery. None of this prepares him for the most shocking discovery of all. He uncovers evidence that Sherlock is Poe's real killer... etc. etc.*

This feels like a fairly natural and intuitive way to write a story. It is the way we would describe the plot of a movie to a friend. There's a term in screenwriting for this way of describing the story of a movie. If it's about a page long, we call it a synopsis. If it's longer, say five to twenty-five pages, we call it a treatment. For someone new to screenwriting, a story synopsis might be the best way to approach plotting. It has lots of advantages. It is both intuitive and natural and it doesn't require specialist knowledge to do it well.

Although writing a synopsis is a good starting place. It doesn't provide enough detail to solve most of the issues. It's just too big a jump to go from one page of planning to one-hundred pages of script. So, what else can we do?

This is where understanding story structure can be useful. Not as a way of applying a formula, but as a way of breaking the story down into key moments. To make sense of this, I need to introduce the idea of a story being broken down into smaller pieces called Acts. A story has a beginning, a middle and an end. Therefore, we can break stories into units that conform to that understanding. This is what most screenwriters do. The beginning of the film we call Act One, the middle part of the story we call Act Two, the ending we call Act Three. I don't think there is anything too contentious about that as an idea. People who believe passionately in structure go further than these basic ideas. They believe stories always conform to the same shape. Some structural ideas are the natural outcome of a story having a beginning, middle, and an end. If a story has a beginning, we need to introduce our audience to that world. Every movie is a strange and foreign land. Our job is to introduce the audience to the culture and the interesting people who inhabit it. This is why screenwriters talk about introducing the ordinary world. The ordinary world is our fictional world. A world with its own rules and geography.

If a story is a series of challenging circumstances. Early in our story, our primary character needs to be provoked and challenged. Screenwriters refer to this moment, as the inciting incident. It's just a way of saying the hero of the story needs to face a challenging situation to get the story started.

Most three-act movie structure needs more than one challenge for the protagonist. Those big challenges and reversals of fortune between winning and losing are predictable. We can predict when they will happen in the script. We will look at structure later in the book. For the moment, we just need to understand one thing. Structure is a way of breaking the story into predictable lumps.

Beginning = Act 1, Middle = Act 2, End = Act 3.

As a writer we can use act structure to change our synopsis writing. We change it to reflect our new understanding. So, we write the heading Act One and then write down what happens in that part of the story. Then we write Act Two and do the same. This is how we start to understand how a plot if formed.

The second piece of terminology I want to introduce is the idea of a sequence. A sequence is a distinct lump of story. Let me give you an example:

Dr Watson follows Sherlock to a series of opium dens and brothels. There he witnesses his friend engage in one self-destructive depravity after another. This forces him to re-evaluate past events. Events that seemed innocuous at the time, but which have huge significance now.

This is a series of events which challenge Dr Watson and transform his life. His lifelong understanding of his friend is shattered. A new truth is revealed. This lump of the story would need to be told through a series of scenes. We might use flashbacks to explore the past. We witness Sherlock Holmes's fall from the pedestal on which Watson has placed him. And, this transformation, of Watson from true believer to sceptic, is a key part of what happens next in the story. As such, we can think of this lump of story as a distinct sequence which also has a beginning, middle and end.

One way to look at a plot, would be to break our prose description down into about twenty-five sequences. Given we have already broken the story down into acts, we could assign so many sequences per act.

The practice of breaking a story down into acts and sequences, is a method I call sequential plotting. Some writers put sequence descriptions onto file cards and pin them on corkboards. Some writers just create a list and call them beat sheets. There are lots of ways to use these plotting methods. The first step is to grasp the basic idea of breaking the story down into manageable lumps.

write the script (at last!)

This is the moment most writers can't wait to get to, writing the script. If we have used our step-by-step process, we will be well prepared to write. We have honed our idea. Our research of the fictional world gives us a powerful visualisation of that world. Our characters will be fascinating. And, our plot will be planned into acts and sequences. The writing of our script can now focus on writing the best possible, cinematic version of each scene. This isn't saying we won't alter and explore the story as we write, we will. The process allows us to do the story justice. Good preparation turns into good writing.

A lot of writers try to avoid development work because what they want to do is the actual writing. They want to get the scenes in their heads on the page. This is a mistake and a misunderstanding of what writing is. It's a mistake because it makes the writing harder and poorer. The creative, fun part of screenwriting takes place in the pre-writing process. Writers who don't do development work before writing, inevitably have to do it for their rewrites.

In the most basic terms, writing a script is writing scenes. A scene takes place in a specific place and time. Once we know where and when, we decide what happens? Which characters are there and what do they do? What does your main character experience? What challenges do they have to overcome and how do they achieve it? Who do they encounter? What do they say? What do they witness? What do they discover?

Let's imagine our hero is chasing a terrorist through a train station. The audience may already know why she's doing this. They may understand the consequences of our hero not catching the terrorist. Imagine this sequence is described this way. Our hero chases a terrorist through the train station. She wants to prevent them from giving the suitcase to the bomb-maker. She manages to get them only to discover the suitcase is empty.

If our hero captures the terrorist without any effort, it's not very satisfying. This is true even if it matches our plot. A more filmic solution would be a chase. Some kind of cat-and-mouse game where the terrorist uses their wiles and the terrain to lose the hero. The audience experiences the struggle. We are writing for the audience. We control their experience of the fictional world.

At the same time that we're writing for the audience, we're also writing for the actors. We need to give them actions to perform and lines to say that do more than move the story forwards. In a very real sense, each story is an exploration of our character's experience of being human. This struggle is not a generic struggle. It's not an average person chasing another average person. It is about the specifics of our hero's strengths and weaknesses. Strengths they match against the strengths and weaknesses of their opponent.

So, what is a screenplay?

It is a series of scenes which provide a specific time and place in which the story unfolds. It is a visualisation of the events which unfold in each place. Where are we? What happens? Why does this matter to the audience? A lot of writers talk about the hero's journey as if this is all that is going on in our story, but it isn't. An equally important journey is the audience's journey. A film reveals its story through action. These actions take place in a series of distinct places and times. We call those units of place/time scenes. Screenwriting is turning a story into a series of scenes. The goal of a screenwriter is to do the following:

Create an overall concept that can be summed up in a couple of lines

Create a believable and interesting world for the story to take place in

Inhabit that world with compelling and engaging characters

Create a plot which explores the complexities and struggles of what it means to be human.

Tell our story cinematically

Inspire the entire production team to do great work

To achieve these goals, it makes sense to allocate time and effort to each challenge. That is why I use process-driven development techniques to write scripts. We can't inspire the production team if we don't write cinematically. We can't write cinematically if we don't know what the plot is. We can't write a plot if we don't know who the characters are. Plots are driven by character. We can't create characters if we don't understand the world they inhabit. And, we can't understand the world of our story if we don't have a clear film concept.

—

24

CHAPTER 5
The Script

If you want to write a script, it's really important to understand what a film script is.

In this chapter I want to cover a couple of things:

What does a film script look like?

What does it mean to write a script for the production team?

What does it mean to write a script for the actors?

What does it mean to write a script for readers?

Early-career screenwriters often don't understand what a film script is or how it is used. Far too many people guess what a film script is and then write what they imagine. This is fine if the plan is to make the film yourself. You can write any way you like providing you never have to show it to anyone in the industry.

A film script is a very specific kind of document. A document that has to do a lot of things. Our script must be formatted and presented to industry standards. There are strict rules about what information must go into a script and how it is presented. In the industry, we call that formatting. Our script needs to provide information and inspiration to everyone on the production team. Everyone from the video editor to the wardrobe team uses the script as a source of information. Information presented in a way that's easy for them to find.

Scripts are formatted to make life bearable for the production team. Our script also gives the actors the information they need to do their job. This means screenwriting is writing drama. And, despite being a very technical document, the script also has to be readable. There are at least a thousand scripts rejected for every script accepted. Writing a script which compels the reader to turn the next page is an essential part of the writing process.

Writing a script to meet the technical needs of a production team is difficult. To make it genuinely dramatic, and a compelling read, is daunting. These are tasks many writers fail to achieve. If we don't understand what a script really is and what it is for, we'll never write a good one.

what does a film script look like?

Anyone wanting to write a novel knows what a novel looks like. The kind of people who write novels also tend to read novels. Anyone educated in the English-speaking world has read novels and plays at school. The way we learn how to read and write gives us all experience of what prose looks like. Film scripts aren't prose. Writers setting out to write their first film script may have never seen or read a film script. This puts them at a serious disadvantage. One of the first scripts I ever read was Bruce Robinson's *Withnail and I*. It was, and still is, available as a book. It's one of the most enjoyable books I've ever read. It's also one of the worst templates for what a film script is supposed to look like. This isn't because Bruce Robinson is a bad screenwriter. He's not. He's one of the all-time greats. However, his approach to screenwriting is idiosyncratic. There are a lot of jokes in the script that can't possibly make it into the film. Jokes made exclusively for the reader. When I was an early-career screenwriter, I adored both the film and the book. My early scripts emulated Bruce Robinson's semi-novelistic style of screenwriting. A habit I didn't break until I was told off by a B.B.C. producer. She did me a favour. Her rebuke forced me to go out and learn how to format scripts.

Learning script formatting isn't as easy as you'd imagine. Screenwriters are encouraged to read a lot of film scripts by script-mentors. On one level, it's good advice. We have to learn what a script is by reading existing scripts. One of the ways people get access to scripts is via the Internet. There are a few "free script" sites out there:

> Drew's Script-O-Rama
> Simply Scripts
> Screenplays for You
> The Daily Script
> The Screenplay Database
> BBC Writer's Room

Although these sites are a valuable source of screenplays, they aren't all as useful as you might imagine. The scripts you get access to are unlikely to be copies of the original script. In a lot of cases, you are reading a transcript created by someone who watched the film. When you do get access to an actual script, it is likely to be a production script. Production scripts and the script a writer creates are profoundly different. If the online script you read has numbers for each scene, chances are that this came from a production script. Scenes in film scripts are never numbered until the script goes into production! Online scripts are useful, but they can't be used as templates for formatting or writing scripts.

Let's look at small section of script. This, essentially, is what a script is supposed to look like.

```
EXT. GALLOWS, NEWGATE PRISON: DAY

ELIJAH THORN (44), London's dandy hangman, muscular, but well
dressed, quickly and efficiently tightens the leather straps
binding the arms and feet of CONDEMNED GIRL (18).

Condemned Girl shakes with fear, her face blank with shock.

Elijah Thorn gently guides her over the trap.

                    ELIJAH THORN
                 (whispers to con)
          Hush now, my sweet.

Elijah Thorn throws the hood and noose over her head.

                    ELIJAH THORN (CONT'D)
          The mercy of the Lord awaits you.

Elijah Thorn pulls the release lever - the trap springs open -
Condemned Girl plummets to her death, as the rope snaps
tight.

                              CRASH TO BLACK:

                              FADE IN:

INT. 1889: PASSAGE BETWEEN THE OLD BAILEY AND NEWGATE PRISON:
DAY

Young Prisoner shuffles through the shadow of the hanged
girl.
```

I can guarantee there are people reading this who don't like the formatting of the above script. Disagreements about script formatting exist because the film industry isn't a single, unified entity. The film industry is made up of tens of thousands of production companies. These companies work in hundreds of different countries. Different production companies and producers have different ideas about industry standards. I once worked with a producer who didn't want any physical descriptions of characters. He didn't like being told how to cast the movie. Another producer liked props (items that are part of the story like a SUITCASE or MACHINE GUN) to be in CAPS. I thought it made the scripts difficult to read. But it was his rodeo, so he got his scripts the way he wanted. It isn't possible to plan for every single producer's idiosyncratic needs. The best any writer can do is to understand the basic rules of script formatting. We should know how the script will be used by the production team. Our aim is to produce a script that is acceptable to anyone working in the industry.

what does it mean to write a script for the production team?

Film production happens in four distinct phases. They are Development, Pre-Production, Production, and Post-Production. The script is used differently in each phase. This has an impact on how the script is written.

development

There are very few people involved in the development phase. Yet, this is the most important phase for the writer. The development phase is all about getting the script right and attracting investment. This process starts with a script. This script is often a "spec" or speculative script. A speculative script is one where the writer comes up with the idea. They then write the script on their own time. The writing is self-financed. Basically, the first investor in any movie is the writer. They can invest months of their life getting a script to the point it is ready to show.

To progress, the script needs a producer. The producer is the person who makes the business plan for the film (the script). They steer it through the process of becoming a product and taking it to market. The development stage of a movie takes a speculative script and turns it into a viable product. The producer's job is to attract the right kind of director, cast and financial investment. They do this by asking for rewrites and changes. At the end of the development process the script is locked. In many cases, this is when the writer's involvement with the movie ends. This doesn't mean there won't be alterations and re-writes. It's just that the original writer may or may not be part of the creative process.

pre-production

The producer now has a script they want to turn into a movie. They start pulling together the creative team they want. They attach a director and a cast. They hire a line producer (who creates a budget) and heads of various departments. These are the people who will use the script. The script acts as a springboard for a collaborative creative process. A process that happens under the direction of the director and the producer. When we talk about writing for the production team, this is what we mean. Each of the heads of department has to be able to make sense of the tasks they have been given. The Line Producer needs to know exactly how many actors are needed. She'll also want to know how many days they are required. For this reason, there are very specific rules about how we refer to characters in scripts.

A script guides the pre-production team in their creative decisions. A screenwriter's job is to give the right information, whilst not dictating how they do their jobs. We might indicate how a character is dressed. We want to give the reader clues about their social status and culture. However, we don't go into specific descriptions of clothing. The role of the writer is to inspire the creatives in the pre-production team. It's not our job to impose our vision on them.

production

The production phase starts when people turn up to the first location and start filming. The start of that process is called "The first day of principle photography." This is worth knowing, because that is normally the day the writer gets paid.

During production, the script is the plan everyone works to. Production is also the moment the script takes on its most important roles. The script is the template for the actor's performances. During the pre-production phase, the script is merely a technical, planning document. Now it also has to inspire the actors to give meaningful dramatic performances. This is also the phase we discover whether the script really works or not.

post-production

The film is now shot. It exists as thousands of tiny pieces of video or film. The post-production team now have to assemble the bits into the final product. The editor cuts the movie. Sound is mixed and sound-effects added. Music is composed. Special effects, colour alterations and titles added. The people involved in those creative processes use the script to achieve this. At this stage, the script is like the picture on the lid of a jigsaw. It tells the post-production team roughly what the movie should be like. They then take the pieces and assemble them into the best film they can, which may or may not be the same as the script.

In pre-production, the script is used to create budgets and creative decisions. During the production as the plan for the filming of the drama. Our script tells the post-production team how to assemble a movie from the little pieces of film shot.

what does it mean to write the script for actors?

Early-career screenwriters tend to have one of two different ideas about what a script is. The first is, they imagine it's a list of shots that make up the final film. It absolutely isn't that. Screenwriters don't include shots in their scripts. The other idea early-career screenwriters have about scripts is that it's like a play. It tells the actors what to say. This is a better starting point. It is true. Part of the job of a script is to tell the actors what they do in a scene and what they say. There is a problem with this view of screenwriting. It can lead to scripts that are page after page of dialogue. Whilst it's true that stage plays tend to consist of pages of dialogue, that's not true of screenplays. Although a film tends to centre around what the characters do and say, that's not what a film is. A film is a combination of locations, costumes, sounds and music. All of these aspects influence how the audience experience what the actors do and say. Yes, a film script does tell the characters what to do (action) and say (dialogue). However, writing drama is more complicated than this. To write for actors we need to understand how actors work and what they need from the text. Screenwriters also need to understand what drama is. We must master the art of storytelling and the language of cinema.

what does it mean to write for readers?

Let's assume that we understand our responsibilities to the production team. We can write a technically competent script. Let's further assume that we understand drama and the world of acting. We can write for actors. We might assume that those two skillsets alone would be enough. But, if we can't also write something that is compelling to read none of our skills will matter. The first, and most important, job a screenwriter has to do is to write a readable script. We want the reader to read our script. And, when I say read it, I mean read it from page one to the end. A screenwriter needs to hook their reader into the movie from the very first page. We then need to hold their attention for every single page after that.

Movie scripts have to be significantly more compelling than a novel. There are a couple of reasons for this. The first is simple. A script has a lot of technical restrictions on presentation and writing style. Scripts, as literature, are less readable than prose. The very things that make them work as scripts make them difficult to read. Bruce Robinson's script for *Withnail and I*, is very readable. The very things that make it easy to read are also the ways it fails to be an industry standard script. We can't make the text easier to read by adding in jokes that are for the reader, rather than for the production.

Producers are the people who read scripts. This is the second reason they need to be compelling to read. Not all producers are natural readers. The film industry is very different from the publishing industry. People who publish books tend to like books and see reading as a good thing. This is not universally true of film producers.

The task of writing a great script is a genuine challenge. It has to conform to technical requirements that make it hard to read. Despite this it has to be compelling to an audience who may not actually like reading. This why screenwriters often decide to take a break from the industry to write a novel. The novelty of writing for people who like to read is appealing. I completely understand why screenwriters sometimes long for the freedoms of writing prose. Serving the technical needs of the production team can be tedious. Writing coherent drama is challenging. Writing compelling cinema for producers is the hardest challenge of all.

The biggest problem for early-career writers is that they don't really understand what a film script is. Now we know. A film script is a technically demanding document designed to act as a plan to create drama. A technical document that also has to be easy and compelling to read. So, if a script is a template for film drama, what is drama? That, as it happens, is a really interesting question.

CHAPTER 6
Drama

In the last chapter, we discovered one of the main purposes of writing a film script is to create drama. We write scripts to be performed rather than read as literature. This means, one of a film script's jobs is to tell the actors what they need to do and what they need to say. In this chapter, I want to look at what this really means to anyone writing a script. It's more complicated than we might imagine.

Let's start with a list. These are the questions a screenwriter needs to be aware of and able to answer about their own work.

What is the role of conflict in the creation of drama?

What is the role of the exploration of human nature in drama?

What is the role of morality in the creation of drama?

What role does forcing characters to overcome problems play in creating drama?

How important is it for a writer to force characters to face their vulnerabilities?

What role does the idea of a dramatic theme play in creating drama?

To write drama a screenwriter needs a working knowledge of all of these questions. And, a film script is always drama.

what is the role of conflict in the creation of drama?

The first thing most writers learn about writing drama is that all drama is conflict. For anyone involved in theatre or acting this is basic knowledge. It's a core part of how actors approach the craft of acting. This means, anyone writing for actors has to understand conflict. It's a vital part of any screenwriter's education to know how conflict is drama and drama is conflict.

This may be a new idea to anyone coming to screenwriting from a non-arts background. A lot of screenwriters struggle with this concept. When we consume drama, we don't think about dramatic conflict. We are too busy submerging ourselves into the action and the characters. It's also pretty difficult to define what dramatic conflict means. Conflict is a word we all understand; it means an argument or a fight. Many screenwriters take this literally. They write a lot of arguments and fights into their scripts. Although a physical fight or an argument can be an expression of dramatic conflict, that isn't what it is. Conflict in drama rarely mean a fight or an argument.

In an earlier chapter, I gave us a definition of what a story is.

> *A story is what happens when a specific group of characters are forced to overcome a series of challenging circumstances.*

This definition of story is entirely based on the idea that drama comes from conflict. I can make this clearer by rewriting the definition.

> *A story is what happens when a specific group of characters come into conflict with a series of challenging circumstances.*

So, what do we mean by a set of challenging circumstances? Dramatic conflict is any opposing force that creates a challenge for our characters. This can be anything a human being can experience as challenging.

Let's imagine we want to write a film about climbing a mountain. This presents a lot of high-stakes challenge. We can increase the stakes and the challenge by setting our story in a remote part of the world. Somewhere where there isn't any mountain rescue. This idea gives us what we need to write drama. We could easily write a script where two men struggle against the elements. In this case, the dramatic conflict comes from the environment.

Now, let's imagine something goes wrong. One of the climbers falls. He is dangling over a cliff and too injured to climb back up the rope. Not only that, his weight starts to pull his climbing partner towards the cliff edge. Let's think about the huge list of challenging circumstances in this one moment.

Our climber is hanging from a rope over a huge drop, that's pretty challenging and dramatic

He's also too injured to save himself, that's also challenging and dramatic

His climbing partner is desperate to save his friend, which is pretty challenging

They are both being pulled over the cliff and moments away from falling. This is challenging and dramatic.

These two men are in conflict with nature. They are in conflict with their own physical limitations. They are fighting gravity and their desperate need for personal survival. They are also both desperate to save each other.

This one moment in a mountaineer's life is a perfect example of what dramatic conflict is. The two men involved aren't fighting each other, nor are they arguing. They are fighting for their survival in ridiculously challenging circumstances. As we can see, conflict is about the struggle our characters have to make. It is the thing that forces them to struggle. And, this challenge doesn't have to come from another character. It doesn't have to be a fight or an argument.

As writers, we should be able to imagine how this dramatic moment plays out. We could resolve it in any number of ways. In an action movie, they would make a heroic effort. The injured climber would be pulled back to safety. What I haven't told you is this scenario comes from a true story. Joe Simpson wrote an incredible book called *Touching the Void* about this moment. Anyone who wants to understand the relationship between challenging events and drama should read it. It's a great story. I'm not going to spoil it for you by telling you how it resolves. I urge you to read it for yourselves. It contains a very important lesson for screenwriters. The lesson is that real life is often much more interesting than most fiction.

Our characters have to face challenging circumstances. There also needs to be some jeopardy involved. Completing a difficult crossword within a time limit is a challenging circumstance. However, there isn't a lot of jeopardy in it. If there are twenty people taking the same test, and only one gets the dream job, the jeopardy increases. If the person taking the test absolutely must get the job or suffer, the scene becomes more dramatic. If they face prison, death, or exposure as a spy for failing, the stakes are increased. Increased stakes mean increased drama. A screenwriter should always ask what are the characters in conflict with and what is at stake for them? If the characters aren't facing a challenge and there isn't anything at stake, it isn't drama.

what is the role of the exploration of human nature in drama?

All drama is an exploration of what it means to be human. If we ask ourselves what subjects films are made about, a pattern emerges. Love and betrayal are common subjects. As are war, sex and obsession. Fame, money, greed and power. Individuality and social responsibility. The lust for power, the lust for success and plain old lust. Fear, murder and genocide also crop up quite a bit. Evil, God, insanity and politics are firm favourites. Revenge, truth, morality, survival and death are very popular. The complete list is considerably longer than this, but I hope you can see the pattern. Each of these are distinctly human ideas. Even when a film is about cats or talking animals, it is really about what it means to be human. That's because the second we ascribe human values to the characters, it's no longer about the animals.

Stories are always an exploration of what it means to be human. More than that, stories always reflect the personal passions and obsessions of the writer. Actually, the same is true of the consumer. People engage with the aspect of humanity that most fascinates them. So, if a person only watches love stories, it's fair to say they have a fascination with romance. A person who loves action movies wants to explore the power of the individual as a source of good in the world. I encourage screenwriters to reflect on what fascinates them and why? What is it about those kinds of stories that really engages you? A script will always uncover our beliefs about human behaviour. When we write a script, we face the same question over and over again. When this specific character is placed in this specific situation how will they react? Our job is to write something that furthers the story. We need to write something which the audience finds believable. We do this by understanding people's motivations and actions. What will a person do and why are they doing it? And when we do this, we reveal our own view of the world and how it works. This will make more sense if we look at an example.

A young woman is asked to hide a gun by her boyfriend. He tells her that both of their lives depend on her keeping the gun hidden for three days.

As screenwriters we have to decide how our character will respond to this challenge. This isn't an easy task because there are a lot of possible reactions. She might be the kind of person who refuses to take the gun. She might take the gun and hide it really well. She might take the gun and hide it really badly. She might take the gun and sell it. She might hand the gun over to the Police. She might take it and then use it to kill her parents/her boyfriend/a random stranger. We have to imagine what kind of person she is. What we imagine will depend on two things. What we believe people are capable of and what we believe about this character. Screenwriting is drama. Drama is driven by the unique reactions of our characters to challenging circumstances. The choices they make tells the audience what kind of person they are.

The only real difference between a hero and a villain is the choice they make when faced with the same moral dilemma. Batman gets to be a hero because he refuses to kill, the Joker is a villain because he revels in it.

what is the role of morality in the creation of drama?

The first stories told in American cinema were often simplistic morality tales. The good guy wore a white hat. The bad guy had a big moustache and a black hat. Someone, usually a damsel in distress, was the object of their conflict. This model of hero (protagonist), villain (antagonist), and damsel in distress (stakes character) is still used by many writers. A lot of the books about screenwriting start from this assumption. That a film's story will be about those three characters.

The protagonist/antagonist/stakes character approach is also an idea we find in a story structure called the hero's journey. The hero's journey is an idea put forward by Joseph Campbell in his book, *Hero with a Thousand Faces*. Campbell believes a protagonist's adventure must conform to the same pattern as heroes in ancient mythology. This is an idea we'll revisit when we get to the chapter on structure.

For the moment, let's ignore the structural elements. Let's look at how stories about heroes inevitably become mirrors of the storyteller's morality.

> *If a protagonist (hero) is the primary character, then the story is an exploration of what it means to be heroic. If the primary source of conflict is a villain, the story is an exploration of being a bad guy.*

Great screenwriters take time to think about what it means to be heroic. Poor writers just copy existing ideas about heroism, without giving them a thought. One of the reasons so many films feel formulaic is because they clone their heroes and villains. When no thought is given to the moral questions at the heart of a story, the end result will feel lacking and cliched.

For the last eighty years writers have reimagined Batman and the Joker. These stories have pulled apart the idea of what it means to be a hero.

The first Batman story appeared in 1939, with the first appearance of the Joker in 1940. These two characters have flourished because the comic book industry hires great writers. These writers have made a relentless effort to explore the moral complexities of these characters. Their work has given us some of the best stories in comic book history.

Batman presents writers with a lot of moral dilemmas to play with. Almost everything Batman does is both immoral and illegal. Batman breaks into people's homes, kidnaps people, assaults and tortures them. He isn't part of the legal system and isn't accountable to anyone. Being innocent until proven guilty means nothing to him. He has no respect for due legal process or prohibitions on duress. In the real world, Batman would be a genuine monster, not a hero. A lot of modern Batman stories tackle these problems head-on. They have something interesting to say about the darkness at the heart of Batman. To understand how the morality of a hero can be the heart of a story, read Frank Miller's, *Dark Knight Returns*. I also recommend Grant Morrison's, *Arkham Asylum*.

Some of the people bringing Batman to cinema have also recognised this evolution. They too have looked at the morality of Batman and the Joker. They show complex characters defined by their beliefs about humanity, good and evil. In my opinion, one of the most successful of these was Christopher Nolan's, *Dark Knight*. Christopher Nolan/Heath Ledger's Joker is iconic. One reason for this is his surprisingly coherent worldview. When the Joker says to Harvey   Dent,

> *JOKER: You were a schemer; you had plans and look where that got ya... I just did what I do best. I took your little plan and I turned it on itself. Look what I did to this city with a few drums of gas and some bullets. Do you know what I noticed? Nobody panics when things go according to plan. Even if the plan is horrifying. If tomorrow I tell the press a gangbanger will get shot or a truckload of soldiers will be blown up, nobody panics, because it's all part of the plan. But if I say one little mayor will die. Well, then everyone loses their minds. Introduce a little anarchy, upset the established order and everything becomes chaos. I'm an agent of chaos. Oh, and you know the thing about chaos. It's fair.*

These aren't the nonsensical rantings of a psychopath. This Joker has a manifesto and a coherent philosophy. Nolan's film isn't about a battle between a good man and a bad man. It's really about the battle between two very warped ideas about morality. In many respects, Batman's world view is no more defensible than the Joker's.

The Dark Knight is also a good example of how moral dilemmas create compelling drama. Bruce Wayne (Batman) is challenged by the Joker to take off his mask and reveal his true identity to Gotham. The Joker threatens to kill another person, for every day Batman doesn't hand himself in. This puts Batman in an appalling moral dilemma. If he hands himself in, he will save lives, but his ability to protect the city will end. But if he doesn't give himself up people will die. A screenwriting friend and I used to call this kind of dilemma, stuffed if you do, stuffed if you don't (only we didn't use the word stuffed!).

These kinds of impossible choices are central to any story with a protagonist. The way a hero solves moral dilemmas reveals what kind of hero they are. And the higher and more personal the stakes, the more dramatic the story. Every protagonist is unique. As is their moral code. Our job is to test their morality. Is the hero really a good woman? Is the bad guy really a monster?

does a character overcoming problems create drama?

The first time I sat down and tried to define the concept of story, I came up with this:

A story is what happens when people are forced to deal with a set of problems

This definition didn't feel accurate or useful. I couldn't get past the idea that this also describes the dynamics of a TV quiz show. The first change I made was to replace the word people with the phrase, specific characters. Characters are not people; a character is the illusion of a person who exists within a story. It's often a mistake to treat characters like they are real people. A character isn't a person. It's the illusion of a person created for dramatic effect. We'll get into this subject in greater depth when we look at character development. For the moment, it's enough to understand that characters aren't real people. They can only exist within a story. My next attempt at defining what a story was:

Story is what happens when a specific group of characters are forced to deal with a set of problems.

Although this is an improvement, it's still not completely accurate. We all face problems every single day. This morning, when I got up, I realised my favourite pair of jeans were in the wash. I had to pick something else to wear. This was a problem because I wanted to wear that particular pair. Although I can imagine a film based on overcoming this problem, it doesn't sound dramatic. It's not dramatic because as problems go, it's pretty easy to solve. All I did was pick a different pair of trousers. It wasn't a challenging problem and there wasn't a lot at stake. But, by altering the situation we can turn what appears to be a mundane problem into one that is dramatic.

After a terrible car accident, John is forced to live in a wheelchair. Severely depressed by his disability, he refuses to look after himself. Instead, he relies on his sister, Molly, to do everything for him. She arrives every morning and cooks breakfast. She gets his clothes from the cupboard and helps him to get dressed. One morning, Molly doesn't show up. Suddenly, John discovers everything he needs from his food to his trousers are all out of reach. For the first time since the accident, John is forced to face his disability. He must overcome the challenges of living in a wheelchair.

The task of selecting, getting and putting on a pair of trousers can be challenging and dramatic. It's about putting the right character, in the right circumstance. For John, having to fend for himself forces him to face the physical challenges of being disabled. He has to face the consequences of his refusal to adapt to life after his accident. What we've added are three important elements:

The problem has become a genuine challenge to this character because of who they are

The stakes are a lot higher for this specific character

The challenge to the character isn't just physical. It also reflects their internal struggle

Giving your protagonist problems to solve doesn't automatically create drama. To create drama, we have to tailor the problem to the character's circumstances. We raise the stakes for them personally. We make sure the challenge reflects an aspect of their internal struggles.

Drama is always about the personal struggles of unique characters. It is this idea that took me to the definition I now use:

A story (drama) is what happens when a specific group of characters are forced to face a set of challenging circumstances

Our movie's plot is more than just a series of problems for the central character to solve. Instead, our plot has to be uniquely challenging to this specific character. It matters who they are and what's at stake for them as an individual. Their struggle in the world reflects their deeper internal struggle. Although a plot can be seen as a series of problems for the central character. They have to be the right problems. We have to create problems tailored to the individual vulnerabilities of the character.

how important is it to force characters to face their vulnerabilities?

There is a direct link between character vulnerability and the question of what's at stake. Understanding this link is the key to good screenwriting. Exposing our character's vulnerability is more important to drama than conflict. So, let's try to understand what vulnerability is and what effect it has on drama

Gunfights are popular in movies because it's obvious that there is something at stake. In a gunfight, there is the possibility the central character will get hurt or die. At the most basic level, a character's vulnerability to injury or death creates drama. However, vulnerability is always unique to the specific character. Let's compare the vulnerability of three different characters in the same situation.

Which of the following characters is the most vulnerable and has the most at stake in a gunfight?

> Superman
> A highly trained soldier
> A nine-year-old child

We know Superman is bullet-proof, so there is absolutely nothing at stake for him in a gunfight. The stakes for the soldier are higher. She could get hurt or die. However, she's trained for this world. So, her real vulnerabilities aren't exposed in this scenario. However, a nine-year-old child in a gunfight is horrifically vulnerable. They are the least able to protect themselves. For both Superman and the soldier, a gunfight is a demonstration of their strengths. It doesn't expose their real vulnerabilities. A gunfight doesn't present them with truly challenging circumstances. When the child is in a gunfight, the stakes and the drama become real. If you watch enough action movies this idea may feel familiar to you. In an action movie, the invulnerable hero often saves someone who is weak and vulnerable? In the industry, this person, the damsel in distress, is called the stakes character. They are, quite literally, the object that is at stake for the hero.

Giving the protagonist a vulnerable person to save isn't particularly good writing. Having an actual fight is the least interesting way to create conflict. A damsel in distress is the least interesting way to expose vulnerability. It's also a stupidly misogynistic way to create a story. We can do better than that. It's possible to write heroic figures with relatable personal vulnerabilities. We just have to make the effort

Risk of death is the least interesting form of personal vulnerability. Vulnerability is always about the risk of harm, but the nature of that harm isn't just physical. Emotional vulnerability is just as important to drama as physical vulnerability. One way to reframe the idea of what's at stake for a character is to ask what is the emotional cost? We can force the protagonist to pay an overwhelming emotional cost. At the end of Roman Polanski's *Chinatown*,

Evelyn Mulray is forced to reveal her family's darkest secret. She admits her daughter is the product of an incestuous relationship with her father. This confession leads to a tragic ending. Evelyn is gunned down by the police. In a very real sense, the entire movie is driven by Evelyn's need to protect both her secret and her daughter. Although Evelyn is killed, the gunfight isn't the real source of drama. The source of drama is the threat/harm (vulnerability) of her daughter. A threat posed by the possibility that their family history may repeat itself. One way to think about *Chinatown*, would be to say that it is an exploration of the cost of sexual abuse and incest. It is the idea of the cost, which takes us to the final aspect of drama, theme.

what role does the idea of dramatic theme play in creating drama?

If you were to ask someone, "What is this movie really about?" there are a lot of different ways to answer. You could tell them the logline. You could tell them the plot. But, please don't! It's the worst way to describe a film. Or, we could talk about the film's theme. That, in my opinion, is the right answer. But what is a theme?

Let's imagine you want to write a love story. For some people, the concept of love would serve as their theme. This is because themes are simple and universal human experiences. Falling in love is a universal and simple human experience, which is why it is often at the heart of stories. However, for me, the concept of love is too broad to work effectively as a theme for screenwriting. What I want to know, is what aspect of love does this story explore? So, for instance, the idea of infidelity might be fertile ground for a story. In which case the theme might be an exploration of the cost of infidelity.

We can create a theme for our script by adding the phrase the cost of in front of a universal human experience. Let's try this as an experiment.

Take a moment and try to create an idea for a movie that explores jealousy. What kind of mental work you are doing, as you do this? Is this easy? Are you drawing from your own experience? Are you thinking about other movies or TV shows where jealousy drives the story?

O.K. Now, let's try this again. But this time we're going to use add in the phrase, the personal and emotional cost of. Take a moment and create an idea for a movie based on the theme, the personal and emotional cost of ambition. Was that a different experience for you? Did you find it easier or harder? For me, it's always easier for me to find ideas when I work from a theme based on cost.

Deciding on a theme for our writing goes to the heart of what it means to be a writer. A writer's choice of theme tends to reveal a lot about who they are and what they really care about. That's why it is the answer I expect from writers when I ask them about their scripts.

"What's your new script about?" ... "Thanks for asking, it explores the emotional cost one woman has to pay to get revenge on her abusers."

When we think about the roots of drama, conflict, exploration of human nature, morality, overcoming challenging circumstances and vulnerability. A good theme encapsulates all of these aspects.

The emotional cost one woman has to pay (vulnerability) to get revenge (morality, human nature, challenging circumstances) on her abusers (conflict).

It's not enough for the theme of a movie to act as the springboard for our ideas. It also has to inform every aspect of the writing. We ask ourselves, does this scene explore this character's struggle with the theme? Is my protagonist forced to pay a horrific price to move forward her plans for revenge? Is the plot putting her in circumstances which prevent her from being successful? Is she forced to make horrific choices? Choices that expose her vulnerabilities. If the answer isn't yes, then the scene doesn't belong in the script.

To write a good film script the story must be more than a string of events. It has to work as drama. Drama is created when we expose our characters to a challenging set of circumstances. Circumstances which expose their vulnerabilities and test their morality. In my experience, a good script needs all of those elements. Scripts without a theme tend to be unfocused. Scripts where the character's vulnerabilities aren't challenged tend to be bland. Scripts which don't have anything to say about moral dilemmas tend to be cliched. Scripts without conflict tend to be boring. And, scripts without a set of challenging circumstances don't have a plot.

A writer who understands what drama is will always have more freedom. A writer who understands process can defy conventions and experiment in their storytelling. They can create challenging stories without losing their audience.

CHAPTER 7
Process & Story

When we write a script, we have to create a story. So, it's a good idea to ask the question, what is a story? As writers we should have several answers to this question. We need a technical definition. If we don't know what a story is, how can we write one? We also need a larger, cultural understanding. We might ask ourselves, what is a story for? The final question we need to ask ourselves is, how is a story created?

It is difficult to separate the concept of story from what it means to be human. Storytelling is a universal human behaviour. Every tribe, no matter how remote, has a storytelling tradition. It is possible to find cultures without agriculture, trade or written language. But it is impossible to find human beings who don't tell stories. In our modern lives, we can choose from a million, professionally-crafted stories every single day. Despite this, we still tell anecdotes and personal stories to friends and colleagues. Human beings are animals defined by our need to communicate. Storytelling is one of the most common forms of communication.

Storytelling is innately human. However, writing a movie requires more than our natural sense of storytelling. We might tolerate a poorly told anecdote for a couple of minutes. But we have higher standards for a movie. In the last chapter we looked at what makes drama. Now we need to look at the relationship between drama and stories.

A cinematic story is more than a list of universal plot-points. The idea that a story is defined by its structure isn't the whole truth. However, some structural ideas are unavoidable. So, let's start with the basics.

how we learned what stories are?

When we are children, the stories we hear all have a definite beginning, once upon a time. Children's stories also have a very definite ending, and they all lived happily ever after. Our earliest understanding of stories is shaped by this idea. We learn that a story has a very definite beginning and a very definite end. As we grow older, we discover stories don't have to have a happy ending. Some stories don't have a simple journey from start to finish. Some stories have to unfold over many episodes. Yet, buried deep in the DNA of storytelling is the basic idea that a story has to have a beginning, a middle and an end.

The other thing we know about stories is they happen to a character or characters, in a world specific to the story.

Once upon a time, in a magic forest, there lived a fabulous pig-princess

Children's stories start by introducing the character the story is about. They also tell you where the story is set. So, we know the story is about the fabulous pig-princess and she lives in a magic forest. This information may seem too obvious to mention. But it is worth looking at because it is universally true. To create a story, we need at least one character, a setting for the story to take place, a beginning and an end. These ideas automatically lead to a basic form of story structure. A story begins. We introduce our characters and the world they inhabit. Things happen. Then the story resolves itself into a satisfactory ending.

We can lay this out into a list of things that happen:

> We introduce the audience to the fictional world and our characters

> The characters face a series of challenging circumstances

> The story resolves into a satisfactory ending

Most of the theories of how to write a movie take these basic structural truths and add to them. They reverse-engineer ancient mythology or the plots of successful movies. I'm being generous when I call this process reverse-engineering. It is, in fact, the process of looking for patterns in stories and then claiming the pattern is universal. In the chapter on structure, we'll look at some of these structural theories. We'll figure out why screenwriters need to be aware of them. For the time being let's keep it simple. Our story introduces characters in their fictional world. They face a series of challenging circumstances. The story ends when it resolves in a satisfying way.

Story structure isn't a cure-all. It doesn't fix bad screenwriting. The way we create good scripts is by understanding the process of creating a story. A process-driven approach focuses on a series of simple tasks or steps. Doing these tasks will create a story. We don't need a formula, structure or template. A process-driven approach creates a story by following the steps. We know if we do, the will story appear organically from the process.

CHAPTER 8
The Ideas Phase

Earlier, we learned the process has four phases. They are, the ideas phase, the research phase, the planning phase, and the writing phase. Before we look at the individual steps in the process, we need to dig a bit deeper into each phase. The next four chapters do precisely that. Let's start at the beginning, the ideas phase.

ideas and theme

The process of creating a story starts with a raw idea. The one thing we can be sure of is this idea won't be fully formed. In my experience, an idea for a script often starts with a *that's interesting* moment. That's interesting moments come in many forms. I remember watching the first Christopher Nolan Batman movie, *Batman Begins*. Batman's costume made the stuntman's movements stiff and mechanical. The lack of grace bothered me. Batman wasn't moving like Batman. That moment of frustration sparked an idea. I wanted to write a script set in the world of free-running or parkour. I now had an idea for a script. An idea triggered by a moment of dissatisfaction.

It doesn't matter where the idea comes from or what form it takes. What matters is that we have an idea. The first thing we do with this idea is to get it down on paper. Ideas for scripts rarely happen when we're looking for an idea. That's why it pays to carry a notepad. Ideas for films tend to crop up when we're working on other things. Getting the idea written down preserves it. We come back to the idea, when we're ready to develop it.

Once we have an idea, we ask the question, what is this story about?

In the last chapter, we looked at the role theme plays in drama. I suggested a film's theme is the best answer to the question what is this story about? A film's theme is an exploration of the personal and emotional cost of a universal human experience. In a process driven approach theme is the foundation of the story, not the structure. Traditional screenwriters sometimes struggle with this. It goes against their belief in structure. All I can say is, a thematic approach works. It's a more reliable foundation than structure.

My Parkour story idea was a gut response to my disappointment in the movie, Batman Begins. I knew I wanted to write a film with action sequences that were acrobatic and natural. But I wanted them to take place in a working class, urban environment. So, what kind of theme would best serve that kind of story? The process encourages us to play ideas. We try out different ideas before writing.

Let's generate some potential themes. Our story will explore the personal and emotional cost of:

Fighting for justice

Revenge

Protecting your reputation

Individual freedom

Escaping gang-culture

Protecting your family

Escaping your family

This list can be as long or as short as we like. I normally suggest writers create at least ten different themes. Experience tells me the first couple of ideas will be the most cliched and obvious. The most interesting themes tend to pop up as the fourth or fifth idea. When we create lists like this, we are also creating related sub-themes. Although a story only really needs one overarching theme. Our central idea often acts as an umbrella for related ideas. The ideas of protecting our reputation sits comfortably with ideas of revenge. We keep all of these ideas. They may be useful later in the process.

Our next step is to make a decision. Which theme appeals to us the most? Let's say, we decide to explore the personal and emotional cost of escaping gang-culture. This becomes our protagonist's struggle. We can also pick a sub-theme for our antagonist. Their struggle will be to protect their reputation. Another character may try to escape their family and another one is seeking revenge. We are using this simple list of themes to create our cast. By doing this way, we create characters with conflicting objectives. This is how we plan to write drama. It is also the way we start to build a story.

Every step in the process is designed to spark ideas for every aspect of the film. We've been working on the theme. It's already starting to suggest ideas for characters. We are making choices that will affect the plot and locations. We may already be imagining specific scenes. Any ideas that pop-up as part of the process, should be written down in our notebook.

Scripts have two different loglines. One is used to pitch our script to producers. It is usually less than forty-words long. It encapsulates the core of the concept. I don't have a lot to say about them. I don't work with the kind of producers who need that kind of pitch. I pitch my projects by lifting the phone and saying *"Hey, I've got an idea I want to run past you."* So, I don't write tight pitching loglines. However, I'm a real fan of the other kind. They are compass loglines. A compass logline is a development tool. Something we use to help us write. It is a short description of the story which tells us who the story is about, their world and the most challenging circumstance they have to face. So, for example:

> *When an ageing movie star is bankrupted by his seventh divorce.* (This is who the story is about*). He is forced to take the lead role in the worst horror movie ever written.* (This is his world). *The movie is a career-ending fiasco. But, with no way to escape the contract, he decides to fake his own kidnapping and death.* (This is the primary challenge he has to face)

The logline tells us who the film is about, their world and their primary challenge. Developing a compass logline is the thing we do after deciding on our theme. It's called a compass logline because it will guide us through the writing process. It is when we turn our idea into a working film concept. We do this by answering these four questions.

Who is this film about?

Where does it take place?

When does it take place?

What is the story really about?

The work we've already done to create a theme neatly answers one of the four questions. So, going back to the story we're developing, the questions now look like this.

Who is this film about? - Don't know yet.

Where does it take place? - Don't know yet.

When does it take place? - Don't know yet.

What is the story really about? It explores the personal and emotional cost of escaping gang-culture.

Like every other part of the process, this is an opportunity to look beyond the first idea that occurs to us. First ideas are a double-edged sword. They represent our natural instinct about a project. At the same time, they can also be the most obvious and cliched response. A lot of the creative process is about playing with ideas. Playing with ideas is the way we find new projects and make tired concepts better. To play with our idea we create a random list of periods we could set a story in.

> The present
> 1987
> The Victorian era
> The future
> 1918

And now some places.

> London
> Tokyo
> A fictional dystopian city
> Somalia
> Alaska

The process always generates ideas that wouldn't exist without this effort. It's one of the reasons I love to work this way. My first feeling about the gang-culture story was to set it in the present day. I still like that idea. However, the idea of setting it in 1987 opens up a different set of opportunities. In 1987, I was living in a part of London rife with gang-culture. 1987 is a time I know I can write about.

Setting a story in the Victorian era is also a natural fit. I have written a few dramas set in Victorian England. I am naturally drawn to that era. I've also already amassed a huge collection of research on Victorian street gangs.

I have a life-long passion for science-fiction. The future would be an interesting time to set this story. I love Sci-fi but have never written a script in that genre.

The last date on the list, 1918, is an in-joke. I put it in because it's already been done. The TV series Peaky Blinders is about the gang-culture in the region where my family grew up. My great-grandmother was a publican in that period and that place.

So, our exploration of gang culture could be a look at modern urban-gangs. It could be about Hackney Yardies in 1987. It might be set amongst Victorian street-gangs. Alternately, I could spend time trying to develop an idea like Peaky Blinders. Even this last idea isn't a total loser. Even if our project's concept is similar to a famous series or film, by making changes we can create something new and fresh.

Let's imagine that we have our heart set on a story exploring gang-culture in 1918. Even though it's already been done, brilliantly, by Stephen Knight. We don't have to give up on our idea yet. Peaky Blinders is set in Small Heath, Birmingham. It is centred around the growth of the Shelby family empire. What makes it compelling drama is not just the period and its theme. The whole drama is driven by being set in Small Heath, Birmingham. That and the specific nature of the Shelby family. It's a portrayal of gang-culture set-in working-class poverty, heavy industry and horse racing. The setting and the characters drive the story. There will always be room for any story that takes the audience into another world. A story about different characters.

We can radically change a project by moving it into a new fictional world. Let me show you how. I'm going to suggest we move the story to post-war London. In the 1920s, London was an incredible city. It was the era Evelyn Waugh described in his book the Bright Young Things. A decadent and promiscuous club culture sprang up. A culture which threw together bohemians, artists, addicts, criminals and the aristocracy. Flappers, jazz, booze, drugs, promiscuity and a decadent sexuality existed in post-war London. This offers fertile ground for drama. One that explores the personal and emotional cost of escaping gang-culture. This already is a radically different world from the one in which Peaky Blinders is set. With a little more work on the idea, we could narrow the setting to something specific. Again, we can generate a list of ideas. I always encourage writers to look at multiple options. To save time, I'm just going to put forward the idea I most favour. We are going to set this film in a high-class brothel and nightclub called The Mermaid.

Our new concept now looks like this.

Who is this film about? - Don't Know

Where does it take place? - The Mermaid, a high-class brothel/club in the West End of London

When does it take place? - After the First World War, in the time of the Bright Young Things
What is the story really about? - The personal/emotional cost of escaping gang-culture.

By picking a new setting new stories emerge. We have started to create something new and different.

The final question to answer, before writing a compass logline is, who is this story about?

The work we have done so far narrows our choices. We can't put any old character into our period and setting. However, there is still a lot of choice. Again, creating a huge list of characters is a useful way for a writer to spend their time. But, when it comes to central characters there is another consideration. As a writer, what kind of characters do I want to work with? In the same way writers tend to be drawn to specific themes, the same is true of characters. The world of film and television is vibrant precisely because writers are unique. They bring their distinct tastes and interests to the work. Nobody writes poignant iconoclasts better than Charlie Kaufman. (*Syndoche New York, Adaptation, Eternal Sunshine of the Spotless Mind*). No one creates believable relationships like Nora Ephron. (*Sleepless in Seattle, When Harry Met Sally*). Yet there is still room for writers like Sam Rami (*Evil Dead*) and John Hughes (*The Breakfast Club, Home Alone*). Each of these writers brings something unique to the industry. They are all great writers. What makes them different are the diverse themes and the characters they write about.

Part of our development is finding the themes and characters that inspire us. The process encourages writers to explore and play with ideas. That's how we find the ones we are passionate about. The process of writing a screenplay runs parallel to our personal development. There comes a point where we know what kind of characters are in tune with our psyche. So, let's add a central character into this mix. We will look at character development later in the book. For the moment, I'll just throw a character in as an example.

Who is this film about? - Lady Esther Martin, a nurse returning from WWI

Where does it take place? - The Mermaid, a high-class brothel and nightclub in the West End of London

52

When does it take place? - After the First World War, in the time of the Bright Young Things

What is the story really about? - It explores the personal and emotional cost of escaping gang-culture.

The process takes our writing to places and concepts we wouldn't have found any other way. Our initial idea was very different to what we have now. The raw idea was to write an urban-action script. We planned to use free-running to get fluid action sequences, a sort of *District 13* meets *Ill Manors*. By playing with the (who, where, when + what is the theme) we have created an idea for a historical drama. One that explores the emotional and personal cost to a nurse returning from WWI. We are writing about what happens when she falls into London's club culture. A world of drugs, jazz, sex and crime. A story set in a London brothel and nightclub. Having done this work, we're now ready to write a compass logline.

> *When Lady Esther Martin returns from WWI, her experiences as a battle-field nurse have changed her. Unable to fit back into her old life, she stumbles into a world of decadent parties, jazz, drugs and crime. At the heart of this new life is The Mermaid. A high-class brothel and nightclub. The Mermaid serves as the playground for the aristocracy, criminals, artists and the utterly debauched. Her medical expertise soon attracts the attention of Madame Badet. A criminal who draws her deeper into the life. She soon finds herself working as the club's de facto abortionist, drug dealer and mob doctor. In a moment of clarity, she decides to get out of this life and The Mermaid. She discovers joining was easy but getting out may well cost her everything.*

This would never work as a logline to pitch the project. It's far too long. However, that's not our aim here. Our aim is to understand the story we are creating. This is a rough sketch of our story. A sketch that will evolve and change in the development process.

CHAPTER 9
The Research Phase

Once we have an idea that inspires us, we shift our attention to the research phase. By playing with our ideas, we have developed an idea we love. We have a central character, a period and a place for our story. We even have a rough sketch of our story, in the form of a compass logline.

Now we have to dig deeper into our fictional world. And the way we do this is with research. But this is research with a difference. It is specific to screenwriting and the creation of a fictional, cinematic world.

researching the ordinary world

When I wrote the compass logline in the previous section, I cheated. Not intentionally. It was a result of the way the concept developed. I was able to write that compass logline because I have a fair amount of knowledge about that era. 1920s London club culture fascinates me. Writers tend to develop ideas in worlds that we have already researched. But, our interest in a particular culture, period or group of people may not be enough. It is almost guaranteed we will not know enough to write a story set in that world. The next part of the process addresses that issue.

I don't believe writers should write what we know. It's too limiting. Writers should write what we are passionate about. One of the ways we identify what we are passionate about is by paying attention to the things that fascinate us.

The one thing that shines through a great script is the writer's fascination. They bewitch us with their love of the culture/period/ people they write about. One of the most valuable things stories do is to give us entrance into worlds we know nothing about. Spike Lee's *Do the Right Thing* is more than a story, it's an invitation into a world I have never experienced. The same is true of movies like *City of Gods* or even a cop movie like *Serpico*. I'm never going to experience what it was like to be an undercover cop in New York, in the 1970's. Waldo Salt and Norman Wexler's *Serpico* transports us into that world. It is our responsibility to be passionate about the fictional worlds we create. The ordinary world of our story is just as important as our characters and our plot.

The creation of a vibrant fictional world happens through fascination, research and imagination. This part of the process is extremely flexible. The research methods have to suit the individual writer.

Our research will be effective, if we understand the task we're undertaking.

Although we aren't ready to write out script, we are preparing for that, we need to know what our locations look like. We need to know how this world works culturally. How do people dress? How do they act and how they talk? When I talk about the world of the story, that's what I mean. One way to define a cultural group is by their habits. If we know their rules and their code of conduct, we can write about them. If we know where they go and what they do, we can recreate that. If we know how they talk, we can write dialogue. When a writer talks about the fictional world, they don't mean a specific place, they mean a culture. So we ask the following questions.

What do these people do?

What is it about them, as a group, that binds them together?

Where do they live?

What are the rules and morality of their lifestyle/culture?

What are their daily challenges?

What, as a culture, are their strengths?

What, as a culture, are their weaknesses?

How do they dress?

How do they talk?

What does this world look like?

How does this culture relate to our theme?

This list of questions may be daunting to some people. This kind of information is very different from the kind you'd use to write an essay about something. It's not as bad as it looks. Although we're exploring a strange land, our theme is always about universal human experiences. And that is what we always come back to.

Let's imagine our theme is the personal and emotional cost of infidelity. We would ask, in this culture, how do people manage to have affairs? If we are writing about New York executives, it might be about late nights in the office or sneaking off to a hotel. If our story is set in a coal mining village in 1880, a couple might be meeting in the alley, behind the pub. If we then ask, what is the moral code about infidelity in this culture? Well, in our New York executive world perhaps it's OK provided you don't fall in love. In our Victorian Pit Village, it might be the most shameful and destructive thing two people can do. The impact could be on the whole community. After all, men in mines depend on each other to survive. Jealousy and resentment in that environment might be a life and death issue.

The three factors that create a fictional world are fascination, research and imagination. The most important of those three factors is imagination. The storyteller's job is to create a fictional, imaginary world. This is true even when it's based on real people and real events. This doesn't mean that research isn't important. It is. It just needs to be research with a purpose.

The most useful sources of inspiration for a fictional world are autobiographies. First-hand accounts often give the best insights into the day-to-day workings of a culture. The trick with autobiographies is to ignore the story and to pull out useful details. As writers, we have to be careful not to steal from existing copyrighted work. We can't take whole sections from a book for our script, unless the book has fallen out of copyright. What we can do, is get a feel for how people behave, what's important to them and how they speak to each other. As I wrote earlier, it's about pulling out useful details. Again, this is where a project notebook is useful.

Here's a list of the kinds of resources I routinely use to research the ordinary world of a project.

Personal experience and observation

Biographies that take me into the world I want to write about

Documentaries on the world I want to write about

Magazine articles

Newspapers specific to the place I want to write about

Photographs (via Pinterest, Flickr, Google and the Internet Archive)

Fiction written by people who come from that world/culture/group

YouTube (particularly video produced by people from the world I am researching)

Visits to key places in the story

Interviews with people from the culture/lifestyle/group

Movies already set in the world/culture/lifestyle

The research we do into our fictional world should be enjoyable and inspiring. Remember, one of the key ingredients is our fascination. If the research feels like work, we should consider reworking our concept.

Writers who aren't fascinated by the world they are creating aren't going to tell great stories. How can we expect to hold our audience's attention, if we're not interested in the subject matter?

Every writer needs to find a way of researching that suits their way of working. I really like to start with documentaries. Then I source photographs. Only when I have a feel for the era or culture do I move onto biographies. Even then, I tend to dip into sections of books rather than reading the entire thing. My focus is always on the imaginary world, rather than any attempt to emulate reality.

Some writers are more concerned with the facts of a situation and I respect that approach. But, in fiction all stories happen in imaginary worlds. Because of this, I am more focused on information that inspires me, rather than facts.

Screenwriter's research isn't anything like the kind of research we did at school or college. It isn't about collecting facts or comparing arguments. It is, instead, a completely creative process. It is entirely about chasing our imagination.

Imagine we are on a bus. A clown on a bicycle rides past the window. He's carrying a watermelon under one arm. Something about this image fascinates us. So, we take out our notebook and write it down. When we get home, we go to Project Gutenberg online and do a search for biographies of clowns. We find *The Autobiography of a Clown* by Isaac F Marcosson. We download it to our Kindle. We Google Isaac F Marcosson. We discover he was a journalist who wrote a lot of interesting books. We copy and paste the list of books into a document and save it to our research folder. Then, we nip over to Librivox and discover *Autobiography of a Clown* is available as a free audiobook. So, we download it onto our phone. The book, we discover is really about Jules Turnour. So, we Google him and go straight to images. There are some great photos of Jules Turnour. One of these photos leads to a website called *Pat Cashin's Clown Alley*. It is an old blog full of archive materials about Victorian clowns. We skim a couple of posts and bookmark them for later.

This may read like a classic case of writer's procrastination. A writer wasting their time by disappearing down the rabbit-hole of the Internet. But, that's not what's happening! This dance between the real world, literature, photos and obscure blogs is the way writers research. If we want to create worlds which mesmerise audiences, we must trust our fascination.

In the past, it was common for artists and writers to talk about having a personal muse. The idea of muses, demi-gods who inspire writers and artists, comes from Greek mythology. You don't hear a lot of writers talk about this anymore. This is because it seems like a pretentious idea. It's almost a cliché. The lazy, feckless writer lying around waiting for their muse to inspire them to write. I see the idea of a writer's muse from a process-driven point of view. To me, a muse just another way of describing a writer chasing their fascination. It is that sense of wonder and excitement as we discover something that inspires us. It helps us to imagine new worlds and new stories. Serious writers understand that experience. I believe in the idea of the writer's muse. Writers who nurture and chase their fascination create intense and compelling fictional worlds.

For every writer, there is a point when they feel ready to move onto the next step in their process. When we do this, when we are ready to move on, this won't be the end of our research. There is a constant to-and-fro between getting words on the page and research. On my last script, I had to hunt down documents on current police procedures. I needed to know how they deal with mental health problems. I have my office set up, so I have two screens. I write on one screen. I use the other for planning documents, notes and my web browser. I was still researching as I wrote. But the research was only for the kind of details that add authenticity to a script.

We have to learn when to drop down the rabbit-hole of research and when to drag ourselves back to writing. The experience of writing is vastly different from the experience of researching. Chasing our fascination is exhilarating. Our brain gives us a lot of positive strokes. As such, it's fairly addictive. I experience writing as more of a trance state. It's actually really difficult to describe the process of writing. For me, the very introspection I need to describe it doesn't exist when I'm writing. In essence, research feeds the ego, and the physical process of writing destroys it. This doesn't mean writers are egoless! Far from it. But, when I write, I lose myself in a profound manner.

Writing is difficult because the mental state required comes from within the writer. Writing is quite a lot like sport, in that we need to develop our strength and our mental resilience. However, rather than hitting the gym, a writer needs to find their way into the right mental state. And, the way we do that is by writing.

CHAPTER 10
Planning Phase. Characters

Our research has given us confidence in our ability to create a fictional world. We know how it works and what it looks like. We are ready to start planning. And, the first part of the planning phase is to populate our fictional world with characters.

character development

Character development is central to storytelling and the writing of drama. It's impossible to create a plot without understanding our characters. Character development is the single most important step in creating any story.

> *A story is what happens when a specific group of characters are forced to overcome a series of challenging circumstances.*

By chasing our fascination, we have created a world for our story. We researched the kinds of people who live in that culture/lifestyle/group. We discovered how they live their lives. The next step in the process is to populate our story with characters. If our story is set in the world of medicine it's not enough to have a character who is a doctor and another who is a nurse. What we need is the specific nurse and the specific doctor for this story. We create a cast of characters. Characters who inhabit the world of our story. Characters who will create drama, given the right circumstances.

Earlier, we made a decision about our primary character. We did this to answer the question, who is this story about? Traditionally, the central character, the character the story is about, is the protagonist. Structural approaches to writing screenplays latch onto this idea. They force their stories to focus on the struggles of the protagonist. They demote other character's struggles to the role of sub-plots. There are writers who believe the only way you can tell a story is to do it this way. They believe in a single, central protagonist. There are other ways to write stories. I know this for a fact. The lone protagonist is only one way to approach storytelling. It's not the only way. For some stories it's right. Sometimes it isn't. Sometimes we want to tell stories about an ensemble, not just a single protagonist. Let me give you an example of a movie which demonstrates this idea:

> *When fading rock legends Spinal Tap embark on a comeback tour, they are forced to face a dwindling fanbase. It's possible they are no longer relevant or capable of being stars.*

The entire band in Spinal Tap serve as the answer to the question, who is the film about? The same is true of ensemble movies like Love Actually:

> *As Christmas approaches, eight potential couples, are forced to accept their true feelings. They must overcome the barriers life has placed between them and the people they love.*

We can write successful, mainstream movies without adopting a central protagonist. This doesn't mean those films lack structure. It means the writers used structure intelligently. Structure is a tool to aid plotting. It's not a prescriptive template. It's also not the foundation of our story. Stories are always an interplay between our characters and the plot. To create a story without the limitations of a plot-template, we have to think about stories in a different way. A story is the dramatic interaction between characters and the circumstances. Character development is central to this process. It doesn't have to be about a protagonist's journey through the plot. Our story can come from the way our cast of characters interact with each other in the world we've created for them.

A character is not a person! Even when a character is based on a real person, that character doesn't behave like real people. Characters behave like characters. It's always a mistake to think of characters as an attempt to imitate a real person. It's also a very limiting way to think about them. Instead, it helps to see each character as a dramatic mechanism. By this, I mean each character is a device to create drama and to explore the theme of the story. It doesn't matter how realistic a character is, if they don't work dramatically. It also doesn't matter how outlandish or unrealistic characters are. All that matters is they work dramatically. What matters is the drama not the realism.

At the heart of character development is an understanding of how drama works. This is the reason we looked at drama before looking at stories. Stories are formed from the drama that flows from our characters. Let's just remind ourselves about the mechanisms of dramatic writing.

> Conflict
> Exploration of human nature
> Morality
> Forcing characters to overcome problems
> Forcing characters to face their vulnerabilities
> Exploring a dramatic theme

We've looked at these ideas before as sources of drama. Now let's look at them as the mechanisms to create stories.

conflict

A character can experience conflict and they can also be the cause of it. Think about the traditional idea of a protagonist and antagonist. It's easy to see that the conflicts experienced by the hero are a direct result of the villain. Logically, the same is true the other way around. The conflict experienced by the villain comes from the hero. In simple protagonist/antagonist stories drama comes from the character's conflicting objectives. If the villain wants to steal a nuclear missile, the hero's goal is to find ways to prevent them.

> *A character's job is to prevent other characters from getting the things they need or desire.*

We know this isn't universally true because sometimes characters help each other. So,

> *A character's job may also be to help another character get the things they want or desire.*

Characters prevent or aid other characters from achieving their goals. To write drama we need to know what our characters want and desire at each point in the story. We can design our casts' needs and desires to bring them into conflict with each other.

Let's imagine our story is about three people stranded in the desert. They all appear to have the same need and desire. They all want to survive and find their way to safety. It appears, at this point, that this story's source of conflict will be from the environment. But we can change this. If they discover there is only enough water for two of them to survive this will create conflict. If our characters are honest and compassionate, our story could be about them all pulling together in a joint effort to survive. Those characters might be well observed and realistic, but how dramatic is it? However, if characters are mechanisms to create drama, we can design them to increase the conflict. Maybe one character tries to seduce the strongest person. They want a protector. Maybe the weakest character steals all of the water. He abandons the other two. There are any number of ways these three characters can create more conflict. We can design our characters flaws, to create more drama.

In most drama, characters face a mixture of environmental conflicts and those created by other characters.

Dramatic characters are driven by their needs and desires. These needs and desires prevent other characters from getting what they need.

We can design the ability to cause conflict into our characters. When we do, we create more drama and better stories.

problems

Conflict is another way of saying challenging circumstances. Sometimes the challenging circumstances come from other characters. Sometimes it is environmental. However, if a character runs into a problem and just gives up there isn't a story.

> *And the mirror on the wall replied, "Snow White is the fairest of them all." The Wicked Queen sighed and shrugged. "Well," she thought "she's half my age and she's got great bone structure, you can't argue with that." So, she made a cup of tea, slapped on some moisturiser and got an early night.*

Characters, all characters, exist within the story to solve problems. They will struggle. Some characters will fail and pay the price for failing. Some characters aren't allowed to give up, even if the audience believes they're beaten. In real life, we can float through life without having to deal with a relentless barrage of challenges. We can choose to walk away from problems. Dramatic characters don't get that luxury. Dramatic characters are forced to face challenging problems. What makes one character different from another may be as simple as the way they solve these problems. Let's imagine there has been a murder. The murder scene and the setting are identical in every scenario. Now let's give three fictional detectives the same problem.

> Detective Columbo immediately spots a problem with the evidence. He guesses the identity of the murder. He then questions the suspect until he gets the evidence he requires.

> Dirty Harry arrives at the same scene. He beats up some criminals and is soon in a violent conflict with the suspect. A suspect he'll shoot after many setbacks.

> CSI's Carl Grissom arrives at the same crime scene. He gathers

forensic evidence. Eventually, he uncovers the criminal after a lot of very clever scientific analysis.

What this exercise demonstrates is the way a story is driven by the way a character solves problems. Columbo is highly-skilled at puzzles. He gets his results by lulling the antagonist into a false sense of security. They always underestimate him. Dirty Harry is a hard man who isn't afraid to get his hands dirty. He gets his killers by being single-minded and relentless. Carl Grissom is a scientist. He solves crimes by finding the evidence other people either can't see or understand. Remember, each of these detectives arrive at the same crime scene. It is the way they solve problems that drives each story in its own unique direction.

Basically, the way a character solves problems is central to every story.

For a story to work characters have to attempt to solve the problems presented to them. The way they do this will be defined by their skills and their attitudes. To create a dramatic character, we need to understand their skills and strengths.

morality

A writer's job is to know what their character will do next. We must predict how this character will react whatever the circumstance. To write drama, we have to answer two questions about our characters. What will this character do next? What will they say next? In a film script every action and every line matter. But, some actions and some lines of dialogue matter more than others. One of the most rewarding moments in drama is when a character has to break their moral code.

> *We create a character who is both a doctor and part of a very religious community. This character believes abortion is immoral and repugnant. And then her under-age daughter is raped. The daughter begs her mother for an abortion. Our character refuses. It's not an easy decision because she loves her daughter. It's something morally she can't do. Her daughter then tries to commit suicide. She'd rather die than give birth to the baby of the man who raped her. What does our doctor character do next?*

Good drama challenges characters to reveal what they will do and what they won't do. Will the spy resist torture? Will the cop plant evidence to convict a murderer? Will the soldier run into gunfire to save a fallen man? Will the lone juror prevent the jury from reaching a verdict despite peer pressure? Will the white lawyer in a racist community defend an innocent, black man? The quality of a drama is often defined by how characters respond to these dilemmas. The most challenging circumstance for any character is the moral dilemma they most fear.

Developing a character means understanding what they believe. We need to know what they care about, what they won't do and their breaking point?

One of the highest forms of drama happens when a character is forced to face a horrific moral dilemma. Understanding what a character will do, what they won't, and their breaking point is a vital.

vulnerability

Vulnerability has two very distinct usages in English. It means the ways in which a person can be physically harmed. It also means the extent to which someone will open up emotionally. When writers discuss drama, we often talk about what's at stake for the character. There is a strong link between the stakes, what a character may lose in a situation, and their vulnerability. When you think about it, this applies to both meanings of the word. Drama loses its impact if the audience believes there is nothing at stake.

> *We create a character who has a dreadful secret. She doesn't care who knows and she's so rich it can't harm her financially.*

If a character can't be harmed by the revelation of a secret, there is nothing at stake. They aren't vulnerable and the drama vanishes. Dramatically there is nowhere to go with this scenario. That's because this threat doesn't expose any of her vulnerabilities. Let's try again.

> *We create a character who is an ambitious politician. Two days before the election she discovers a journalist plans to expose her darkest and most shameful secret.*

The stakes in this second scenario are a lot higher. A lifetime's work, her reputation, her career and her family could be destroyed. Just as she is about to seize power, she realises she has become vulnerable. It should be easy to create a story that flows from this challenging circumstance. The way she responds will define her as a character. Will she turn out to be heroic? Will she go against the advice of her team by exposing her secret to the public? Or, will she feel compelled to take drastic measures to protect her secret? In a sense, it doesn't matter because each decision is fertile ground for drama.

Characters without vulnerability destroy drama. This leads us to an aspect of a writer's life that doesn't get written about enough. A writer, inevitably, has to have some kind of take on why human beings do the things they do. We don't have to become psychologists. But writers do have to come to some kind of opinion about what makes people tick. It may appear, I am contradicting something I wrote earlier. If characters are not people, why do we need to understand the psychology of their behaviour? It is important to remember that all drama is written to be performed by actors. A written character is merely a blue-print for an actor. Writers need to understand human behaviour because it is how actors create characters. For some actors, acting is about finding ways to empathise with their character.

There is a common belief in the acting profession

Every character is the hero of their own story.

This is a useful way for writers to think about the characters we create.

Characters have to believe they are doing the right thing. This is true regardless how perverse, immoral or deranged a character behaves. What is the difference between a terrorist and a freedom-fighter? Well, freedom-fighters believe they are the good guys. The believe this even if you see them as a terrorist. When we cast an actor as a terrorist, they have two choices. They can either knock-out a one-dimensional version of a bad guy or they can do their job properly. They do that by seeing their character as the hero of their own story. The actor portraying the terrorist may need to understand why they planted the bomb. Is it an act of revenge? Are they driven by their religious beliefs? Are they motivated by their understanding of international politics? Maybe they are a vulnerable person who is being manipulated. They could even be someone who once believed in the very thing they are now attacking. A person whose world-view has changed.

All these reasons to carry out a terrorist attack answer one question. What has happened to this person which has brought them to this decision? Or, in simpler terms, why are they doing this? Actors use two ideas to encapsulate this. One of them is character motivation, the other is character backstory. Character motivation is just another way of saying, why are they doing this? A character's backstory is one of the ways an actor understands why characters behave the way they do. The backstory is the history of the character before the start of the film. The central idea here is

Characters make decisions in the present because of their past experiences. A character's past is their backstory. Actors often search for character motivation in the backstory.

A character's backstory will not be part of the story we are telling. The audience doesn't need to know that a character went to a private school. They don't need to know she was routinely humiliated and bullied. Or that she comes from a working-class family. But the writer needs to know these things. The actor needs to be able to piece together a backstory from the script. This is where it gets slightly complicated. Because the writer's backstory and the actor's backstory, for the same character, may be very different. One of the reasons I like to direct my own scripts is because I know the backstory I had in mind when I was writing.

Backstory and character motivation are important. The relationship between the writer, the script and the actor is one of the hardest aspects of screenwriting to understand. Even well-established screenwriters struggle with this.

> The writer imagines and creates a backstory for each character

> The backstory provides the internal, emotional motivation for the character's behaviour in the script

> The backstory is not part of the story!

> The actor is given the script, reads it and tries to understand what motivates the character

> The actor invents a backstory that matches their character's actions within the story

> The actor's backstory may or may not match the writer's original backstory

I know this sounds complicated, but it isn't as bad as it sounds. Both the writer and the actor need to understand what motivates a character to behave the way they do. The writer creates a backstory for the character. That backstory allows the writer to predict what a character will do or say in any situation. The actor also needs to understand what motivates their character. The actor's process is a mixture of detection and invention. Actors hunt for clues in the script. They need to understand who their character is and what motivates them. The actor then creates their own backstory to fill in anything they can't get from the text. This complexity happens because the writer is rarely part of the production. The only communication between the writer and the actor happens on the page.

Writing drama is writing for actors. Good screenwriters develop techniques to reveal their character's vulnerabilities and inner-life. We'll look at those techniques in greater depth later in the book. Our job is to reveal the inner life, motivation and backstory of a character through subtext and the things they do. It's not that complicated to understand, but it's difficult to master.

Good character development creates good stories. This is only true if we create a cast of characters with high-levels of dramatic potential. If we don't create characters with dramatic potential, we can't write great stories.

We create characters with high-levels of dramatic potential by seeing them as dramatic mechanisms. They are not real people. The goal of character development isn't to chase realism. It is to create characters whose behaviour will create drama and good stories. But, how do we do that?

High-levels of dramatic potential come from characters who have the following attributes:

> Their needs and desires prevent other characters from achieving their goals

> They have an interesting skill set and can solve problems

> They have personal vulnerabilities which can be challenged and exposed

> They have a core-morality that can be tested to breaking point

> Their motivation to act is driven by their inner-life and beliefs

> Their present-day actions are driven by their backstory

We can simplify this. To create characters a writer needs to know:

> What the character needs and desires

> The character's skills and strengths

> The character's weaknesses and fears

> The character's moral code and its limitations

The character's motivation (why they do what they do)

The character's backstory (how their past drives them to act in the present)

create a cast not a character

I like to write for actors. I tend to write scripts where the story is created from the conflicting motivations and needs of the cast. I see characters as dramatic mechanisms. I design characters so conflict is inevitable. You can't do this if you create characters in isolation. We need to create a dynamic cast of characters.

Structural approaches to screenwriting create a plot of challenging circumstances for their protagonist. One of the side-effects of this approach is the mechanical use of minor characters.

To a structural writer it doesn't matter why the character Terrorist 2 is trying to blow up the bridge. It only matters the protagonist has to try and stop them.

The end result of that kind of thinking are films that are emotionless and sterile. They are more like watching someone else play a video game. They are films where every character, except the protagonist, is both disposable and empty. Decades of structural screenwriting makes these kinds of movies far too common.

Process-driven screenwriting creates drama from the dramatic potential of the entire cast. Our character's motivations, needs, desires, fear and vulnerabilities collide. Process-driven screenplays can be as complex as we want. We create stories that explore human strength and frailty. These roles tend to be more attractive to actors. Process-driven scripts find drama in the complex interactions of the characters.

If we create characters with high-levels of dramatic potential we will find our story in that potential. Stories based on the conflicting objectives, needs, fears and vulnerabilities of our cast. The cast is itself a story machine. The dramatic collisions of the characters we have created is inevitable. We don't need to create a plot. We can look at the dramatic potential of our cast and decide which of the stories on offer will make it to the page.

CHAPTER 11
Planning Phase. Plot

Once we have a cast of characters and a world for them to play in, we find stories naturally emerge from the work we have done.

At this point, we are ready to play with our plot.

characters, the story and the plot

We took our raw idea and figured out what dramatic theme we wanted to explore. We then dove deeper into the idea and decided who it was about, where and when the story will be set. Then, we researched the fictional world. We decided where it is set and learned enough about it to get a feel for how it works as a culture. In the last step, we populated that world with a cast of characters. Characters we designed to give us high-levels of dramatic potential. We now know enough about those characters to be able to predict how they will act in any circumstance. If we've done the job well, we should also understand their motivation. We are now ready to think about the journey this story will take.

This is when we make a conscious choice of how we want to structure our plot. Process-driven screenwriting doesn't forbid structural templates. Instead, it puts structure into perspective. There are a few different structural models out there and each of them have their uses. We'll look at these in more detail in the chapter on structure.

> *Structural screenwriters build stories from plots. Process-driven screenwriters build plots from the forces that drive stories.*

When a process-driven screenwriter is ready to create a plot, a great deal of the work has already been done. We've already taken hundreds of creative decisions. At this stage in the process, the plotting can be as tight or as loose as the writer needs it to be. A writer can either create a tight, traditional plot or skip this step completely. We can choose to work out the story on the page.

This will sound insane to any writer used to structural approaches. This is because structural screenwriters rely on the plot to act as the foundation of their story. They use an established plot shape as the base from which they explore character and theme. Process-driven screenwriters use character and theme as the foundation for their stories. This means they can be more flexible and experimental.

Most fiction writers experience moments when their characters take over the story. To an early-career writer this might sound weird. But it's true. When we are writing, our characters sometimes surprise us. They don't do the thing we planned for them. A great deal of the creative process is subconscious. When writers tap into that it feels like the story exists outside of our mind.

Ultimately, a writer has to figure out a way of plotting their script that best suits them. Here are a couple of ways a writer might approach plotting from a process-driven point of view.

> On the page - No formal plot. Instead the writer trusts their innate ability to tell a story

> Structural - The writer creates a traditional, structured plot

> Sequential - The writer breaks the story down into sequences. They plan each sequence without a formal structure

> Experimental - The writer focuses on aspects of cinema that challenge conventional narrative

on-the-page plotting

Process-driven screenwriting provides a ridiculous amount of security for the writer. The writing of the script becomes easy. We can concentrate all our efforts on getting the most from each dramatic moment. This is because of all the creative decisions we took in the previous phases.

Process-driven screenwriters are capable of writing very solid first drafts. The kind of first drafts structural screenwriters can only achieve after three or four rewrites. That kind of safety is a curse as well as a blessing. It is possible to end up with a script that works flawlessly, but it may not be the best thing we'll ever write.

To write something astounding most writers need a degree of uncertainty. One way to get that uncertainty is to plot on-the-page. When we write like this, each scene has a natural relationship with everything that's happened before. The downside is, if we start a script without a clear idea of how it's going to end, there is a very real possibility that our story could become a rambling mess. At this point, structural screenwriters will point at us and laugh. Despite this, there is a lot to be said for writing a first draft where we plot as we write. We can think of this as an exploratory or vomit draft. We use it to throw up unexpected moments and ideas. By writing actual scenes, we get to play with the characters. We explore the fictional world. Then, we go back and write a more plotted second draft.

structural plotting

If we need to get a script written to a deadline, structural plotting is the way to go. Especially when the producer needs something that will tick all their boxes.

A process-driven screenwriter, with a structural plot, can churn out a good, fast, first draft. This is how I work on gun-for-hire scripts. Projects where someone is paying me to fix/write their idea. If we are disciplined, it is possible to turn around a script from idea to first draft in about twenty-days. That's five days of prep and fifteen days writing the script.

There are a few different structural approaches we can use.

> Three Act
> Four Act
> Hero's Journey/Story Circle
> Save The Cat
> Fabula/Syuzhet
> and many, many other variations

There's a lot of crossover between these different ways of structuring a story. We'll look at them in depth in the chapter on structure. For the moment, all we need to know is that most structural approaches do two things. They break the plot down into smaller parts. They also make claims about what each of those parts is supposed to achieve. All I want to do in this section is to introduce us to the ways a plot can be broken down into smaller parts. We can look at the mechanics of structure later.

There are at least four different ways to break a story down into smaller parts.

> Acts. An Act is a large unit of drama, which can have its own beginning, middle and end
>
> Sequences. A sequence is a lump of story that covers a dramatic event over multiple scenes
>
> Beats. A beat is a dramatic event

Plot points. A plot-point is a key moment in a plot, according to some structural theories

Scene. A scene is the action that happens in one location, at one time

scenes

The eventual goal of a screenwriter is to turn their story into scenes. A scene answers the question what happens in the story at this location, at this time.

When it comes time to write the script, a screenwriter's job is to tell their story by writing a series of scenes. Scenes are so central to the craft of screenwriting the next chapter is dedicated to them. It's important to understand what a scene is and how to write one.

story beats

These are the most intuitive way of understanding a story. Imagine you ask a child to tell you what happened in their favourite film. What they might tell you is

> *There's this princess. She lives in this castle but she's sad because she wants to go to the dance. Her best friend steals a magic wand so they can go to the dance. Then they try to make a ladder so they can escape the castle. But they don't know how the wand works and they keep making pigs. Soon the castle is full of pigs. Then her father comes home and he's really cross… etc. etc.*

When you think about it, this is a list of the events that happen in the story. Story beats are exactly the same thing, but organised into a list.

plot points

Most structural approaches to screenwriting suggest stories have a universal form. That stories must have certain key moments in them. Talking about plot points is part of the language of screenwriting, so we need to know about them.

The most common plot points are: ordinary world, inciting incident, call to action, first act break, mid-point, second act break and denouement. We'll look at this more in the chapter on structure.

sequences

A story sequence is a piece of dramatic action, usually played out over several scenes. At first glance, sequences might look the same as beats or plot-points. They're not the same. Sequences don't always conform to plot-points. A sequence often has several story beats in it.

> *Our central character breaks into the company vault to steal the plans to the nuclear weapon. This part of the story might start in her van. Then it moves to the compound fence. She goes past the security team guarding the doors. Then into the building. This leads her to the vault itself.*

Immediately after this, the story moves onto a new part. Perhaps a sequence about the character whose job it is to recover the stolen plans. To write this sequence, we'd have to write anywhere between six and ten scenes. It also has more than one story beat. However, we can easily understand how all those parts are one lump of the story. Sequences are really important to screenwriters. It's the easiest way to think about a plot, if we aren't working to a specific structural approach.

act

Stories are broken down into several acts. The most common versions of this in screenwriting are Three Act and Four Act. An act is a large section of story that works as a unit. This will make a lot more sense when we get to the chapter on structure. There is a very strong link between the idea of acts in screenplay structure and plot points.

sequential plotting

Sequential plotting is the middle ground between plotting on the page and structural plotting. This approach works best for writers who want to tell their story intuitively. Our story must be expressed as a list of *this happens, then this happens*, and *then this happens*. Sequential plotting happens when a writer creates a list of what happens in each sequence. This list of events becomes the plot.

Sequential plotting allows us to decide on the shape of the story before we start writing. We can do this without having to conform to a structural theory of storytelling. Sequential plotting is the best way for screenwriters to write experimental films. Experimental doesn't mean chaotic. Sequential plotting allows us to plan our story. We decide the audience's journey from start to finish. But because it's not structural, it also gives us freedom to step away from conventional thinking. We decide the order in which each part of the story is revealed to the audience. This gives writers a lot of creative freedom. It also provides the safety net of having a plan, regardless of how unconventional the plan may be.

There is an old method of plotting, favoured by a lot of Hollywood writers, called the file card method. Writers would make a list of their plot-points, beats or sequences and put each one on a file card. They would then pin them to a cork board. They would use this opportunity to see their story in sequences. They could arrange the cards in one order and then make decisions about their story. They could reorder their sequences easily. It became easy to decide whether the story worked better, if told in a different order. It was also easy to pull out sequences and replace them with new ideas. This is a technique developed by structural screenwriters. But, this way of thinking about a plot, as sequences that can be reordered or even replaced is really useful to experimental screenwriters. If used as a tool for sequential plotting, it becomes a powerful way to experiment.

experimental plotting

Not all films are driven by their narrative. It's a mistake to see a story or a film as one narrative point after another. Cinema is capable of very much more than that.

Most of what screenwriter's learn about writing comes from other, older art forms. The fact that films are drama means screenwriting borrows a lot from theatrical traditions. The idea of dramatic stories having acts originates in Roman Theatre. Roman performances had breaks every half-hour, so the audience could stretch their legs. Despite sharing a lot with theatre, cinema is a completely different art form. There are some aspects to writing cinematic which are unique to cinema.

The education of most screenwriters tends to focus on traditional views of screenwriting. What tends to be lacking is any sense of what cinema is as an art form. This isn't helped by the power directors have over film production. Writer's in the film industry are taught to concentrate on story and drama. We are expected to leave the creative vision of the film to the director. Directors are taught to immerse themselves in the history and language of cinema. There is an obvious problem with this split in creative expression. It stifles the development of cinema as an art form. The most interesting and innovative film directors tend to be writer/directors. This isn't accidental. Writer/directors approach cinema without separating drama and cinema. It is this way of thinking about a film which leads to experimental plotting.

The real challenge for the next generation will be to bridge the gap between storytelling and cinematic art. I can't tell you how that will happen because it will need to be experimental. I do know this. Narrative is more flexible than we imagine. Cinema is capable of achieving more than we currently believe possible.

what is a story?

We started these chapters on the phases of the process with a question. What is a story? I suggested structural definitions of a story as a universal list of plot-points isn't that useful. Instead, we explored the possibility that stories arise out of process.

The process-driven approach starts with a raw idea. That idea is then played with as the writer looks for a theme. The theme being an exploration of the personal and emotional cost of a universal human experience. From that theme, the writer then plays with questions about with the who, where and when of the story. Playing with multiple answers to these questions lead us to write a compass logline. We now know what our story is about. The next part of the process is an exploration of the fictional world or culture the story will take place in. We chase our fascination to discover a world worth showing to our audience. Once we are comfortable in the fictional world, we create a cast of characters with high-levels of dramatic potential. We design characters with complex needs. We create their skills, vulnerabilities, a core morality and a backstory. We understand their motivation. At this point, stories emerge from the work the writer has already done. The writer then decides how they want to plot their story. We do this secure in the developmental work we have already done.

We have a raw idea

We play with that idea and search for themes which explore the cost of a universal experience

We play with answers to the questions who, where and when the story takes place

We combine the theme and answers to our concept questions to write a compass logline

We chase our fascination and research the culture of the ordinary world

We create a cast of characters with high-levels of dramatic potential

We decide what plotting approach to take: on the page, structural, sequential or experimental

This is how we use a process to create a story. It gives writers more freedom and more control than any other approach. Although it may sound prescriptive, it isn't. Writers can find their own way to achieve each part of the process. They can even rearrange the order in which they take on the tasks.

In later chapters, we'll look in more detail at each part of the process. We'll also look at different techniques to approach the steps. But, before we can dig further into the process, we need to understand what a scene is.

CHAPTER 12
The Scene

Our script is a blueprint for the production team. It is a dramatic text for the actors. It is a piece of literature. A script is also a series of scenes. To write a scene, we need to meet the needs of the crew, the actors and the reader. So, let's start by looking at what the production team needs from writers.

writing a scene for the production team

In the film industry, we write scenes because the scene is a unit of production. When we write scripts in scenes, it is for the benefit of the production team. So, what is a scene?

A scene is all the action which takes place in one location, at one time.

Let's imagine a story where a man and a woman need to meet up. They don't know each other, so it needs to be somewhere public. They decide to meet in a coffee shop. This coffee shop becomes a place they meet on several occasions. These meetings happen at different points in the story.

Everything that happens during that first meeting, in this coffee shop, is a scene. The scene heading would look like this.

```
INT. COFFEE MANIA. THE MALL. DAY
```

Our story progresses. They each face a series of challenging circumstances at other locations. Then they meet up for a second time.

Everything that happens in that second meeting, at the same coffee shop, is a scene. The scene heading will be identical to last time, even though this is a different scene.

```
INT. COFFEE MANIA. THE MALL. DAY
```

Despite the fact that these scenes take place at the same location, they are different scenes. That is because they happen at different points in the script. Despite this, they have exactly the same scene heading. This is because the production team will shoot all the scenes at any given location at the same time. Films are shot out of order. All the scenes in one location are filmed on the same day/days.

The most basic fact we need to understand about film production is this. A lot of people have to travel to the same location, at the same time, to shoot a scene. This means production is always controlled by where and when the action takes place. This is why scripts MUST be written in scenes. It also means a scene MUST be restricted to the action in one location.

> *One scene = one location.*

There are exceptions to the one scene/one location rule. Sometimes it's necessary to intercut between multiple locations. We do this to follow simultaneous actions taking place in different locations. In the chapter on formatting, I'll explain how to do this. For the moment, just accept the basic fact that one scene = the action in one location, at one moment in time.

The most basic job in screenwriting is to break the story down into scenes. We need to do this in such a way that makes sense to the production team. They also need us to be consistent in the way we name locations. Computer programmes analyse the script and identify how many locations there are. The programme also works out how many scenes happen at that location. It is easy to mess this up:

```
INT. HARMON'S BAR. NIGHT
INT. THE BAR. NIGHT
INT. HARMON'S JOINT. NIGHT
INT. HARMON'S. NIGHT
INT. THE PUB. NIGHT
INT. HARMON'S PUB. NIGHT
```

If we read a list of scene headings like the one above, we can guess they are all set in the same location. We know this because we recognise that a pub, a bar and a joint are the same things. But, to the computer programme these are all different places. And, even a human reader can't assume they are all filmed at the same location without checking with the writer. This isn't acceptable.

If we write a script with scene headings that are inconsistent, the line producer will phone us up. They are not going to be happy! They will force us to check that all these scenes, with different scene headings, are the same place. The more of this they have to do, the less they will like us as human beings. It's unprofessional to do this. And it is easily avoided.

Another way to annoy the production team is to write action into a scene that can't be filmed at the location!

> *Our scene opens with Sally in the kitchen. She sees Brad outside in the garden. She goes out to meet him, but he's gone. She runs to the garden gate*

and looks down the street. She sees Brad walking to the shops. She follows him. Brad goes into "Dandy's Transvestite Clothing Store." Sally can't see through the window, so she goes in and finds Brad trying on a corset.

In the mind of the writer, this may feel like one dramatic moment. It may feel like it's all one scene. There is a coherent thread of action. However, for the production team, this action takes place in several locations.

Our scene opens with Sally in the kitchen (interior - location 1). *She sees Brad outside in the garden* (exterior - location 2). *She goes out to meet him, but he's gone. She runs to the garden gate and looks down the street* (exterior - location 3). *She sees Brad walking to the shops. She follows him. Brad goes into Dandy's Transvestite Clothing Store* (exterior - location 4). *Sally can't see through the window, so she goes in* (interior - location 5) *and finds Brad trying on a corset.*

This simple dramatic sequence takes place in five different locations. The production team needs it written as five different scenes. But why five? It may feel like there are only three locations: Sally's house, the Street, and Dandy's Transvestite Store. To understand, we need to know another fact about film production. The exterior of a building and the interior may not be filmed in the same geographical locations. Imagine the location manager has found a house and garden in the real world. This is where they will film the exteriors of Sally's house and garden. However, they have decided to build the interiors in a studio two-hundred miles away. This means the interior shots and the exterior shots of the same sequence won't happen on the same day.

If this all sounds complicated, here's an easy way to understand the rules.

You write a scene heading to tell the production team where to put the camera and lights. If the camera and lights need to be moved to a different place, we create a new scene heading. This includes moving them from outside to inside or vice-versa.

Let's rework the Sally and Brad sequence so you can see how it works.

```
INT. SALLY'S KITCHEN. DAY.

Sally sees Brad outside in the garden.


EXT. GARDEN. DAY

Sally goes out to meet him, but he's gone. She runs to the
garden gate and looks down the street. She sees Brad walking
to the shops.


EXT. STREET DAY

She follows him.


EXT. TRANNY STORE. DAY

Brad goes into Dandy's Transvestite Clothing Store. Sally
can't see through the window.


INT. TRANNY STORE. DAY

Sally goes in and finds Brad trying on a corset
```

In the chapter on formatting we'll learn how to format a scene for the production team. At the moment, it's enough for us to understand that scene is something specific. It is a unit of production. It's vitally important for us to break the action into scenes. Those scenes need to conform to the production team's needs.

what is a scene, dramatically?

Although a scene is a unit of production, it is also a moment of drama. Writing to meet the needs of the production team is the easy part. The hard part of screenwriting is creating effective, cinematic drama. The real work of writing a film script only happens when we start writing scenes.

A scene is a moment of cinematic drama that occurs in one location

Understanding how to write cinematic drama is the life's work of a screenwriter. There aren't any easy answers to this. So, in this section, I want to try to give you some ideas to think about.

We need to understand why we're creating cinematic drama. Why aren't we just writing cinema? To understand this, we need to think about how cinema works.

It is possible to shoot footage of the most incredible sunset. We can shoot it in the most beautiful location on Earth. That moment of film will be deeply cinematic. Cinema is an art form which has similar aesthetic tools to any visual art. It is about colour, composition, subject and use of light. We can create visual moments that are breathtakingly beautiful. If we add the right soundtrack to this eye-candy, we may create something that is deeply cinematic. It works on a sensory level. However, that doesn't make the moment dramatic. To be dramatic that visual and auditory feast needs to mean something. It needs to work within the context of the story.

> *The sun sets over the Croatian coastline. The colour of the sky and the sea merges so it looks like a line of tiny islands are disappearing into the heavens.*

That is a cinematic moment.

> *Henrietta lies in her bed, her face ravaged by time. Her breathing is laboured. She stops her nurse from drawing the curtains. She begs her to open the doors to the balcony, so she can see out across the bay one last time. The sun sets over the Croatian coastline. The colour of the sky and the sea merge, so it looks like a line of tiny islands are disappearing into the heavens.*

This is that same moment given a dramatic context. It's not just a beautiful visual moment. It is both the last thing our character sees and a visual metaphor for her death. If a screenwriter's job is to do anything, it is to create cinematic moments that have dramatic context. In other words, cinematic drama. This brings us to the central problem of screenwriting. How do we write scenes that are both dramatic and cinematic?

I want to be clear about this. It is not the writer's job to direct the film. It is the writer's job to write drama that makes use of all the cinematic opportunities. These are two very different ideas.

directing on the page

A lot of first-time screenwriters imagine a film script is a description of all the shots needed to make the film.

> Close-up of a telephone. It rings. A woman's hand reaches over and picks it up.
> Mid-Shot of Elaine as she answers the phone. "This better be important!"
> Close-up of an alarm clock that reads 4.32 am.

I can understand why someone might want to write like that. They have a visualisation of the movie they want to see. So, they write down the instructions of what to shoot. Even though it's understandable, it's not how we write film scripts. Writers never give shot instructions. To achieve the same effect a screenwriter might write something like this.

```
INT. KASBAH HOTEL. CAIRO. NIGHT

Elaine is asleep. Her alarm clock reads 4.32 am, but even at
this hour, we can hear the distant hum of Cairo's nightlife.

SFX: PHONE RINGS

Elaine fumbles for the phone, still half asleep.

                        ELAINE
            This better be important!
```

This scene implies the same thing as the one where we directed on the page. Doing it like this gives the director creative freedom to decide their own shots.

What's important is that writers need to tell stories using visual storytelling techniques. We don't ignore the cinematic elements of screenwriting. We have to develop ways to write cinematically, which also give the director space to do their thing. A good writer inspires the director. A bad screenwriter tries to impose their vision on the production team.

understanding the dramatic potential of cast, locations and props

It is possible to write a scene where the only thing we concentrate on is what the actors do and what they say. In theatre, it is not unusual to perform plays without scenery or costumes. The actors all wear simple, black clothing and the stage is a black box. The idea is to draw drama from the characters. It is all about what the actors do and what they say.

Screenwriters are often told to concentrate on what the actors do and say. However, cinema rarely takes place in a simple black box. Any cinematic scene is a combination of many factors.

The physical opportunities and threats presented by the location

The dramatic opportunities and threats presented by the characters present

Any objects (props) in the location the characters can interact with

The meaning of the objects. (props, costume, architecture, vehicles)

The meaning of actions

The meaning of what is said

Cinematic drama is created from the dramatic potential of each of these elements. So, it's important to understand how each of these elements works. This may seem like a lot to think about, but it can be simplified down to the idea

> *Our job is to create drama and meaning using the location, props and the cast available in any scene*

In the chapter on drama, we pinned down six forces that drive drama. They were, conflict, human nature, morality, overcoming problems, facing vulnerability, and theme. This last one, exploration of dramatic theme is really important.

> *Our story is an exploration of the personal and emotional cost of sexual obsession*

The touchstone for writing any scene is the theme. In this case, the personal and emotional cost of sexual obsession? But this isn't the only information we have. We also have our compass logline.

> *When the world's most successful female adult film producer decides to go into the reality TV business, her trademark mixture of voyeurism, sex and violence set in the seedy world of Eastern European sex tourism soon builds an audience. However, under pressure from her ruthless business partner to create an immediate global sensation, she decides to gaslight one of her central characters into committing suicide, live on-air.*

We have researched the world of our story and created a cast of characters. These characters have a lot of dramatic potential. To write our first scene, we have to decide where the story starts. We assume our readers and audience know nothing about this world. They don't understand the people in it, or the story that's about to unfold. For that reason, our opening scene is doing a lot of different things. It introduces our fictional world. It starts to introduce our cast. And, it sets the story in motion. Despite this, everything we do relates to our theme and is driven by our compass logline.

```
EXT. SKYBAR. BUDAPEST: JUST BEFORE DAWN

The view from the roof terrace bar is spectacular. The first
tinge of blue breaks the night across the skyline of
Budapest. Below, the streets are empty.

SFX: BAM! A SINGLE SHOT RINGS OUT.

Pigeons rise, they appear on the skyline, silhouetted
against the first rays of sunlight.

ON THE BAR'S ROOF TERRACE:

Behind a glass wall, sprayed red with blood, a room full of
PARTY GUESTS. Overpriced Milan fashion draped over Eastern
Europe's beautiful people. They stand open-mouthed, like
statues. In the background, the BARTENDER whispers
frantically into the telephone.

CASSIUS (38) A gunshot thug in a blood-drenched Armani suit.
He slides down the glass wall and collapses.
```

This is the opening scene of a script I wrote ten years ago. A script created from the theme and compass logline above. Let's look at the dramatic mechanisms involved.

```
EXT. SKYBAR. BUDAPEST:  DAWN

The view from the roof terrace bar is
spectacular. The first tinge of blue breaks
the night across the skyline of Budapest.
Below, the streets are empty.
```

Like every scene, we start with a scene heading. This gives us our location, the Sky Bar in Budapest. It also tells us whether it is night or day. In this case, the timing is precise. It's dawn. As we write the first line of action, we put the reader/audience into a specific location. They are looking down over the city of Budapest, as the sun is rising, from the deck of a roof terrace. There is a lot going on with this selection of time and place. Budapest is one of Eastern Europe's destination cities for sex tourism. Given our theme and logline, it's a natural setting for this story. And yet, our first view of the city isn't at night with our characters prowling sex clubs. We see the city from a bar's roof terrace as the sun is coming up. This is both the start of a new day and, possibly, the tail-end of a wild night. What this moment holds, more than anything else, is the kind of stillness you only find as the sun is coming up. It's that moment just before the bakers, street-cleaners and shop-owners start to wake up the city. And then…

```
SFX: BAM! A SINGLE SHOT RINGS OUT.
```

```
Pigeons rise, they appear on the skyline,
silhouetted against the first rays of
sunlight.
```

The pure stillness we've created is destroyed by the sound of a single gunshot. At any other time of day, this sound would be lost in the noise of the city. It's an intrusive, violent and unexpected sound for this time of the day. The reader is only ten seconds into the script. They already have their first sense of this fictional world. The reader knows they have been presented with a significant moment. Something has happened. A gunshot. The reader doesn't know why it's happened. They just know it's important to the story.

```
ON THE BAR'S ROOF TERRACE:

Behind a glass wall, sprayed red with blood, a
room full of PARTY GUESTS. Overpriced Milan
fashion draped over Eastern Europe's beautiful
people. They stand open-mouthed, like statues.
In the background, the BARTENDER whispers
frantically into the telephone.
```

This isn't a new scene. We're still in the same location. When we see ON THE BAR'S ROOF TERRACE: in a script, it tells us where within a complex location the action is happening. These are called sub-slugs.

When we research the fictional world, we study the culture in which our story takes place. We understand a culture is the way a group of people interact with their environment. This paragraph of action introduces us to the ordinary people of this fictional world. In Budapest, the average wage is two-thirds less than wages in the rest of Europe. The people in this scene are the ones who can afford to buy designer clothes and to party all night in an exclusive bar. Despite their obvious privilege, their night has turned ugly. They have just witnessed a murder. The sound of the gun-shot disrupts the stillness of the morning. The spray of blood up the glass wall destroys the illusion of sophistication. We see the first consequence of this first dramatic moment. The bartender is on the phone. People are being told. Maybe it's the police, maybe it's someone else even more dangerous?

```
CASSIUS (38) A gunshot thug in a blood-
drenched Armani suit. He slides down the glass
wall and collapses.
```

The gunshot forces us to wonder who was shot and why? The spray of blood up the glass wall of the bar tells us the murder is happening right here, right now. This is how we introduce to our first character, Cassius. We now have an answer to the question, who was shot?

There's a lot of information embedded in this one cinematic moment. The audience is getting a sense of our fictional world. The party goers are rich and beautiful. The dead man isn't beautiful. He is thuggish. Yet, he is dressed in clothes just as expensive as everyone else. Is he an intruder into this world? Or is this world considerably darker than it appears. Perhaps this isn't a world of the idle-rich, fashion, parties and beautiful people. Maybe it's a world of murder and crime. If we remember our theme, an exploration of the personal and emotional cost of sexual obsession, this moment fits. The idea of the idle rich as debauched and depraved isn't a new one. Their culture would be a fertile arena for that theme. This death immediately establishes the high-stakes nature of the emotional and personal costs. This is a world in which people get murdered.

We are one scene, fourteen lines and less than twenty-seconds into our story. We have established the city our story starts in, Budapest. We have established the culture/ordinary world, rich and beautiful party animals. And, we have given the audience their first hint this world is darker than it appears. Very little of this storytelling has come from traditional sources of drama. Instead, we are creating a trail of ideas for the audience to follow. A great deal of the work is being done by the assumptions the audience make based on the visual clues we give them. Let me give you an example.

```
A room full of PARTY GUESTS, wall-to-wall
overpriced Milan fashion, draped over Eastern
Europe's beautiful people.
```

As screenwriters, we have to describe the world the story takes place in. We do this so the production team can recreate the world we've imagined. At the same time, every description should also communicate something significant to the audience.

Screenwriting relies on the fact that people make assumptions based on appearance. We all do this. If we see a muscular man covered in Nazi tattoos, we make judgements about him. We do the same with everyone we meet. In the real world, we communicate things about ourselves by the way we dress, the places we go and the things we do. It is like a shared code that allows us to function as a society. It's not perfect, because our beliefs about other people depend on our values. When I see the tattooed Nazi, my value system tells me to avoid him. Another person, with different values, will see the same person as a potential friend (Yucky but true). Screenwriters have to assume we share a common understanding with our audience. Every description we make of a place, person or thing is more than just an instruction about what to shoot. It is an opportunity to communicate with the audience.

As we write we ask ourselves several questions. What will this specific location mean to the audience? What will they think about these specific people? What does this specific car or these clothes tell the audience about this character? One of the biggest mistakes a screenwriter can make is to focus on the drama of what people say and do, at the expense of communicating concrete ideas. The most common way to do this is by using generic locations

```
BAD = INT. WAREHOUSE. NIGHT
```

Locations like this don't communicate anything to either the reader or audience. A generic location raises more questions than it answers. Is this a clean, new warehouse? Or is it an abandoned wreck? Is it the kind of warehouse you find at a harbour? Or, is it on an anonymous industrial estate?

```
GOOD = INT. WAREHOUSE 49. EAST RIVER, NEW
YORK. NIGHT
```

Good locations are specific and communicate something about the story. The same is true for everything else we write. Every choice matters because every choice gives the audience information.

writing drama

Traditionally, screenwriters start with a list of plot-points. They crack open the first page of their script and read the first plot-point, Elaine is murdered. They then write a scene or several scenes to cover this piece of action. The biggest weakness of structural screenwriting is it encourages plot-driven stories. There isn't any focus on writing drama. Just because we've written a scene that nails our plot-point, it doesn't mean we've created drama. This is because drama comes from conflict, the exploration of human nature, overcoming problems, vulnerability, moral dilemmas and theme. A scene that doesn't contain at least some of those elements isn't going to work as drama.

Let me show you a scene that hits our plot-point but doesn't work as a scene.

```
INT. HOTEL. NIGHT
Elaine is asleep in her bed. Rodger enters the
room. He shoots her and leaves.
```

It would take all day to list the ways this scene fails. It isn't drama. It doesn't convey any meaning via the set and setting of the action. We don't know who Elaine is, who Rodger is, or why it matters that she is killed? When I read a scene like this, it tells me the writer doesn't have anything to say about the world of their story. They don't understand their characters. This isn't good enough. The actors playing Elaine and Rodger need to know their character's motivations. The audience also need to know more about the scene. They need to know what any action means and why it matters?

We have to understand our scene on many levels. We have to understand why each character is doing what they are doing. At the same time, we also have to be aware of what the scene reveals to the audience. In practice, this means each moment of a script is driven by four questions:

> What will this character do in these circumstances?
> Why are they doing this?
> What does this moment mean to the audience?
> Why does it matter to the audience?

To fix this scene, we to answer these four questions. If I asked you to do that right now, do you think this would be easy or difficult? I get writer's block just trying to answer the questions for this scene. There's a reason for that. That's because we haven't done any preparation for this scene. We don't have the answers prepared. Right now, I don't have the first clue who Rodger or Elaine are, what the story is about, or why this matters? Without the process, writing this plot-point is like pulling a story from the void. There's nothing to build drama from! Despite this, I will give it a go. If only as an exercise in messy writing. This means, I will try to create characters, motivation and meaning as I write… here goes!

```
INT. KASBAH HOTEL. CAIRO. 1973. NIGHT

The hotel room is a mess. Every surface is littered with
empty bottles of booze, women's clothes, books and
magazines. Only one area is organised. Facing the window is
an old table. On it, a battered travel-typewriter,
surrounded by neatly arranged folders. There are stacks of
photographs weighed down with tourist trinkets and a neatly
stacked manuscript. It is weighed down by a Nikon camera.

Elaine is on the bed, fully dressed. She is face down. More
passed out than asleep. There is a full ashtray on the bed
next to her, a cigarette still burning down, balanced on the
edge.

On the desk, the papers rustle slightly as they are caught
by a breeze.

SFX: NOISE FROM THE KASBAH INCREASES

The window to her room slowly opens. Elaine stirs a little.
Her hand knocks the burning cigarette from the ashtray onto
the bedsheets. It starts to smoulder.
```

```
The cigarette falls onto the bed and starts a small fire,
the smoke irritates Elaine. She regains consciousness with a
start. She slams her hand down onto the fire to beat it out.

Rodger quickly pulls a gun from his pocket and tries to
screw in the silencer!

Elaine turns around. She searches for something to
extinguish the smouldering embers on her bed. She reaches
for a glass of water. As she reaches for the glass, she sees
Rodger, the gun in his hand.

Rodger rapidly screws in the silencer. He points the gun at
Elaine. But, before he can shoot, she grabs the glass and
hurls it at his face.

SFX: BLAM!

Rodger's first shot goes wide and destroys a lamp. Dazed,
with blood running down his face, he takes aim again. Elaine
hurls herself at him. He shoots and she collapses at his
feet.
```

Like most messy writing, this scene is over-written. Despite that, this attempt works better than the previous version. It is better because my intention wasn't just to hit my plot-point. Instead, I tried to create drama from the characters and location. I also wanted the audience to learn something significant about Rodger and Elaine. And, at the same time, present them with unanswered questions. Questions to be resolved later in the story.

What do we learn about Elaine in this version of the scene? Well, it looks like she's some kind of photojournalist or writer. This appears to be the only organised part of a chaotic life. The area where she writes is organised. The rest of the room is chaotic. We also learn she is a drunk. Her life seems self-destructive. There are empty bottles everywhere. The lit cigarette on the bed tells us a lot about her. When Rodger turns up to kill her, he comes across as highly-skilled and professional. He gets into the room silently. He easily deals with a problem caused by Elaine's chaos. It's only by accident that he is discovered. The scene implies Elaine is working on an important story. Why else send a professional killer? The manuscript on the table may be the reason she's murdered. It doesn't matter if this it's true or not. It is the meaning the audience draws from the scene which matters.

This scene puts Elaine into conflict with Rodger, her alcoholism and a lit cigarette. There is a good chance Elaine would have died in the fire, regardless of whether Rodger showed up or not.

Rodger is in conflict with Elaine, the chaos in Elaine's room and fate. He's is genuinely unlucky. It's not his fault Elaine is drunk and has a lit cigarette on the bed. He is discovered, not because of a flaw in his professionalism. Elaine just turns around at the wrong moment. We also get a window into Rodger's morality.

Does this scene use the key sources of drama?

> Exploration of human nature - **Yes**. Elaine's battle between order and alcoholism is implied
> Overcoming problems - **Yes.** She overcomes the fire. Rodger overcomes the environment and her.
> Vulnerability - **Yes,** Elaine's vulnerability is exposed
> Moral dilemmas - **No,** but Rodger's morality is exposed, which might set-up a future dilemma
> Theme - **No**, because I have no idea what the theme is for this scene

This scene is an improvement on the sterile nothing of the first version. But, it's still not a great scene. Rodger, in this scene, is a one-dimensional cliché of an assassin. He is nowhere near being a fully formed character. He is a plot-lever. A plot-lever is a robotic, disposable character, who turns up in a scene to make sure the plot-point happens. In a lot of scripts, Rodger would be KILLER 1, or something else equally generic.

There is another problem with this scene. An alcoholic journalist being murdered for uncovering shocking story is a cliché. It's been flogged to death in cinema and TV. There are hundreds of films where a journalist is murdered for uncovering a shocking story? It is normally the moment that incites an action hero to go after the bad guys. And, journalists are almost always drunks in the world of film and TV.

Although this scene uses the right tools to create drama, it's not good drama because it's a collection of clichés. And, it's a collection of clichés because I wrote it without doing the necessary development work. Most writers, if forced to pull drama from thin air will reach for their first idea, and that idea will be a cliché. And this is where most structural screenwriters fail. Creating characters and drama from plot-points is like lifting an elephant with candy-floss.

How can we find conflict in the environment if we haven't researched the fictional world? How can a writer expose a character's vulnerability if the character is a cliché? How can a writer create heart-breaking moral dilemmas, if they don't understand their character's fears? How can we write a scene if we don't understand the theme? And, how can we write a coherent story if we don't know where it's set and who it's about?

so, what is a scene?

For the production team, and the writer, a scene is all the action that happens in one location, at one time. It's that simple.

For the actors and the writer, a scene is the things characters do and say in that location, at that time. For a scene to be dramatic, everything in a scene has to be driven by the forces which create drama. We concentrate on the conflict, exploration of human nature, overcoming problems, vulnerability, moral dilemmas and theme.

To the audience and the writer, a scene is a moment of cinematic-drama. Everything we write needs to be loaded with meaning. Each choice of character, costume, location, prop, action and line of dialogue matters. The audience makes assumptions and learns as they travel through the story. They want to understand what everything means. At the same time, they are also deciding whether it matters to them. And it needs to matter to the audience or we will lose their attention.

Writing a scene is primarily about understanding the technical requirements of the production team. However, beyond that, a scene has to be both dramatic and meaningful. In order to do this well, a writer needs to understand the following:

The forces that create drama.

> Conflict
>
> Exploration of human nature
>
> Overcoming problems
>
> Vulnerability
>
> Moral dilemmas
>
> Theme
>
> How to convey meaning.

Character action and dialogue

Costume choices

Location choices

Props

And, finally, we need to arrive at the scene having read thought about our story. And, we do this by putting our idea through the process.

Playing with and developing our raw idea

Choosing a theme. An exploration of the personal and emotional cost.

Writing a compass logline. Who is the story about, when and where is it set?

Researching the fictional world. The culture in which the story is set

Developing characters - What will they do in any situation, what they will say, why are they doing it?

Planning our plot-points - What happens at this moment in the story

If we do the development work before we write, we arrive at each scene with all the tools to create great drama. Without it, we have to pull our answers from the void. I've written scripts both ways, structural and process-driven. Process-driven is better.

CHAPTER 13
The Sequence

The production team thinks about scripts as a series of scenes. Writers tend to think about stories in sequences.

In the last chapter, we looked at the challenges a screenwriter faces when writing scenes. Screenwriters have to write scenes because that's the job. It is what the production team need. A scene isn't a particularly useful way to think about stories. A more natural way to think about a story is in sequences.

> *A sequence is the action needed to play out a plot-point, usually written as several scenes.*

There are four different ways a screenwriter can approach planning their story. We were introduced to these in the chapter about the planning phase. They are, on-the-page, structural, sequential, or experimental. To create a story, we have to understand plots. And to understand plots we have to understand sequences. Every plotting method is about planning sequences. Each sequence is a plot-point and a challenging circumstance. We turn our plot into a story by writing the scenes necessary to complete each sequence. Let's have a look at how this might work in a simple story. One where we have a traditional protagonist.

> *Marty owns the only business in Amsterdam which sells professional xylophones. The biggest orchestra in the city needs a replacement xylophone for a concert that night. Marty's business is close to bankruptcy. This one order is the difference between staying in business and folding.*

Let's give this idea a suitable theme.

> *The exploration of the personal and emotional cost of trying to please your family*

Marty is our protagonist. We can assume he's trying to save the family business out of a sense of duty rather than his love of xylophones. We have already created his primary challenge. His primary goal is to save his family business. He can achieve this by delivering a xylophone to the other side of Amsterdam. We can think of this primary challenge as the global goal of a character. Our story is how they achieve this goal. In this case, the central question is whether Marty manages to save his business? So, how and what challenges will he face along the way? That's what we need to decide. The one thing we can be sure of is Marty won't succeed immediately or easily. Let me show you why.

> *Marty gets a phone call from the Royal Concertgebouw Orchestra. They must have a xylophone delivered to their concert hall in the next twelve hours. Marty has just what they need in stock. He and his father load it into the van. They drive to the hall without incident and deliver it with time to spare.*
> *THE END*

This isn't a story. Stories are formed by difficulties and complications. Our characters have to overcome problems to achieve their global goal. This means, for this to become a story we have to engineer a series of challenging circumstances. These challenges come from the environment, other characters or internal flaws. If he gets stuck in a traffic jam, that's an environmental challenge. If his father hides the keys to the van, that's a character challenge. If Marty gets too drunk to drive, the challenge is his internal flaw.

To understand the relationship between sequences and stories we just need to accept one idea. A sequence is the action required to face and overcome a challenging circumstance. Once we understand this screenwriting gets easier. Plots created from challenges generate drama and stories. That is what we want.

Let's go back to Marty. He's had the phone call requesting a xylophone for tonight. We are not writing a scene. So, we don't ask "what will Marty do?" That question drives the writing of scenes, not sequences. The most important sequence question is what is the next challenge for Marty? We create challenges to write a plot. Marty's response to these challenges, what he does, is what we turn into scenes. In basic terms, the sequence creates a challenging circumstance. The scenes we write are the character's response to that challenge.

To write drama, we need to create the right challenge for this part of the story. We need to bring Marty into conflict. We expose his vulnerabilities or force him to make a moral decision. And in every sequence, we explore the central theme.

Let's make Marty's father his first challenge. Marty's father has promised the xylophone to someone else. This person hasn't paid a deposit. But all Marty's father cares about his reputation. His word is his bond. As far as he's concerned that xylophone isn't available.

One way we could lay this out would be like this.

___

96

Sequence One. Marty gets a phone call requesting an emergency xylophone for the orchestra. It must be delivered in the next three hours. He knows there is one in stock, so he guarantees it'll be there. When he goes to load the xylophone into the van his father stops him. His father has already promised it to an old friend.

We have defined Marty's first obstacle. The way Marty overcomes this problem creates our scenes. The resolution of one challenge also needs to launch us into the next. Marty's problems and his solutions will form a pattern. Sometimes he will succeed. Sometimes he will fail. We call this the rising and falling action. Sometimes our characters win (rising action), and sometimes they fail (falling action). This idea will become more important to us in the chapter on structure. Structural approaches plot the rising and falling action into a standard pattern.

simple and complex plotting

In process-driven screenwriting, the plotting process can be simple or complex. A simple story is created when a single protagonist overcomes a series of challenges. Each sequence has one obstacle for the protagonist to overcome. A complex story is where many characters face multiple challenges, at the same time. We can create a simple story creating a simple list of sequences.

sequence	challenge
1	Marty gets a phone call requesting an emergency xylophone for the orchestra. It must be delivered in the next three hours. He knows there is one in stock, so he guarantees it'll be there. When he goes to load the xylophone into the van his father stops him. His father has already promised it to an old friend.
2	Marty contacts his father's old friend. He agrees to let Marty have the xylophone, but only if he'll drive him to the other side of city to collect a fish tank. And, he needs to do this right away.
3	Marty drives the old man to collect the fish tank. It's massive! They can barely get it into the van. And, to stop it getting broken they have to drive back at 10mph. It's going to take hours.

4	Marty get's to the old man's house with just enough time to get the xylophone to the orchestra. But, the old man needs to get it up four flights of stairs. He lives on the top floor. Marty can't abandon him
5	They struggle to get the tank up the stairs. But when they get to the top, Marty sees his van being driven away. It's been stolen!

Simple plots are nothing more than a list of sequences that follow the protagonist's journey through the story. If there are sub-plots these may get their own sequences or be embedded in the protagonist's journey. A simple list is less useful when we try to create complex plots. Especially plots that have an ensemble cast. However, let me show you a way to approach this.

> *Let's create a story with more complex sequences/plot-points.*
> *Rubin, Charlie, Ruth and Joan each win tickets to a luxury river cruise. As their ship travels down the Rhine, they are each forced to face the insanity of their banal life choices.*

Of course, we'll need a theme.

> *The exploration of the personal and emotional cost of avoiding risk and adventure.*

What we have been doing, with this kind of planning, is to create a challenge for each character in each sequence. This means our first sequence (or plot-point) includes the challenges for all of our characters. All the events in the first row make up our first sequence.

Plot Point 1	Rubin	Charlie	Ruth	Joan
Amsterdam. The day they arrive to start the cruise.	Rubin sees his childhood sweetheart in the Van Gogh museum. He avoids her.	Charlie tries to buy a postcard but can't find exactly what he's looking for.	Ruth goes straight to the cruise ship unpacks her clothes and writes a letter to her sister which lies about her brilliant day	Joan finds a cafe, buys a pot of tea and reads a book.
Plot Point 2				
First night on the ship, on the way to Cologne	Rubin discovers his childhood sweetheart is the chef on the cruise.	Charlie is forced by the organisers of the competition to choose a random activity to experience in Cologne.	Ruth is forced by the organisers of the competition to choose a random activity to experience in Cologne.	Joan refuses to pick an activity and demands a flight home.

In this first sequence, our characters arrive in Amsterdam to start their trip. Each of them immediately avoids a call to adventure because it's outside their comfort zones. Rubin is avoiding romance and his past. Charlie is terminally indecisive. Ruth hides the fact she didn't explore the city. Joan avoids life by living in the fantasy world of literature.

The second sequence takes place during the first night on the ship. Again, it is all the challenges in the second row.

Rubin discovers he is stuck on a small ship with the woman he avoided at the museum. Charlie is forced to take a randomly selected adventure, which he finds distressing. Ruth is also forced to agree to a randomly selected adventure, which she wants to avoid. Joan, throws a tantrum, refuses to participate and demands to be sent home.

This complex story is created by interweaving the journeys of four different, thematically-linked characters. We plot it by creating a challenging circumstance for each character in each sequence. As we know, well-designed characters prevent each other from reaching objectives. They also help each other overcome challenging circumstances. We don't have to plot for a single protagonist. Using this method our story can be as complex as we want it to be. This is an idea we'll look into in more detail when we get to the chapter on plotting. In process-driven screenwriting, multi-character plotting is the norm. Even if we're telling a simple protagonist driven story.

sequences, page estimates and script length

Planning in sequences like this makes writing a script very predictable. Let me show you why.

We are creating a story which takes place on a river cruise. A cruise which goes to a series of cities. We also decide to create two sequences for each city. One in the new city and one on the boat. Before we even start writing, we can estimate the length of our final script. We can even predict the number of scenes it will take to complete. To do that we need to know one fact.

A single page of formatted script = one minute of film

Sequence	Plot-Point	pages/mins	scenes
1	Arriving in Amsterdam	12	10
2	First night on the boat	8	5
3	Unwilling adventures in Cologne	15	13
4	Second night on the boat	8	6
5	The unfortunate incident in Koblenz	10	8
6	Third night on the boat. The night we hide in our cabins	12	5
7	Nuremberg, the uprising	10	15
8	Fourth night on the boat, consequences	15	18
9	Vienna, (this means nothing to me)	6	3
10	Adventure is embraced at the airport home	8	3
totals		1 hr. 44	86

This kind of estimating is important if we are writing for television. If the film has to be thirty, forty-four, forty-eight or sixty minutes long, there is no point creating a plot with twenty complex sequences. A twenty-sequence story will be at least ninety minutes long. This is simple maths. We know how many sequences there are. We can estimate the number of pages to write each sequence. Therefore, we know the length of the script.

This way of planning is also useful when we write a first draft. Let's assume we have created the estimates in the table above for our script. We believe the first sequence will need twelve pages. When we start writing, we discover our estimate is wrong. Our first sequence takes twenty pages, instead of twelve. This is useful information. It allows us to step back and make some decisions.

We might not care about the overrun. This is a first draft. Lots of writers prefer to write long on a first draft. They edit back in the rewrites. We might decide to edit our first sequence back, so it conforms to our twelve-page target. Or, we might decide to edit our plot. Maybe we need to tell this story in fewer sequences. The important thing is, we have choices. And, we have these choices because we have a plan.

I always create sequence estimates for my projects. I always underestimate how many pages I'll need to nail a sequence. I'm the kind of writer who likes to edit and hone a sequence before moving onto the next. The ability to predict and control a script's length as we write is really useful. It is often easier to fix as we write, than it is to fix in a rewrite.

truth, deceptions and foreshadowing

A sequence is more than an opportunity to move the story forward. It's also how we control the audience's experience of the story. To do this, we need to separate the fictional world from the plot. This starts by understanding what the fictional world is.

The fictional world = The world of the story.

We can think about the world of the story as if it exists as a real place. Our characters were born in that world. They grew-up, had formative experiences and became the people they are right now. In other words, we can imagine our characters experience life just as we do. This is true even if that world is very different from our own. The world we imagine doesn't have an audience. The things that happen, happen. Our characters behave in ways that are natural to them. This world exists in our minds as a simulation. This may seem like an odd way to think about the fictional world, but there are good reasons for a writer to do this. Let's create a fictional world.

> *Gideon lives in a world of crime and gangsters. He is a killer, but he manages to hide this from everyone because he is also a Police Captain. He uses his position to undermine the work of the police. He will murder witnesses or destroy evidence for the right price. He keeps getting promoted because he always frames someone for his crimes. His arrest rate is phenomenal.*

Gideon isn't a real person. He is a character we have created, who lives in a world we created. As process-driven screenwriters, we know what he does, who he is and why he does it.

When we come to create our story, we have choices. One choice would be to follow Gideon's journey. We can let the audience experience this fictional world through Gideon's struggles to murder people and get away with it. We choose to see this world from Gideon's perspective. But it's not the only story available to us. Let me pitch you an alternative that also takes place in the same fictional world.

> *Detective Barbara Holt is assigned to protect a gangster turned witness. On the first night, a sniper takes advantage of an easy shot into the safe-house. Concerned that someone may be on the take, she takes her suspicion to her Captain, Gideon Starr. He takes her seriously. They agree to discover which of their colleagues is the dirty-cop. They also agree to keep their investigation a secret.*

When we switch to this perspective, Gideon is still a killer and a dirty cop. But in this version, the audience knows something Detective Holt doesn't. They know Gideon is the killer and she is in danger. They will experience the drama of Detective Holt's jeopardy.

This isn't our only choice. We can also tell this story from Detective Holt's perspective. In that version, the audience doesn't discover Gideon is the killer until the detective does. This is an entirely different experience for the audience. In this version, the story is a puzzle for the audience to solve. Will they figure out who the real killer is before it is revealed?

Here we have three different perspectives of the same fictional world. The thing that is different in each is the what the audience knows and their journey through the story. The sequences we would create for each story would be very different. This is important because our definition of a plot is changing. This isn't about our character's journey through the story. This is about the audience's journey. And the audience's journey is just as important as the journey taken by our fictional characters.

Process-driven screenwriting helps us to create vibrant and fascinating fictional worlds. Worlds filled with characters who have high-levels of dramatic potential. But, as we can see, there is another creative level to this. Once we have created our fictional world, we get to choose how the audience experiences it. We can hold back information from the audience and deceive them. Does this mean writers can lie to the audience? No! Writers should never lie to the audience. It's not OK to make fools of them. Nobody wants to leave the cinema feeling either stupid or believing the writer cheated. When we mislead the audience, we have to give them a chance. The truth always needs to be part of the deception. The way most writers deal with this is to foreshadow any surprise or revelation. To foreshadow something is to hint at something before it's made obvious.

A good example of how foreshadowing works come from the movie *Fight Club*.

(Spoilers) In Fight Club we enter a world where men fight each other in club basements. This story is told from the perspective of an unnamed narrator. He is both an insomniac and in a dead-end, corporate job. His life changes when he meets Tyler Durden, a flamboyant soap-salesman and anarchist. The pivotal plot moment in the movie is when the narrator discovers Tyler Durden is his own alter-ego! They are the same person.

This is a big reveal. The audience have always experienced the narrator and Tyler Durden as two separate characters. The characters are played by two different actors. Even though this approach misleads the audience, the film never lies to them. Everything is true from the perspective of the narrator. And, importantly, the big reveal is foreshadowed all the way through the film. Tyler works as a projectionist. He splices "subliminal" frames of porn into family films. The director of the film foreshadows the fact that the narrator = Tyler. He does this by cutting subliminal frames of Tyler into scenes.

The foreshadowing isn't only in the directing, it's also in the writing. There are a huge number of clues for the audience to pick up on. It is entirely possible for the audience to figure out the truth before the reveal. And, there's a reason for this. Even when the perspective of a character is misleading, it still has to conform to the truth of the fictional world. The world of story has to be consistent. The audience doesn't know Tyler and the narrator are the same person. His girlfriend in the story, Marla, does experience them as one person. She is confused by his weird behaviour. She struggles with the hot/cold nature of their relationship. Her truth runs through the movie. But it only makes sense to the audience once the truth is revealed. Providing the writing remains true to the fictional world, the truth will always leak out.

The only lies that work in a screenplay, are the lies characters tell each other. Even the lies characters tell each other must always be true to the world of the story and the characters.

In the world of literature, it is common to experience the story from the perspective of someone who is misleading. These kinds of stories even have a name, they are called unreliable narrator stories. Unreliable narrator stories are less common in cinema. This isn't because they're ineffective, the opposite tends to be the case. Unreliable narrator stories create the kind of movies people rave about. The reason unreliable narrator stories aren't common is because they are hard to write. We need total insight into the characters. We also have to be able to see the true world of the story through the distorted worldview of our narrator. It's difficult for structural screenwriters to cope with unreliable narrators. This is because unreliable narrator stories require two parallel plots. The one the audience experiences and the real one. Structural plotting isn't designed for that kind of writing. I have some good news for anyone wanting to write that kind of script. A process-driven approach to screenwriting gives us the tools to tackle this kind of story. One of the tools that allows us to do this is our visualisation of the world of story. If we are able to separate this from the perspective the audience is given, we can navigate our way through these stories.

sequences and time

The ability to separate the world of story from the audience's experience has another use. It gives screenwriters the power to mess with time. There is a theory about the way we manipulate time in stories created by Russian writers. It's called fabula and syuzhet

> Fabula = the sequence of events as they happen to the characters within the true world of the story

> Syuzhet = the order in which the events are presented to the audience

Although there is a chronological order for the character's journey, the audience doesn't have to experience events in that order. It's possible for the sequence of events in the world of story to be different from the audience's experience. This is because the audience's point of view can move backwards and forwards in time. In the industry, we call steps back into the past flashbacks. We call a step into the future a flash-forward. What many writers don't realise is the effect non-linear storytelling has on stories. So, let's look at the difference between linear and non-linear storytelling:

> *Goldilocks goes for a walk in the woods and gets lost. Hungry and tired she finds a small house. No one answers. The door isn't locked. She goes in. In the kitchen, there is a table with three bowls of porridge. She tries each one and chooses the one she likes. The other two taste weird. She feels tired and decides to rest in one of the chairs in the living room. She loses control of her body as she throws herself into the smallest chair, breaking it. She isn't feeling well and needs to lie down. She goes upstairs, tries the beds and falls asleep in the one she likes best. When she comes around, she's surrounded by bears and the smallest one is crying.*

This is the story of Goldilocks told in linear time. We reveal it to the audience in the same order Goldilocks experiences it. When we do, the fabula and syuzhet are identical. However, it is possible to tell this story out of order, in a non-linear manner.

> *Goldilocks comes around in a strange house, in a strange bed, surrounded by bears. The bears drag her downstairs and show her their living room. All their furniture is smashed. Goldilocks remembers staggering through this room in a drugged haze. She remembers destroying the furniture. The bears demand compensation. They demand Goldilocks becomes their slave until she's worked off the damage. Goldilocks remembers walking through the woods. She remembers how misleading signs forced her towards the house. The front door was unlocked. She remembers the sound of a small bear giggling in the wood as she entered the house. The bears drag Goldilocks into the kitchen and force her to clear the table and do the washing up. As she's cleaning the dishes, she sniffs the porridge. It smells odd. She remembers tasting each bowl and not liking two bowls. She confronts the bears, and demands to know if they drugged her. Mother bear admits it was all a trap, but before Goldilocks can escape, they gaffer tape her to a chair.*

In the new version of Goldilocks, we have disconnected the fabula and the syuzhet. The story isn't Goldilocks' linear journey from getting lost to sleeping in a small bear's bed. Instead, the story is about how Goldilocks figures out she's been fooled into becoming a slave.

separating the world of story from the audience's experience

It's interesting to see time, linear or nonlinear, as only one factor amongst many. We can separate any aspect of the true world of the story from the narrative. We saw this when we looked at unreliable narrator stories.

In simple terms, the audience doesn't have to experience Time as a linear journey (the story can use flashbacks and flash-forwards) The audience's experience of the world of the story doesn't have to come from a reliable narrator

The plot or narrative doesn't have to be linear. We can mislead the audience. These factors affect the way we plan our sequences. When we first looked at sequences, we only looked at the challenging circumstances. Or, in other words, our planning was done as if the world of the story and the plot were the same thing. The idea of non-linear time and unreliable narrators changes the way we plot. We decide the order things are revealed to the audience. We decide about the truth of the perspective offered to them.

Writer's don't have to limit themselves to these two choices. Being a screenwriter means thinking about what is possible. I am sure there are other ways to separate the world of story from the audience's experience of narrative. It's not for me to suggest what those separations might be. That is why we need to experiment. However, the glue that binds the story and the audience together is the underlying truth. Providing the audience leaves with their trust intact, it's possible to take them on any journey we want.

planning non-linear and unreliable narrator sequences

Let's assume we want to write a story told from the perspective of an unreliable narrator. A story that unfolds in a non-linear manner. This appears to be a complex plotting problem. And, if we tackle it from a structural, build-from-the-plot approach, it is. However, process-driven screenwriting makes complex stories easy to manage. Nonlinear, unreliable-narrator stories are no exception.

Unreliable narrator stories rely on the writer's understanding of the truth. We need to know the truth hidden by the unreliable narrator's perspective. We research and create our fictional world. Writing an unreliable narrator story isn't difficult if we do the right planning. It works providing we know the reality hidden behind the false worldview of our narrator. And, we also need to understand why our narrator sees the world in such a warped way. One way to organise this kind of planning is to break our sequences down into two columns. One column explains what's really happening in the world of the story. The other shows the way our narrator sees the world.

World of the Story	How our Protagonist sees
John is moved to a new mental hospital	Emperor Napoleon is taken in exile to an island
John is locked in a cell. He demands paper and a pen	Napoleon inspects the room and decides to write his memoirs
John creates a stick figure drawing of a battle with a crayon	Napoleon writes about his invasion of Russia

This is an extreme example of a schism between the world of story and the narrative. The difficulty when writing this would be how to leak the truth into the narrative. Remember, we always need to foreshadow the eventual reveal. The audience needs the opportunity to figure it out before the reveal.

non-linear

Creating a non-linear storyline involves adding another step to the process. We plan our sequences in linear order, so we understand the chronology of the story. The next step is to reorder events in the way you want each part of the story revealed to the audience.

Let's create an example.

the linear time in the world of the story	The order in which the story is revealed to the audience
Helen wants to play the drums	Helen is interviewed about her rise to fame
Helen takes terrible jobs to buy her first drum kit	Helen remembers forming the girl band that made her famous
Helen joins her first band but is treated dreadfully by the boys	Helen remembers joining her first band but is treated dreadfully by the boys
Helen forms a girl band and becomes famous	Helen remembers terrible jobs she did to buy her first drum kit
Helen is interviewed about her rise to fame	Helen remembers her childhood and wanting to play the drums

The order in which we put the sequences alters the meaning of the story. The linear and non-linear versions are different. The linear version is the story of a girl who creates fame and success for herself. She does this after overcoming poverty and sexism. In the non-linear version, this is the story of a woman who has achieved fame. She now longs to reconnect with the pure, childlike joy of playing the drums. She wants it to be how it was before all the struggles and the fame.

what is a sequence?

Let's see if we can come to some useful conclusions about sequences.

It's hard to talk about sequences without talking about plots. It would be a mistake to think of them as the same thing. For a screenwriter, a sequence is

> *The planning and writing of all the action needed to play out a plot-point. These are usually played out over several scenes.*

Sequences are planned. This is why some people make the mistake of treating sequences as if they are the same as a list of plot-points. They are different.

> *John goes to the zoo and fights a penguin*

That is a plot-point. It's a description of what happens. It can function as the description of a sequence but it's not an effective way to write drama.

John is forced to recover the next clue in the treasure hunt from the penguin pool of the local zoo.

This is an effective sequence description. It works because it explains the challenges the character has to face.

writing

When we write a sequence, we do two things. We create drama and decide on the audience's perspective. The drama comes from the character's struggles with challenging circumstances. The audience's experience of the story might be what's really happening. Or, we might mislead the audience. The audience can be misled by characters who hide their true intentions. They can be misled by narrators whose grasp on reality is warped or deluded. Buried underneath any deception has to be foreshadowing of the truth. We have to give the audience opportunities to see the reality beneath the deception. If we don't, they will hate us.

Altering the audience's experience of events alters the story's meaning. This is true of unreliable narrators and non-linear stories. A story about the struggle to achieve success can become a story about lost innocence. It is transformed by altering the order in which the audience experiences events. This is the reason a story's theme is always going to be the touchstone for any creative decision. Each sequence is an exploration of our theme. The order in which we tell the story is also driven by the theme.

Sequences are the real building blocks of cinematic stories. They are the way writers think about and plan their plots.

CHAPTER 14
Structure

what is structure?

The answer to this question depends on who you are talking to.

Some writers believe structure is an absolute truth. They think it is a perfect description of the universal shape of stories. They think stories follow a predictable and unbreakable pattern. Anything that doesn't conform to the universal structure either isn't a story or isn't a good story. A subgroup of these writers believe the shape of stories comes from mythology. This is why you sometimes hear people talking about either the monomyth or the hero's journey.

Some writers believe successful stories tend to fall into a predictable plot pattern. They don't all agree about what the pattern is but their thinking about what makes a story tends to share fundamental aspects.

Some writers believe you can reverse engineer a formula for creating a new movie. They do this by looking at common plot patterns of successful movies. There are the writers who believe they can write a success movie without effort. It will work if they follow the formula or plot template of some "script guru."

There are writers who believe structure is a restriction of their personal liberty. They want to write any way they want!

I am a writer who believes stories tend to conform to predictable plot patterns. Where I differ from most writers is I don't believe we have all the patterns, yet. Traditional plot-patterns are useful for telling some stories. I also believe we can create new story forms. I believe in story-structure, but I don't believe in reverse engineering. Before we can create new stories structures, we need to understand the traditional ideas about structure. We also need to know why we should care about them?

why is it important to understand structure?

Every screenwriter has to let people read their script. Let's say a producer reads our script and that producer shows some interest. The script may go out to a professional script-reader or script-editor. Regardless, it is now inevitable that we'll have to discuss structure. Structure is the way people in the industry give notes when there are problems with the plot.

Producers and script-editors love structure. Notes on structure allow them to sound objective. It allows them to believe they're saying something objectively true. They're not just giving their opinions. The idea of story structure is so embedded in the film industry, we can't escape dealing with it. So, for that reason alone, we have to look at it.

There are other reasons for understanding the various versions of story-structure. Structure can be useful when it comes to plotting. This is especially true when we need to deliver a script to a very tight deadline. If the producer wants a traditional structure, it makes sense to give them what they want.

Structure is a tool and a good screenwriter should know how to use all the tools available.

simple structure

A story is what happens when a specific group of characters are forced to face a series of challenging circumstances

If we accept this definition, the basic logic of story structure emerges. This is especially true if you add the need for a resolution to the definition.

A story is what happens when a specific group of characters are forced to face a series of challenging circumstances in order to reach a satisfactory resolution

This addition is important. From a structural point of view, it tells us our story must have a very definite end. We already know this. Our basic understanding of structure comes from our childhood experiences of children's stories.

Once upon a time, someone lived somewhere. Then, one day, something happened. As a result of this, they had to overcome several problems (which may or may not involve bears). And, they lived happily ever after.

Beginning	Middle	End
Once upon a time, someone lived somewhere. Then, something happens.	As a result, they have to overcome several problems (which may or may not involve bears).	Then they live happily ever after.

When we strip the content out of a story it reveals the shape. Stories have a beginning. Then there is a middle, where all the action happens. Then there is a resolution, where everything resolves. Even within this very simple version of structure certain logical ideas emerge.

Beginning - ACT ONE	Middle - ACT TWO	End - ACT THREE
1. Introduction to the world of story	3. Problems and obstacles	5. Solution to problems found
2. Something happens which provokes or incites the characters into the adventure	4. Bigger Problems and obstacles	6. They all live happily ever after

This is the basis for the simplest structural form for stories.

Act One	1. Ordinary World
	2. Inciting incident
Act Two	3. Challenging circumstances
	4. Even more challenging circumstances
Act Three	5. Solutions found and obstacles overcome
	6. The story resolves

It's hard to argue with the logic of this structure. Our movie starts. We introduce the audience to the world of the story and the central characters. As story is a series of challenging circumstances for our characters. It is inevitable that their adventure will start with an incident. The characters move towards their overall objective. The story becomes a series of challenging circumstances. And, when those challenges are faced, we can come to some kind of resolution. If we remove any of these elements, the story stops looking like a story.

Let's create an example by removing act two from our structure

> Once upon a time, there was a magical princess who lived in a castle. One day, a robber came and stole her favourite horse. She cried because she was sad. The end.

If the princess, or some other character doesn't try to recover the horse there isn't a story. What happens if we remove the third act?

> Once upon a time there was a poor farmer who lived near the castle. One day, a thief stole his pig, so he chased the robber. He couldn't catch him, so he went to the castle to get help. When he gets to the castle, they arrest him for stealing

a horse. He hadn't stolen a horse, but no one believes him. He tries to escape from the castle. The guards catch him. Eventually the horse is recovered. He is released from jail. But now he is a known criminal and no one wants to hire him. So he runs away to sea and becomes a pirate. etc. etc. etc.

Without a resolution the story just meanders from one incident to the next. It is more like real life than a story. In a story, the way a character travels from the start to the resolution is called the character arc. If it is a simple story, where we follow the character arc of a protagonist, this can also be called the story arc.

three-act structure

The most common and traditional structure for screenwriting is called three act structure. When we look at it, we can see three-act structure shares a lot of elements with basic story logic.

ACT ONE	1.	Ordinary world
	2.	Inciting Incident
	3.	First Act Break
ACT TWO	5.	Challenging circumstances
	6.	Mid-point
	7.	More challenging circumstances
	8.	Second Act Break
ACT THREE	9.	The final problem
	10.	Resolution

The difference between basic story logic and three-act structure is three extra plot-points. They are the first act break, mid-point and second-act break. These extra plot points take us from story logic into story theory. Up to this point, our understanding of structure is based on logic. A story can't exist without a beginning, middle and end. They also have to have challenges for the characters. These additional plot-points aren't like that. And because of this, not every agrees how they should be used.

	Hero's Journey	Reversals	Pragmatic
1. Ordinary world	Comfort zone	Ordinary World	Ordinary World
2. Inciting Incident	The first challenge	The first challenge	The first challenge
3. First Act Break	A refusal to act leading to action after additional pressure	A reversal of fortune forces the character into the adventure	Something massive happens raising the stakes
4. Challenging circumstances	Adapt to challenges	Challenging circumstances, little victories	Challenging circumstances
5. Mid-point	Abandon the quest	Huge reversal of fortune	Something massive happens
6. More challenging circumstances	Paying the price	Challenging circumstances	More challenging circumstances
7. Second Act Break	Face the big problem	Hope of victory	The most massive thing possible happens
8. Face the final problem	Sacrifice to win	Final problem	Face the final problem
9. Resolution	Return home a better person	Resolution	Resolution

The first act break can be the moment your character is forced into action after a refusal to act. Or it can be a reversal of fortune, which then forces the character to act. Or something massive happens which raises the stakes. These aren't the same. Yet, each of them reflects the beliefs of a common film theory on structure.

The mid-point can be when the character abandons the quest. Or it can be a huge reversal of fortune. Or, something massive happens.

The second act break can be when they decide to face the big problem. Or, they get hope of victory. Or the most massive thing possible happens.

There is a fair amount of overlap between these concepts. Some structures are more prescriptive than others. What is common to them all, is the idea of regular changes in both the stakes and the fortunes of characters. The challenges our characters face shouldn't all be at the same intensity. Some challenges will be harder than others. Sometimes the character will be winning. Sometimes they will be losing.

story-arcs vs character arcs

For a simple story, with a single protagonist, the story-arc is the same as the character-arc. Structure is a great tool if we want to create the story of single hero. It's not as user-friendly if we want to construct the arcs of multiple characters. It can be done. Linda Aronson's book, *21st Century Screenwriting* is useful on this subject. In fact, she's good on every aspect of structure. I highly recommend her book.

sub-plots

There are advocates of structural plotting who want to do more than follow a protagonist on their quest. They have adopted the idea of sub-plots as a way to add complexity. A subplot is a character arc which compliments the story of the protagonist. It concerns another character or an aspect of the protagonist's life away from the adventure.

> *Sam is a lawyer who specialises in criminal defence. Her primary story arc is about defending someone accused of being a brutal killer. Parallel to that story, she tries to move apartments. And, parallel to that, her mother starts a relationship with the murder's brother.*

So, in the plot of this film we'll have Sam's primary arc (plot A - defend the killer). She's struggling to move apartment (subplot B). And, her mother's poor choice of partner (subplot C). Subplots definitely add depth to a story. It's not an approach I use. That's because I prefer a multi-protagonist approach to plotting.

multi-protagonist

Multi-protagonist plots can be as structural. They just require us to separate out the character arcs.

	John, the Pig who has straw	Dick, Pig who has sticks	Harry, Pig who has bricks
1. Ordinary world	John, the eco-friendly pig decides to build their house made out of straw because it's energy efficient	Dick, the craftsman pig who loves carpentry decides to build their ideal home out of wood.	Harry, the builder pig has always wanted a traditional brick-built home. So, they build it.
2. Inciting Incident	A wolf comes along, destroys John's house and tries to eat him.	Dick gets a frantic call from John about the wolf attack. He offers to give John sanctuary	Harry gets a call from Dick telling him about the attack on John, warning him a wolf is hunting pigs
3. First Act Break	John narrowly escapes to Dick's house	Dick and John barricade the house against wolf attack	Harry looks at the security of his own home and thinks seriously about anti-wolf measures
4. Challenging circumstances	John goes into shock and becomes struggles to function	The Wolf arrives at Dick's house and demands their surrender	Harry rushes to the hardware story to get supplies
5. Mid-point	When the wolf attacks Dick's house John barely survives the second encounter	Dick struggles to save both himself and John, when the wolf destroys his house and attacks them	Harry discovers the wolf has hacked his bank account and stolen his money. He can't get the anti-wolf supplies he needs

It is possible to construct a story where each character has their own experience of the story. Or, in other words, each has its own character arc. We can create character arcs for more than one character in one story. We can do this and still have a coherent narrative. It's even possible to do this when the stories appear to travel different paths. This is an idea we'll examine in depth in the chapter on plotting.

the hero's journey

The most influential structural theory in cinema is the monomyth or hero's journey. This theory originates with Joseph Campbell's book *Hero With a Thousand Faces*. Sometimes we see elements of the monomyth incorporated into traditional three-act structure. We may also see it expressed as four-act structure. This is because the monomyth has four distinct parts. This doesn't present huge problems to people who use three-act structure. As we can see in the table below.

Act 1	Act 2 (before mid-point)	Act 2 (after mid-point)	Act 3
Act 1	Act 2	Act 3	Act 4

Three-act and four-act structure agree on most things. The difference with four-act structure is we separate act-two into two halves. The part before the midpoint and the part after. There are a lot of good reasons for doing this. One of three-act structure's biggest weaknesses is that it has a lot to say about act one (the start). It's also clear about act three (the end). But it has very little to say about act two, the main body of the story. The one thing the monomyth has going for it, is it has a lot to say about the entire arc. So, let's have a look at that.

In a four-act, monomyth, structure each act signals an alteration in the protagonist.

Act 1	The loner	The protagonist is isolated in the ordinary world until he responds to the call to action and enters the next act
Act 2	The wanderer	Having heeded the call to action, the protagonist searches for answers and power
Act 3	The warrior	The protagonist moves from searching for answers to fighting their obstacles
Act 4	The martyr	Only through sacrifice can the protagonist return to the ordinary world a changed person

The hero's journey also has a set of plot points.

1. Ordinary World	The world of the story before the adventure
2. Call to Adventure	The primary challenging circumstance
3. Refusal of the Call	The protagonist refuses to get involved
4. Meeting the Mentor	The protagonist meets their teacher and is guided in the right direction
5. Crossing the Threshold	The protagonist leaves their comfort zone and enters the adventure
6. Test, Allies and Enemies	The protagonist learns the rules of the adventure and is tested
7. Approach	A major set-back occurs forcing the protagonist to change
8. Ordeal	The protagonist faces an obstacle that almost destroys or wounds them
9. Reward	Having survived the protagonist is rewarded with new power
10. Road Back	The protagonist travels towards the final conflict
11. Resurrection	The protagonist is tested in a way that pushes them to their limit
12. Return	The transformed protagonist is returned to their life with new abilities

The monomyth's advantages show when we need to write a story that is heroic. It is also a particularly masculine structure. It's a popular approach in comic books and the part of Hollywood that makes adventure movies. However, it is too prescriptive to be the single universal approach to structure. In fact, the biggest problem with the hero's journey is the term monomyth. The claim that all stories must conform to the hero's journey is both ludicrous and damaging. As writer's we need to educate ourselves. Understanding the hero's journey is definitely part of that education. We also have to decide for ourselves what we learn from it and how we intend to use it.

adapting and altering the hero's journey

It is definitely an interesting idea, that characters change and evolve in each act. If that's the case, why does it have to be the loner, wanderer, warrior and martyr? Can we create our own developmental stages for each act?

Act 1	The conformist	The character is a law abiding respectable member of society
Act 2	The prisoner	The character is put into captivity and submits to the rules until forced to rebel
Act 3	The iconoclast	The character learns to think independently
Act 4	The leader	The character returns to the world with new ideas

This idea rejects the central claim of the monomyth. To do this we have to play with the idea of mythologies not yet imagined. We dare to think about our character's journey as transformative. And, we do this without restricting the possibilities. I believe this is a valuable idea. There's also no good reason why we have to restrict ourselves to the four transformations Campbell pulled from his source material. Let's create another one.

Act 1	The mother	The character is a nurturing person who cares for others
Act 2	The victim	The character's life is destroyed by powerful forces
Act 3	The child	The character's community her help to recover
Act 4	The activist	The character becomes an example to other who have suffered in the same way

Or, radically

Act 1	The hero	The character is well meaning and acts heroically
Act 2	The avenger	The character's motivation shift to revenge
Act 3	The criminal	The character's struggle shifts from revenge to fighting law and order
Act 4	The villain	The character completes their fall into depravity and evil

This allows us to think about our character's journeys as transformative. It's a valuable idea. And, there's no reason why we have to restrict ourselves to four transformations.

Act 1	The psychotic	The character is revealed to be suffering from delusions and mental illness
Act 2	The inmate	The character is revealed to be the victim of institutional power
Act 3	The fake	The character is revealed to be faking their illness
Act 4	The manipulator	The character is revealed to be manipulating her captors
Act 5	The punished	The character is overwhelmed by the power of the institution
Act 6	The escape artist	The character reveals her ability to escape the institute
Act 7	The criminal	The character demonstrates her true criminal nature

Act 8	The lover	The character's motivation is revealed to be her love for another
Act 9	The fugitive	The character is forced to run from everything she cares about in order to survive

In this version, not only have we shifted from four acts to nine, we've also altered the perspective. We aren't describing the character arc of a lone hero. Instead we are looking at the arc of the story for the audience. It's important to remember that plot and character arcs aren't the same thing. This is an idea we looked in the previous chapter.

Writers need to understand structure is a tool rather than a formula. We have complete freedom to play with it, change it, alter it and to experiment. It either aids our understanding of the story we are telling or it doesn't. When we are creating a plot there is no reason why we must write in three acts. We can break it up into as many lumps as we like. Characters don't have to go through a transformative experience in each act. But if they do, it doesn't have to be the four prescribed by Joseph Campbell.

so, what is structure?

Structure is the way writers talk about the plots and plot-points. It is impossible to write a story that doesn't have structure. Our definition of what a story is seems to dictate some structural elements. These come from the logical necessities of what a story is. Apart from the logical necessities, there are also a number of theories about story structure. Theories that suggest how stories are constructed. Some of these are based on mythology. Some are based on other theories. Some of these theories are dubious, at best.

Structure only becomes formulaic if we use it dogmatically. Understanding structural theories is part of educating ourselves as screenwriters. Anyone who claims to have cracked the code! Who suggests that their version of structure is the one and only true method, should be treated skeptically? As with every other part of the process, I trust writers to play with ideas, to rebel against conventional thinking, and to trust their intuition.

Structure is a tool to aid plotting. A subject we'll look at in depth when we get to the chapter on process-driven plotting.

CHAPTER 15
Step 1. Raw Ideas

An idea that is developed and put into action is more important than one that exists only as an idea - Edward de Bono

Before we can develop an idea, we need to have an idea.

The Process is all about the steps we take to develop our ideas. Before that development process can take place, we have to start with a raw idea.

emotionally connecting to an idea

Finding ideas is the most intuitive part of the screenwriting process. The motivation for most people's first attempt to write a screenplay is because they have a great idea for a movie. Their idea inspires them to want to write the script. Being inspired to write by an idea is far more important than you can imagine. Raw ideas are the single most important part of the process.

The power of an idea to inspire a writer is something we must preserve at all cost. Nothing destroys screenwriters faster than ignoring our passionate connection to an idea. Writing the script for a concept we don't believe in is a soul-destroying experience. This is true even when we're paid to write the script.

No one in the world knows more about what inspires you than you!

The most important moment in any film script's existence is when the writer connects with an idea. There are a couple of ways we can think about this moment of inspiration. This emotional connection to an idea is fuel. We are so passionate about this idea we must write it. The inspirational moment also defines us as a writer. The things that inspire me are unique to me. The ideas that make you want to write are personal to you. We need to trust our feelings about our projects. Regardless of what anyone says, writing is not a craft. It can't be learned mechanically. Emotional connection, our passions and fascination are central to the process. Without heart and instinct, we can't expect to write anything meaningful. Audiences want to emotionally connect with the movies they watch. The passion the writer has for their story feeds the audience's need to connect.

originality and instincts

I have a tattoo on the back of my right hand. It's three hexagons, like a honeycomb. There's an illustration of a bee in one of them. I can see this tattoo when I write. It's there to remind me of this fact.

Our ideas are the product of the culture we consume

My tattoo reminds me that ideas don't come from nowhere, they don't exist in isolation. My ideas come from the culture I live in and a hive is a good analogy of a culture. We form our ideas from the sum total of the ideas, stories and experiences we consume. This is true for everyone. Our originality as a writer is entirely dependent the culture we consume. That and our experiences.

A writer who wants to be original needs to consume culture outside of the mainstream. As a writer, we shape our ability to create ideas. This is why there is a strong connection between our fascination and our ability to find ideas worth writing.

It's not my job to tell writers where to find their fascination, but this one thing is true. A writer who only watches the most popular drama on Netflix will not create original ideas. Writers who only consume must-see and blockbuster movies won't ever surprise a reader. It's insane to consume exactly the same things as everyone else and then expect a flow of original ideas.

The way we find original ideas is by chasing our fascination to the obscure corners of our culture. The one thing I can't do is tell you where and how to do this. It has to be our own journey. I believe every writer should create time for reading and research. It doesn't matter how we spend that time. We can listen to obscure podcasts or visit libraries. Travel is good. As is reading obscure Hong-Kong comic books from the 1970's. Or tracking down rare Russian movies. Whatever appeals to us most is what we are looking for. The important thing is the time and energy we devote to our unique interests.

the 20-to-1 ratio

One big myth about creativity is that great writers have better ideas than anyone else. This isn't true. The difference between a great writer and everyone else isn't the quality of their ideas. It is that great writers understand the value of ideas. Great writers understand the 20-to-1 ratio.

On average, we have to generate twenty bad ideas to find one good one.

Once we know about the ratio, we can put our ideas into perspective. It's important for us to acknowledge and look at every single idea we have. Noticing ideas is how we build and strengthen our ability to find new ideas. We have to pay attention. And, we do this by writing down our ideas as they occur. At the moment an idea occurs, it is valuable. This doesn't mean we are going to develop it any further. The important thing is to generate a lot of ideas. It is only once we have a collection of ideas to choose from that we can start selecting. Remember, only one-in-twenty of our ideas are going to be worth developing. When we have a list of ideas, we can concentrate on the process of choosing.

choosing which ideas to develop

One of the hardest decisions for a writer to make is which idea to develop. People screenwriting for the first time often do so because they have one idea they want to write. When it comes to our first script, we really should write the story that inspires us. At that stage, all that matters is we have a story we want to tell. As we develop as writers, we'll find more and more ideas present themselves. Pretty soon, we will have more ideas than time. We can't write them all. The question then becomes, how do we choose which ideas to develop?

Every writer has to find their own way to pick projects. However, there are processes which may help us. I am going to suggest there are four ways to consider raw ideas.

> Instinct
> Commercial value
> Testing
> Develop it

instincts

Of the four ways writers choose their projects, this is the only one that matters. The final decision should always be to write what inspires us the most. The problem with a purely instinctive response is all ideas are inspiring when they occur to us. That's the nature of ideas. Finding an idea for a story is a process of noticing the idea rather than creating it. Ideas present themselves to us because they spark our fascination. So, our initial response is always going to be positive. One of the ways we can instinctively decide on an idea's value is whether it is persistent. Some ideas, just stick with us. We have an idea and we write it down. Then we pull our train of thought back to whatever we were working on. If this idea keeps pulling our attention away from our work, that tells us something. The idea is asking us to notice it. If an idea has a strong pull, we can afford to walk away from it. We see whether time away alters how we feel about it. If we're still fascinated, when we come back to it days, weeks or sometimes months later, it's a good idea.

When I was writing this book, I needed a small piece of script to use as an example. So, I went to my archive folders and picked a project from ten years ago. The excerpt was from a project whose history goes back twenty years. The script is now nothing like the original idea. It has been rewritten more than ten times. Each time the story has shifted and transformed. It's also been more than seven years since I last looked at it. As I read the script segment, I was still as fascinated with the idea and the characters. The pull was as strong now as it was back then. This tells me it's time for another rewrite.

Some ideas have such a strong pull we keep going back to them over and over again. As a writer, we need to nurture and recognise this instinctive pull. It is the source of our originality and our voice. It is what makes us stand out from the other writers.

commercial value

A writer's ability to judge the commercial value of an idea is dependent on how much they know about the industry. Most screenwriters don't have the knowledge or experience to estimate commercial value.

The film industry is one of the most complex and baffling industries in the world. On one level, movies are products. Movie finance can also be a way for rich people to decrease their tax burden. Some movies make money through global domination of the market. Some make money by appealing to niche audiences. And, the vast majority of movies are money pits which never make back the money invested in them. Even those losses have commercial value! Some countries offer deals and finance to companies who film in their region. The way money works in the film industry makes it impossible to think of films as simple products. There isn't a direct link between how good our idea is and the film's ability to make money.

Another common misconception about the movie industry is that it is a single entity. It isn't. The movie industry is tens-of-thousands of production companies, spread all over the world. Each of these companies is an independent business. They each have a plan to make money from the production, sales and distribution of films and TV. Each of them has their own ideas of how to do this. It's important to understand this because it affects the potential value of any idea or script. Each of these companies is run by either a producer or a team of producers who know what kind of ideas they need.

> *Barry has an idea for a zombie movie. The twist is the zombies are the protagonists. They're trying to survive a human apocalypse. He writes the script and pitches the idea to Happy Films. Happy Films specialise in family movies that promote Christian values. To them, Barry's "Day Of The Living" zombie flick has zero commercial value. So, Barry pitches it to Manderville Pictures. They specialise in English period drama. Barry's idea is of zero commercial value to them. He then pitches it to Brainmuncher Movies. They specialise in low-budget horror. They can see commercial value in Barry's idea, providing it can be produced for less than £50,000.*

The concept that ideas have any kind of inherent commercial value is idiotic. Ideas for movies only have value providing they find the right producer, on the right day. Our job isn't to come up with a commercial idea. Our job is to come up with an idea that fits one producer's business plan.

In 2001, I applied to be part of a screenwriting development programme. Every year this company selected five writers to train and mentor. Part of the application process was to pitch the idea you wanted to work on. At the time, I wanted to write a movie about Sherlock Holmes. I had an idea for a story where he is the antagonist rather than the protagonist. When I got to sit down with the producer running the programme, he told me my idea had no commercial value. He said, "No one is interested in Sherlock Holmes, No one will ever make another film about him. It's a valueless idea." Of course, eight years later Guy Ritchie made two blockbuster Sherlock Holmes movies. And, Steven Moffat wrote a multi-award-winning TV series.

The commercial value of an idea changes as the industry changes. I pitched my Sherlock Holmes project six years too soon. And, ironically, I also pitched another Holmes project nine months too late. In 2009, when Steven Moffat's TV series was in pre-production, I also pitched a TV series based on Sherlock Holmes. This time I got my project to the producers too late. By the time people were reading my script, Steven Moffat and Guy Ritchie were greenlit. Commercial value is always about hitting the right desk on the right day.

The worst piece of advice you can ever give a screenwriter is to look to the market to see what kind of ideas to develop. It's bad advice for many reasons. Writers who look to the market for ideas run the risk of dulling their instincts. Even if that wasn't the case, when someone suggests you "look to the market" which part should we look at? An idea's value to the market depends on whether it's a good fit for the production company we show it to. And even that depends on whether it hits the right producer's desk on the right day.

If it's impossible for a writer to predict the needs of the market, how can they choose ideas which have commercial value?

The simple answer to this is, we can't. What we can do is to look inward rather than outward. We trust our instincts and chase our fascination. We present producers with fresh ideas and a unique point of view. If we are lucky, we'll find producers who as fascinated by our ideas as we are. At that point, our ideas will have genuine and lasting commercial value. A value which will increase if audiences share our fascination.

testing our ideas

We have natural positive feelings for our own idea. This is because finding an idea is a bit like finding someone attractive. Our attraction is instinctive and unique to us. The same is true with ideas. We will always be attracted to the ideas that have a personal pull. Deciding which ideas are worth developing sometimes requires some outside help. We need to test the idea. We can do this with minimal effort by pitching it to some people and gauging their reactions. Testing ideas by pitching isn't market research. It's an ad hoc, testing-the-water, version of market research.

Ideas play an important role in the film industry. This is because a movie is a product where sales often come from it being a simple, attractive concept. What film producers want is for anyone who sees the film to tell their friends "Have you seen *Day of the Living,* yet? It's an amazing zombie movie, but it's told from the point of view of the zombies." Producers rely on audiences to pitch the movie to their friends. For audiences to rave to their friends about it the movie, it has to be easy to explain and compelling. These two ideas are important when we test our ideas.

Let's create an example

> *Mock Turtle, is a movie about a girl who leaves home in search of success and fame. She wants to be a dancer but ends up working in a strip-club.*

As writers, we may have a deep fascination about the complex lives of women who work in strip-clubs. We may have good ideas about how to tell this story. We may well be able to create a brilliant script. However, at this point, we're just testing the idea. So, we get in touch with ten mates. People who might like this film. Then we pitch it to them based solely on this idea. We gauge their reactions.

Gauging their reactions isn't as straightforward as it seems. These are your friends and they want to be supportive. They are going to say nice things. When we test ideas, we aren't interested in positive feedback. We're looking for actual enthusiasm. Our friends can fake a "that sounds interesting," or a "that sounds good." What people can't fake is genuine enthusiasm. Trust me, if you pitch people an idea and it blows their minds, you'll know. And, that's what we're looking for. The ideas worth developing are the ones that consistently blow the minds of the people you pitch to.

Even if the pitch test fails, we may still want to work on our idea. We don't throw failed ideas away. A rejected idea may be redeemable once we've done some work on it.

developing ideas

The best way to make decisions about ideas is to use our instincts. This is only one half of the story. The other best way to make decisions about raw ideas is to develop them. This isn't a contradiction. The best way to hone our instincts about idea is by developing ideas.

The process encourages writers to play with and develop ideas. And we do this well before committing to writing a draft. The time we invest in developing ideas is minimal, in comparison with writing a script. This means we can afford to play with ideas as much as we want. It takes very little time to play with an idea. And, it almost always throws up something interesting. Let's try to develop our failed stripper pitch.

> *Mock Turtle, is a movie about a girl who leaves home in search of success and fame. She wants to be a dancer but ends up working in a strip-club.*

We take our raw idea and generate some ideas for themes. An exploration of the emotional and personal cost of...

Failure

Low-self esteem

Sex addiction

Exhibitionism

The power of sexual attraction

Let's use, an exploration of the emotional and personal cost of sexual-attraction as our theme. Now let's rework our pitch.

> *Mock Turtle - When Shelly runs away from home, she has a plan. She swaggers straight into the most exclusive gentlemen's club in the city and demands a job. Using her sexual power like a weapon, she seeks out and seduces the rich and powerful. She's going to make them give her everything she wants.*

This is already a more powerful, compelling idea. And, that's the point, raw ideas are exactly that, raw. And process-driven screenwriting is a way to play with ideas, to hone and reshape them.

If we'd pick a different theme, the idea would be different. Let's pick the emotional and personal cost of low self-esteem

> *Mock Turtle - When Shelly runs away from home, she doesn't have a plan. Desperate for money, she takes the first job offered, bar work in a strip-club. Shelley discovers a world where her body is just another product. A product she has to fight for if she wants to stay in control of her life.*

We are playing a game of "what if?" We take our idea and see what it would look like if we change the theme. We are just playing. But this play has a serious purpose. We are looking for the idea that fascinates us. The one worth writing.

Anyone serious about screenwriting needs to be serious about ideas and their development. The steps in the process are tools designed to help us develop, alter and play with ideas. That's what makes them so powerful.

CHAPTER 16
Step 1. Practical Tools

1. collect and save ideas

The most important thing a writer can do is to collect and save every raw idea that occurs to us. This is one reason writers need to carry a pocket-sized notebook at all times. We also need to learn how to use our mobile devices to record voice-memos. Most smartphones have this ability as standard. The second we have an idea, we need to either write it down or record it. At this stage it doesn't matter whether the idea is good, bad or indifferent. We just make sure we pay attention to it in a way that stores it for later.

The second phase of idea collection is to have either a document or a folder for ideas. We call this our ideas dump. On a regular basis, we transfer the ideas from our notes into our ideas dump. This tiny amount of organisation allows us to create a bank of ideas. Some of these ideas we'll develop straight away. Some ideas we'll come back to much later. Some will never be developed.

It is also important to remember that some of these ideas may be for themes or vague notions. I might note down. I want to tell a story that follows the antagonist's arc. Or it might be something as vague as, research Victorian clowns.

2. create connections

When we generate and collect our ideas, it may look like they are random and disconnected. But if we pay more attention, we'll see how our ideas connect to each other. One of the interesting ways to play with raw ideas is to combine two or three ideas into one.

Idea 1 - a movie where we follow the antagonist's character arc.

Idea 2 - a family attempt to rescue their son from a cult that teaches empowerment through sexual slavery

1 + 2 = A charismatic man sets up a self-help group. But the adoration and eagerness of his followers triggers a downward, narcissistic spiral. He falls into a life of sexual depravity and corruption.

Some of our ideas will be vague feelings about writing. I am currently obsessed with stories where the antagonist is the primary character. So, I take that idea and mix it with a lacklustre "movie of the week" ideas. The end result is one that fascinates me. That's how idea combination works.

3. abandon the search for originality

The easiest way to get writer's block is to attempt the creation of astounding and original ideas. The second we try to force great ideas our minds will go blank. To experience writers block, all we need to do is as follows.

> *Set a stop-watch for sixty seconds. Put a blank piece of paper and a pen on our desk. Start the stop-watch. We now have sixty seconds to put one perfect idea onto the page. It must be utterly original and astounding.*
> *When we tell our minds, we are only interested in astounding and original ideas we stop creating. That's because we're making value judgements. In other words, we are rejecting ideas for not meeting the criteria, rather than generating ideas.*

Now try this second exercise

> *Take a piece of paper and write as many bad ideas for movies as you can. There is no time limit. No idea is too bad or too cliched. In fact, the worse the idea the better.*

When we give ourselves permission to create bad ideas they will flood onto the paper. That's because it's fun to create dreadful ideas. Another thing also tends to happen. Once we open the door to bad ideas sometimes a good one slips. Let's generate a list.

A cannibal opens a restaurant

Zombie ballroom dancing competition

Two pigs invent a way to make tofu taste like bacon

Nazi-hamster destroy all gerbils

The woman who was the model for the Statue of Liberty is deported from America

A dog race across Alaska becomes the cover for a Russian spy ring

A group of computer geeks fake Armageddon using social media

The act of generating bad ideas is always revealing. It pushes us to play with ideas, to approach the work of writing in an irreverent and childish manner. Creative work feeds on the excitement we experience when we play with ideas. In the list above, there are a lot of non-starters. But, I can also see three that genuinely interest me.

4. test them

There are a lot of good reasons for writers to practice pitching raw ideas. It's not a complicated process. Turn your idea into a simple sentence or two and pitch it to friends. The primary reason for doing this is to test the potential of our idea to enthuse an audience. Test pitching ideas is a process that builds three skills. It builds is a writer's ability to turn their ideas into a simple written concept. It hones our instincts. It teaches us how to sell an idea, verbally. Let's play with an idea.

> *This film is about a guy who wants to go to the moon. He's a regular, working guy but it's his ambition. So, he starts building a rocket in his backyard. Everyone thinks he's mad, but he does it anyway. In the process, he creates a plant-based fuel that is so efficient it will solve the world's energy crisis. He's ended global warming. The bosses of the big oil companies send people to sabotage him. But he prevails and manages to be the first private citizen to walk on the moon.*

Over the years, I've listened to countless writers tell me their ideas in a format a bit like the paragraph above. It's a bad way to pitch. I don't want to hear the story. Instead, inspire me with the idea.

Let's see if we can edit this down into something that works better. The biggest problem with this pitch is it feels like two stories. It's difficult to tell whether it's the story of one man's attempt to go to the moon or if it's about a fuel that can save the world. Although these two story elements can work together as a plot, what is our central idea?

> *When one man's dream to walk on the moon drives him to build a rocket in his garage everyone thinks he's insane. He soon discovers it's not just Earth's gravity he needs to overcome, it's all the people who want to stop him.*

We can still use the rocket fuel/oil company idea as part of the script. It's just, at this stage, it's a distraction from the idea we're pitching. That is unless it's the idea we most care about. In that case, we need to redraft our pitch.

One man's dream to reach the moon turns into a fight to save his life and his family, when he invents a revolutionary new fuel. A fuel that will make the oil and coal industries irrelevant.

Pitching is as much about deciding what we focus on as it is anything. Either way, it's definitely about honing our ideas into coherent statements. Practicing this craft is one of the most important skills a screenwriter needs.

Testing our raw ideas helps us build confidence in our pitching. It's good to practice selling our ideas to other people. Most people don't find selling ideas a natural or easy experience. The more we practice, the easier it will be when we have to pitch to people in a position to make our projects happen. As with all things, practice makes perfect.

5. push our ideas through multiple iterations

Ideas are our play things. Good things happen when we play with our ideas. We can use any tool we like to do that. The more we play with an idea, the more ideas we'll create. Ideas are like that, there is almost always a link between this idea and the next one. So, when we alter, adapt or deepen a raw idea we create new ideas. We chase our fascination, hone our instincts and play. Let's try pushing a raw idea through five redrafts where we change a major component in each rewrite.

> A princess is cursed to sleep for a thousand years as revenge for her father's crimes
>
> A scientist is cursed to sleep for a thousand years as revenge for her father's crimes
>
> A scientist is cursed to sleep for a thousand years after an experiment goes wrong
>
> A scientist is cursed with immortality when an experiment goes wrong
>
> A scientist is cursed with immortality and uses it to avenge the death of her father

Change one thing. Repeat that process. We start with the story of sleeping beauty. We end up with an original story about the consequences of immortality.

CHAPTER 17
Step 2. Theme

We've already looked at theme a couple of times in this book. So, we know what a theme is.

> *The theme answers the question, what is this film about? Where the answer is, an exploration of one aspect of what it means to be human.*

So far, we've looked at theme as a way of playing with ideas. In process-driven screenwriting, deciding on a theme is a vitally important step. It will impact every other part of the process. It is the key to writing coherent drama. Theme also determines the kinds of stories we tell.

Let's say, we have an idea for a script about a family who buy an abandoned village in the Italian mountains. We don't have any specific characters or a plot in mind. It's a raw idea. We're fascinated by the idea of abandoned villages. We half-remember reading a magazine article about how cheap they are but don't know that much about them. At this stage, we don't know enough about it to create a story. So, we chase our fascination and do some research. We find an article about people who bought one of these villages. They had a hellish experience. They sank their life savings into properties on the verge of collapse. We also discover some of these beautiful ruins are completely off-grid. No electricity, water, telephone or internet.

After chasing our fascination, in the form of writer's research, we are ready to pick a theme for this story. It's an important decision. No other piece of creative work will have more impact on the screenplay. Our theme will guide and shape every other choice we make. It will influence the characters we create and the scenes we write. To illustrate the power of a theme to alter a script, let's use it as a tool to create some different stories from the same idea. Let's base them on our family who buy an abandoned village.

Theme one - an exploration of the personal and emotional cost of chasing your dream

> *Sam hates his job as a PE teacher. His wife, Alice, hates living in Aberdeen. It's all too cold, wet and grey. So, when they see an advert offering them an entire village for sale in Italy, they make an offer. They remove their kids from school and drive off to their new life. They don't care that they don't speak any Italian, or that they only have £5,000 to survive on. They're sure they can make it work. When they arrive the get a shock. The village has no*

power, water or telephone… and the houses are all on the verge of collapse.
But, the entire family refuses to give up on their idyllic Italian life etc

This seems like the kind of story you'd expect from our initial research. But what happens if we throw a completely different theme at it?

Theme two - an exploration of the personal and emotional cost of manic depression

> *After years of managing his manic depression with pills, Sam decides to try something new. He sells the family house and buys an abandoned Italian village. He persuades his wife that an idyllic Italian life will solve his mental health problems. His enthusiasm carries the family right across Europe to their new home. But when he arrives, it's not as he imagined. He realises he's brought his family to a place without water, electricity or a telephone. His illness goes into a nose-dive and he falls into an almost catatonic depression. Alice finds herself and her kids isolated and desperate. She must find ways for them to survive and to get Sam the treatment he so desperately needs.*

Although there are a lot of similarities, this story has a very different feel from the first idea. It's more than a family fighting hardship and adversity. This is a family dealing with the difficulties of surviving a bad decision. And, at the same time, dealing with a chronic mental illness.

Theme one gave us a *family win against all odds* movie. Theme two offers us a story about a family struggling to survive the cruelty of mental illness. This second theme has greater dramatic potential.

Let's create something completely different.

Theme three - an exploration of the personal and emotional cost of infidelity

> *When Sam discovers his wife, Alice, is having an affair, she begs him for a second chance. She doesn't want to be in a new relationship. She needs their relationship to be more exciting and adventurous. Sam isn't sure, he needs some time to think. So, he goes on a holiday to Italy. Alice is delighted when, a week later, Sam calls her. He's bought an abandoned Italian village. He begs her to come out and join him. They can have chickens, grow their own vegetables and live a simple life. They can start over and save their marriage. As he waits for her arrival, Sam broods on his wife's betrayal. He's changed his mind. He wants to stop her from coming. Then he realises he has created the perfect opportunity for revenge. It would be so easy for Alice to have a tragic and fatal accident. So, he starts to construct a series of fatal traps. His*

planned revenge runs into a brick wall when Alice arrives. She's not alone.
She's with her lover. It appears Sam isn't the only person planning a murder

This is a very different story. Even though the location and the environmental factors are the same. The only difference between these three, very different, projects is the primary theme. When the theme is the cost of chasing your dreams, you get a family drama. When it explores the cost of dealing with mental illness the story changes. When infidelity is the theme, the location's isolation takes on a darker significance.

It still amazes me how something as simple as changing the theme can transform a story. Even when we start with the same initial inspiration and research. Earlier in the book, I suggested first ideas are often problematic. Our first reaction is often the least interesting. It is always the most cliched and most obvious concept. The three examples above seem to back up this belief. The first theme gives us the most obvious approach to the initial idea. It's easy to imagine the script and the film that would result. I would also argue it is the least interesting. The second theme, where the focus moves onto a family's struggle with mental illness is a much stronger idea. It has much greater dramatic potential. Of the three, that's the story I would write. The third theme throws up an interesting idea, it's just not my kind of project. Which leads us to our next point.

our choice of theme defines us as a screenwriter

It is not our ideas that define us as a writer, it's the themes we choose to explore. All stories are explorations of what it means to be human. The best stories have something interesting to say about our humanity. Despite this, far too many screenwriters concentrate on their ideas and their plots. This is unfortunate. There is no easier way to fail than to focus on the idea and the plot. We can't create good drama from an idea and a plot.

Process-driven screenwriting always brings us back to our true nature. When we research, we chase our fascination. When we select a theme, we ask ourselves what do we really care about? This isn't an intellectual decision. It is a visceral choice. We trust our guts. As writers, we have a duty to chase our fascination and to trust our feelings. It is a very personal, individual process. One of the worst pieces of advice given to screenwriters is to look outwards, to the market. That we should think about what sells when we decide what to write. It's bad advice because why would anyone hire us to write a script like Wes Anderson's last project? Wes Anderson already exists. Why would we want to be a copy of an existing, successful writer? The best thing a writer can do is to chase their fascination. We should trust our instincts about what stories are worth writing. The thing that makes a writer valuable isn't their competence, it is their unique point-of-view. It is our unique take on universal human experiences that define us. We find those things by looking inward and trusting ourselves. It is the absolute opposite of looking out to the market. Writers who look to the market for answers are saying, I don't trust my own fascination. I only care about other people's stories. The fastest way for a writer to ruin themselves is to disconnect from their own instincts. Instincts are like muscles; we ignore them at our peril.

When we select a theme, the most important part of that decision is the gut feeling, this is what I am interested in. I have something worthwhile to say about this human experience. Presented with the same research material, each of us will pursue a different theme. We will create different characters and have different things to say about them. One of us may want to explore the cost of chasing love. Another will explore the cost of living in a dysfunctional family. Another, the cost of being a traditional hero in the modern world. Each of us will create something unique and personal, if we follow our instincts. When those scripts go to the market, we are offering a story no one else could have written. The industry will either be inspired by those fictional worlds, or they won't.

Our value to the industry is our ability to write stories no one else would ever write, in a way that is uniquely ours. We only get that kind of ability as a writer when we tune into our fascination. When we pay attention to our passions and the things we care about.

theme and characters - simple stories

The process starts with theme because the theme impacts every other creative decision. Let's see how a shift in theme alters characters in a simple protagonist vs antagonist story.

Theme one - an exploration of the personal and emotional cost of deception

> *A boy is sent to the hills to guard the sheep. They tell him to cry wolf if the flock is in danger. After a while he's bored so the boy cries "WOLF! WOLF!" Everyone in the village grabs their weapons and runs up the hill. The boy finds it hilarious. The adults remind him this is a serious business and not to do this again. But, an hour later, when he knows they'll all be eating their evening meal, he cries "WOLF! WOLF!" Again, the villagers grab their weapons and run up the hill. Again, the boy laughs in their faces. This happens half-a-dozen times. Eventually, the villagers decide enough is enough. The boy won't catch them out again. In the early hours of the*

morning, a starving pack of wolves appear. The boy cries "WOLF! WOLF!" but the villagers ignore him. The wolf kills all the sheep and the boy.

This is the story, in its traditional form. The Boy Who Cried Wolf is a parable about the cost of lies and deception. It is hard to imagine this story as anything else. However, if we change the theme it changes the characters.

Theme two - an exploration of the personal cost of toxic masculinity

A father wants his timid ten-year-old boy to toughen up. "Tonight," says the father, "you are going to be guarding our flock of sheep from wolves, alone on the hill." The boy is terrified! How will he, a small-boy, fight off wolves. His father tells him to stop being such a baby. If he calls for help, his father will run up the hill so they can fight the wolves together. As the sun goes down and shadows lengthen, the boy trembles. He is sure the wolf will attack and kill him. When the wind blows the boy believes the wolves are coming. "WOLF! WOLF!" he cries. His father, annoyed to be dragged from in front of the fire, grabs his gun and runs up the hill. When he can't find a wolf, he beats the boy. An hour later, the wolves really do appear. Again, the boy screams "WOLF! WOLF!" But his father rolls over in his bed and ignores his son's cries.

A change in theme changes the nature of the protagonist and antagonist. In the original, the boy is a naughty prankster. Although it's grotesque, it makes sense that the wolf eats the naughty boy. The boy is the antagonist in this first story.

When we change the theme, the second boy isn't naughty. He's terrified. He is now the protagonist. The real villain of the piece is his father, who exemplifies the theme. The nature of the characters and their function in the story is radically altered by the change in theme.

theme and characters - complex casts

Generating a list of themes for a story does more than provide the writer with a single choice. Often there are links between the themes on our list. Links we can use to create interesting characters and subplots. Here's a list of potential themes we created earlier.

Fighting for justice
Revenge
Protecting your reputation
Individual freedom

Escaping gang-culture
Protecting your family
Escaping your family

We can use the rejected themes as the starting point for creating characters. Let's select the emotional and personal cost of escaping gang-culture as the primary theme. Our rejected ideas become sub-themes. Each the driving force for a new character.

Primary Theme = The personal and emotional cost of escaping gang-culture

Character	Sub-Theme	Rough Overview
Kitty Bandit	Protecting her reputation	Bandit is the gang's up and coming enforcer. She's violent, ruthless and totally focused on making a name for herself
Queen Bee	Protecting her family	Queen Bee runs the gang. She's also the sister of the Duchess. She's all about protecting her family. However, what will she do when she has to choose between her blood kin and the gang?
Pistol	Revenge	Pistol is the gang's top enforcer. Everyone except Bandit is afraid of her. She believes every threat needs to be met with terrible and bloody revenge.
The Duchess	Escaping her family	The Duchess runs the legitimate front business which launders the gang's money. She desperately wants to escape gang life and her sister's influence.
Officer Monroe	Fighting for justice	Officer Monroe is the patrol officer in this block. She really wants justice for the ordinary people whose lives are ruined by the gang
Baby	Individual freedom	Baby is utterly unpredictable. She is part of the gang but doesn't follow orders and will not listen to anyone else. She commits crimes for the fun of it.

These are a long way from being fully formed characters. What this demonstrates is how we can outline a cast of characters based on a list of sub-themes. And, even at this stage, it is possible to see the first glimmers of dramatic potential in each character. We already have dramatic tension. Queen Bee's drive to protect her family is in conflict with The Duchesses' drive to escape her sister. Pistol's need for revenge looks like a source of conflict for everyone. Pistol is also in direct conflict with Kitty Bandit's drive to build a reputation. These conflicts are the foundation of drama and story.

Sub-themes are an interesting starting point for creating a cast. My biggest problem with this cast, as it stands, are the clichés. Character development is a more complex process than creating a puppet to act out a sub-theme. We'll cover this development process in detail in the step on character development. For the moment, it's enough to know we can use the idea of complementary sub-themes to create characters. And, that sub-themes create dramatic potential.

the theme and the sequence

Plots can be created from the right challenging circumstance for each part of the story. Characters respond to each challenge and this drives the writing. Theme is pivotal to this way of plotting. This is because every sequence is an exploration of the theme. It's much harder to keep a story on track when writers don't commit to a theme. Let's try to create a plot without using any part of the process and without a theme.

Sequences	Plot-Points
1	Sally works in a fast-food restaurant, but dreams of becoming a rodeo clown. One day, Trent, a broken rodeo star limps into the restaurant. He wants to know if there's a cheap motel near-by. Sally points to the one over the road. It's clean, cheap and close to the best bar.
2	Sally watches Trent drive over the road to the cheap motel. At the end of her shift she follows him over. He's there with all the other rodeo riders. Sally offers to show them where the best local bar is. They get drunk together.
3	Sally seduces Trent but is gone when he wakes up the next morning. But, when he goes to his pickup, she's waiting with her suitcase. She wants to run away to the rodeo. Trent agrees.
4	As they drive towards the next competition at Marble Falls, Texas, Sally tells Trent about her dream to become a rodeo clown. He laughs at her. She bets him a hundred dollars she will get hired if he gets her an audition.
5	Trent gets Sally an audition. She makes a fool of herself and has to be rescued by Micky, the top clown. Trent tells her go home, he even gives her the bus fare.
6	Sally goes to the bus stop. Micky drives past. Asks her how serious she is about becoming a rodeo clown. She persuades him that it's her dream. He offers to teach her providing she cooks, cleans and gives him an occasional blow-job. She agrees to everything except the cooking. She hates to cook.

There is a plot here and a couple of half-formed characters. It's not the worst story, but it is not great. It's thin and lacking. It doesn't excite me as a story.

The biggest problem is it lurches from one event to the next. We don't learn anything new about any of the characters in any of the sequences. It also feels familiar and predictable. Let's take the same idea, the same characters and think about them thematically.

Theme One = An exploration of personal and emotional cost of chasing fame

Sequences	Plot-Points
1	Sally wants to escape her job a fast-food restaurant and dreams of becoming a rodeo clown. One day, Trent, a famous rodeo star limps into the restaurant. Sally recognises him and start flirting. All he wants is to know, is where he can find a cheap, clean motel. She recommends the one across the road, where she works her other job.
2	After her shift ends, Sally goes over to the motel. She tries to seduce Trent. He's not interested. He wants to know why she's bothering him. She tells him about her dream of becoming a rodeo clown. Trent agrees to take her with him to the rodeo, if she fills his bath with ice. She raids the ice-machine. When she comes back Trent is naked in the bath. As she pours the ice into his bath, he shows her every scar and explains every broken bone. He's only 38 and his body is wrecked, all because of the rodeo. If she still wants to go with him, she needs to meet him outside the motel at 4.30 am
3	Sally is waiting for Trent when he gets to his battered old car. Sally wants to know how come a famous rodeo rider is driving such a terrible car. As they drive, Trent tells her how much he's had to spend on medical bills and about all the times rodeo people have ripped him off. He tries to persuade Sally to get the bus home. She tells him she'll do anything to get her dream.
4	They arrive at the Marble Falls Rodeo, in Texas. Trent introduces Sally to Micky, the top clown. Micky doesn't want an untrained clown on his team. Trent tells Micky she'll do **anything** to get into the rodeo. Micky agrees to give her an audition in return for a blow-job. Sally thinks Micky is joking. She begs Trent to save her, but he tells her everything at the rodeo costs something. She refuses, so Trent drives her to the bus stop.
5	Trent goes back to the rodeo. He reminds Mickey people will pay good money to see a pretty girl stomped by a bull. Sally waits for the bus but doesn't get on it. She's furious. She drags herself back to the rodeo, finds Micky and knocks him on his ass. She demands an audition.
6	Mickey gives Sally an audition. Puts her in the ring with a baby bull. It knocks her on her ass. She gets up. She get's knocked down again. She gets up and gets stomped. Trent helps her up, she's got a broken rib. He laughs… "welcome to the rodeo"

At first glance, the two plots may look similar, but they're not.

140

no theme

The plot without a theme tends to follow a single idea. It's the things Sally will do to get her dream. In the no theme version, Trent and Mickey are stepping stones for Sally's journey. Because of this there is no depth or foreshadowing in the story. We move from one event to another. Sally is also a one-trick-pony. She uses sex to get what she wants, and it always works. Her character isn't challenged at any point, nor does she reveal anything new to the audience. It's a story, but only just.

chasing fame theme

The second plot moves forwards faster. It has more depth and complexity. Sally is only allowed to progress towards her dream after Trent shows her the cost. His broken body and virtual poverty foreshadow her future. Both she and the audience see the real cost of her dream.. Trent's motives for taking Sally to the rodeo are hidden. His stories of how rodeo people rip you off may foreshadow a future betrayal of Sally. Trent's warning about rodeo people becomes real when Mickey demands a blow-job. This is the second time she's shown what the price of her career might be. Sally's attack on Micky shows how she overcomes her first real obstacle. She's a fighter. Her audition demonstrates she's more than a pretty face. She's tough. Although she's proven herself, she's also proved Trent right. "People will pay a lot to see a pretty girl get stomped by a bull."

Theme focuses the writing. By asking, *how does this moment explore the cost of chasing fame?* we are forced to use every character to explore the theme. It is better than chasing our protagonist through a series of events. Even under-developed, half-formed characters have their dramatic potential raised this way. They become more rounded simply by asking how does this character relate to the theme? It's interesting to see Sally grow dramatically in the chasing fame version. But the real transformation happens to Trent. In the no theme version, he is a handy device to get Sally into the world of the rodeo. In the chasing fame version, Trent has greater depth. He emerges as a character with a hidden agenda who may help Sally or destroy her. Or both. We can't tell at this point. The fact we can't tell is important. It's unanswered questions like this which keep the audience hooked into the story.

the dangers of writing to a theme

Any technique or process a writer uses comes with dangers. Regardless of the technique, the danger is always the same.

Dogma is the enemy of creativity

Any technique or formula becomes useless if writers surrender their instincts. My biggest criticism of structural screenwriters isn't that they use structure. It's when they surrender their creativity to a theory. Let's be absolutely clear about this. The belief that stories have to conform to the shape of the monomyth is a theory. The same is true of the idea that we should write film scripts in three acts. Thematic writing is a good approach. It's not a universal panacea. It shouldn't be used as a way to shortcut experimentation.

Theme keeps the story focused and it shapes characters. It's easy to see the benefits. The downside of focusing the writing at so early a stage is it can shut down experimentation.

I believe in process-driven screenwriting. I know my tools work. They work best when I remember to move between messy writing and focused writing. Process-driven screenwriting encourages writers to generate new ideas at each stage. I want writers to play with ideas. However, that's not enough. Screenwriting has to be fearless. We need to foster our determination and our instincts. We need the ability to get messy creatively. To devote a day/week/month to instinctive unplanned writing. If we discover something fascinating, we can come back to a theme and hone whatever we've discovered.

The other danger of theme is it can turn a script into a polemic. Each character can become a puppet to act out the writer's strongly held political or moral beliefs. There is room in the world for films with a strong point of view. But, audiences don't always warm to stories where the characters feel robotic. This is the main reason I like each character to have a unique sub-theme. This is also why character development is the biggest task undertaken in process-driven screenwriting. Our characters are not rhetorical devices. They are drama engines. They drive the drama and the story. The quality of our screenplays will always be entirely dependent on the quality of our characters.

CHAPTER 18
Step 2. Practical Tools

1. use your instincts

When we look at our raw idea, we will have a gut instinct about the primary theme.

Let's look at an example

> *Raw Idea. When one man's dream to walk on the moon drives him to build a rocket in his garage everyone thinks he's insane. As he gets closer to his launch, he discovers it's not just Earth's gravity he needs to overcome. There are a lot of people who want to stop him from trying.*

When I read this, my gut instinct is this story's theme is

> *An exploration of the personal and emotional cost of chasing your dreams.*

I believe the development of our instincts is a vital part of being a writer. The way we develop our instincts is by paying attention to them. We teach ourselves to look at an idea and to get a sense of the theme that feels natural. This gut-level instinct comes from two places. The idea suggests it. This idea is about someone chasing their unusual dream. Our gut reaction also comes from who we are and how we see life.

2. generate a list of alternative themes

Creative processes swing between instincts and play. Once we have identified our gut reaction to an idea, the next step is to play with alternatives. Let's do that with our example.

> *Raw Idea. When one man's dream to walk on the moon drives him to build a rocket in his garage everyone thinks he's insane. As he gets closer to his launch, he discovers it's not just Earth's gravity he needs to overcome. There are a lot of people who want to stop him from trying.*

Let's generate some alternate ideas for themes

Mental illness
Pride
Obsession

Willful ignorance
Dogmatic belief

This list seems to be the motivation of the primary character. With single protagonist stories this will often be the case. The theme is often the protagonist's primary motivation. Is our protagonist building a rocket in their garage because he's mentally ill? Does his pride need him to prove a point to someone? Or, is he a victim of his obsessive nature? It is interesting how the story changes completely as we shift the theme. Building a rocket because of an obsession is different from being a slave to a dogmatic belief.

Alternative themes allow us to look at the raw idea from different angles. The central idea stays the same. The story changes. Playing with our ideas in the early stages pays off when we start writing the script.

3. create a word cloud of human experiences

When we look for themes, the idea narrows our potential choices. This is inevitable because our mind will be looking for links. If we step away from our idea, we can generate a cloud (list) of themes. These will be unrelated to the idea we are working on. We're trying to create a random list.

> *lust, obsession, ambition, fear, trauma, patience, murder, terror, revenge, discipline, study, rationality, spirituality, family, childbirth, warfare, disease etc. etc.*

Even a list this short, generated in about two minutes, can be useful. We can transform our story by throwing a random theme at it and seeing where it takes us. What happens if we pick a theme at random from our list? Let's pick one that seems completely disconnected from the idea.

> *Our story is an exploration of the personal and emotional cost of childbirth*

There doesn't seem to be any link between childbirth and our story about a man who builds a rocket in his garage. However, what if the birth of their first child is the trigger for the man's obsession. Is he running away from the responsibility of being a father by hiding in his garage? Perhaps, he wants to show his child it is possible to achieve anything if you dream big and try hard?

The purpose of this exercise isn't to force change on our idea. It is playing with the idea for the sake of play. In a very real sense, this is a writer's exercise. It's something we do to find new angles on a story.

4. combine themes

Normally we choose to use a single theme. However, this is a creative process. We can choose to link thematic elements in one story.

Again, let's go back to our raw idea

> *Raw Idea. When one man's dream to walk on the moon drives him to build a rocket in his garage everyone thinks he's insane. As he gets closer to his launch, he discovers it's not just Earth's gravity he needs to overcome. There are a lot of people who want to stop him from trying.*

What happens to this story if we combine two themes?

> *Our story is an exploration of the personal and emotional cost of obsession and fear*

When we add in a second, contrasting theme our characters become better drama engines. A character with several conflicting motivations is very dynamic. Imagine our protagonist is obsessed with getting to the moon. He may also be afraid of failure and the effect his obsession has on his family. Is he going mad? Our theme doesn't just apply to our protagonist, it is universal. It applies to the fears of his family and the obsession of the people who want to stop him.

5. explore the positive and negative aspects of your theme

Any aspect of human experience can have both positive and negative aspects. Our ability to write a story depends on the negative and positive aspects of the theme.

Positive LUST	Negative LUST
Sex is good	Sexual obsessions
Emotional connection with another person	Manipulative use of others
Desire drives us to be creative and romantic gestures	Destructive and jealous impulses
Being desired builds self-esteem	Stalking
Recreational pleasure	Selfish use of others for gratification

Even if we only use a couple of these aspects, this exercise is still worth doing. Imagine we have a protagonist who stalks her ex-partner. It's easy to see how we can use the negative aspects of the cost of lust. But, she isn't the only character. Our theme is for the whole story, not just the protagonist. We may want to include a character whose connection to lust is empowering and healthy. A character who acts as a contrast to our protagonist. The most important part of the process is playing with ideas. We play and explore. Then we make decisions based on our instincts. We use what we've learned to focus our writing.

CHAPTER 19
Step 3. Compass Loglines

loglines

In step one - raw ideas, we honed our ideas in and tested them. Rewriting and reworking ideas is how we write a logline. Loglines play a very important role in pitching and selling scripts. It is the first part of the project a reader sees. And, sometimes it's also the last. As writers, we are drawn to some ideas in preference to others. The same is true of commissioning editors and producers. They will not care how well written the script is, if the idea doesn't grab them.

Writing loglines is a very important part of professional screenwriting.

compass loglines

A compass logline isn't the same thing as the logline we use to pitch the script. We write the logline to pitch our script after we finish writing. In fact, every time the script goes out to a new reader, we will rework the logline. A compass logline is different. We write a compass logline at the beginning of the process. It's not written to test or pitch our idea. It's written to point us in the right direction. It's our first fully formed statement about the story.

Raw idea - a group of computer geeks fake Armageddon using social media

Theme - an exploration of the personal and emotional cost of deception

There are a lot of different stories that can emerge from this idea and this theme. The obvious story would be about the people who create a real crisis by faking Armageddon. In that story we'd ask, how they do it, their motivations and the consequences. The first question we need to answer is, whose experience of the world of story we're going to use. Let's try to write a compass logline based if we tell this story from the point of view of the hackers.

Compass logline - When a group of media students in rural Idaho decide to prank their local TV station. They fake Armageddon. Their prank soon spirals out of control when their videos go viral, all around the world.

We get to a compass logline by looking at four questions.

Who is/are the central characters?
Where is the film set?
When is the film set?
What's the big problem?

Raw ideas and theme always offer many different stories. The obvious idea isn't our only option. It is one amongst many. To find alternative stories all we have to do is alter the elements that we use to create our compass logline. So, let's do that. Instead of going down the obvious route, let's try something more ambitious.

Who are the central characters? - Seven people in different parts of the world all affected by the hoax

Where is it set? - A US air base in Japan, New York, rural Idaho, North Korea, a Tokyo ramen shop, in a submarine, and the FBI data centre Pocatello

When is it set? - The present

What's the big problem? -The North Korean military believe a series faked viral videos about the end of the world. Seven different people find themselves drawn into the effort to save the world.

Compass logline - When a kid in rural Idaho makes a fake video it was just a prank. He fakes a US Military attack on North Korea. He's delighted when it goes viral. However, the Korean military don't get the joke. They think it's for real. They put their entire country on a war footing. The world is one wrong move away from global nuclear war. In the following confusion, seven decisions will decide the fate of the world. An FBI agent, an American pilot, a fourteen-year-old hacker, an illiterate Korean soldier, an FBI data-manager, and a Tokyo ramen shop owner, hold the fate of the world in their hands.

This is a very different film from our first idea. Yet, it comes from the same raw idea and theme.

understanding the ideas phase

We tackle the process in four phases. The first phase is when we play with ideas. The second phase is research. The third is development and planning. The final phase is writing. Steps one, two and three are the ideas phase. We play with ideas, try different themes and write alternative compass loglines. Looking at all the alternatives helps us develop our project. It is important that we spend time playing with and explore the ideas at the heart of our story.

We do this at the start because it's hard to do later in the process. We do this work now so we don't have to do it for our rewrites. Idea development is quick, simple and painless at this stage in a script's life. It's much more difficult to do this once we've written our first draft. This isn't because the process is any different. It's exactly the same. When we rework ideas for a rewrite, we have to fight the emotional baggage of our existing draft. If we've devoted six weeks to writing a script, it's hard to make changes. We aren't playing with a raw idea anymore. We are throwing six weeks work into the trash.

Our ideas are the real foundation for the entire story. If we alter one element, everything changes. This is why it's very important for screenwriters to learn how to play with and develop ideas.

Our compass logline becomes the springboard for the research and development phase. It also points us in the right direction. This is because we make two important decisions when we write our compass logline. We make our first decision about who the story is about (characters). We also decide the primary problem faced (plot).

A story is what happens when a specific group of characters are forced to face a series of challenging circumstances

A story has two key elements, characters and challenging circumstances. This means the compass logline is the first moment our story starts to emerge.

rewriting the compass logline

The process may appear linear. We move from one step to the next in order. That's not the case. There is a lot of moving back and forth between steps as ideas and stories evolve. We will rewrite the compass logline, many times, as our story changes. This is because the compass logline is the foundation of our story. So, when we make concept-shifting alterations, we circle back to our compass logline. Let's create an example to show how this might work.

Raw idea - a cannibal opens a restaurant

Theme - an exploration of the personal and emotional cost of challenging society's taboos

Compass logline - When an artist cooks human flesh as part of an exhibition the media outrage is absolute. She's arrested and it seems inevitable that she's going to prison. That is until civil rights lawyer Kim Dane volunteers to take on her case.

This seems like a reasonable starting place. We've taken a raw idea, decided on a theme and created a compass logline that gives us a basic form for our story. We've decided to do a film about an artist on trial for cannibalism. As we move into the research and development steps (4 world, 5 characters, 6 plot) we may discover something that alters our story. The following is a true story from 1884.

1884 - Two sailors, Dudley and Stephens, become shipwrecked by a storm. They abandon their ship and are stranded in a life-boat with another sailor and a young cabin boy. After eleven days the food runs out. Two days later the water runs out. Five days after that, Dudley and Stephens draw straws to decide which one of them should be killed and eaten. But there's an argument and not everyone agrees to draw lots. Dudley and Stephens kill the cabin boy, as he is the closest to death and has no family. They cut his throat. Although only two men take part in the murder, all three survivors eat the boy. Because of this, they are able to survive until rescued, four days later. Dudley and Stephens are then tried and convicted of murder.

Let's assume that this piece of research is so fascinating it alters the story we want to tell. We haven't written a script, yet. It's still easy for us to reevaluate our project. One way we could approach this would be to see this as completely new raw idea.

Raw idea - a story based on the true case of the Crown vs Dudley and Stephens. Two sailors who murder and eat a cabin boy to survive being stranded at sea

It might be this is the route we now want to take. But not necessarily. What if we still like our original idea but we want to alter the story? That is when we rewrite our compass logline.

Compass logline (rewrite) - When performance artist, Kim Steltz reads about Victorian sailors who turned cannibal, she becomes obsessed with cannibalism. The taboos of food and death fascinate her. As she prepares for her biggest show ever, at the New York Museum of Modern Art, rumours start to emerge. People think Steltz intends to cook and serve human flesh as part of her installation. The museum comes under intense media and legal pressure. Curator Pearl Grotlz is forced to deal with an artist planning the unthinkable. And, at the same time, a public outraged by the mere idea of cannibalism.

This is a very different story from our original concept. It explores art, public outrage, media attention and the moral dilemmas of a curator. There's a lot for writers to work with here. The art world courts controversy and part of its history is the exploration of taboos. There are a lot of parallels in art history to draw from. Let's look back at our original compass logline.

> *Compass logline - When an artist cooks human flesh as part of an exhibition the media outrage is absolute. She's arrested and it seems inevitable that she's going to prison. That is until civil rights lawyer Kim Dane volunteers to take on her case.*

When we look at our original idea, we can see how simple that story is. An artist does something unthinkable and society wants to judge her for it. The unresolved issue is whether she will be punished or not. Now let's look at the new one.

> *Compass logline (rewrite) - When performance artist, Kim Steltz reads about Victorian sailors who turned cannibal, she becomes obsessed with cannibalism. The taboos of food and death fascinate her. As she prepares for her biggest show ever, at the New York Museum of Modern Art, rumours start to emerge. People think Steltz intends to cook and serve human flesh as part of her installation. The museum comes under intense media and legal pressure. Curator Pearl Grotlz is forced to deal with an artist planning the unthinkable. And, at the same time, a public outraged by the mere idea of cannibalism.*

This version of the story has a lot more to offer. It will make a better story than the first. This version lets the audience follow the artist's journey. They watch her go from fascination with cannibalism to acting on it. They don't know if she will or won't try cannibalism. They also witness the curator's struggle with the morality of this situation. Will the museum allow the exhibition? What will the public do to stop them? There's a lot of material to explore.

This is how our story develops. We learn something new, we reevaluate and rewrite our compass.

what is a compass logline?

A compass logline is the short paragraph or sentence we write to give a basic form to our story. It's the moment we decide who the story is about; where and when it's set; and the primary issue the characters will face.

A compass logline is also the last step in the ideas phase. This is because we make our first decisions about primary characters, the world of the story and the plot. The decisions we make at this point will inform the more detailed work we then do on those three areas.

The most important thing to remember about a compass logline is we can come back and rewrite it at any point. The compass logline is the foundation of the story. It is important we fully explore and understand that foundation. It's a process worth doing and worth doing well.

CHAPTER 20
Step 3. Practical Tools

1. write a compass logline based on your gut feelings

Before we play with ideas it's important to write down our gut feeling response to the raw idea and theme. This is an instinctive, messy writing approach. We look for the first and most attractive idea to use at this stage. It doesn't matter whether it's a good, bad or indifferent logline. It is our baseline response. All creative work dances between instinct, play, research and craft. To be effective writers we have to engage each of these forces in our work. Writing our instinctive, off-the-cuff logline is part of that process. It's something I encourage writers to do at every stage.

Writing an instinctive compass logline to connect to our gut is a good thing to do. It also allows us to practice writing loglines. The more time we put into writing loglines the more skilled we will become. We must learn to see the relationship between our ideas and all the stories that emerge from them.

2. try lots of different central characters

The easiest way to change our story is alter who the story is about. This changes the point of view from which we tell the story. When we change the central character/characters, we get to see the story from a different angle. Even if we have decided on a central character, we can still play with alternative ideas. If our central character is the best choice, that will still be true after we've looked at some alternatives. So, let's create an example.

Raw idea - zombie ballroom dancing competition

Theme - an exploration of the personal and emotional cost of hanging onto the past

Instinctive compass logline - Australia's champion ballroom dancer, Murray Kline, is infected by the zombie virus. As a zombie, he is banned from all human competition. He's not a quitter. He may be a zombie, but his heart still beats to the rhythm of the Samba. So, Murray organises the first ever zombie ballroom dancing competition

This idea isn't without its charms. I, for one, want to see what zombie ballroom dancing looks like! Before we get carried away with ourselves, let's see what happens when we change the primary characters. So, let's generate a list of alternatives.

The owner of a tv cable network

The contestants of the TV show "Dancing with The Stars"

The clients of a ballroom dancing studio in rural Texas

A local police officer

A zombie hunter

We could write a compass logline for each of those characters.

When the Zombie Apocalypse takes over the world, cable tv owner, Rex Munty, struggles to keep shows on air. All Australia is barricaded in their homes. Rex realises he has a massive captive audience, starving for entertainment. Always the optimist, he decides to turn the apocalypse to his advantage. He stages the first ever zombie ballroom dancing competition.

The TV show "Dancing with the Stars" goes into lockdown when the Zombie Apocalypse hits the city. The producer, Carly Smith, decides the show must go on regardless. But, things get out of hand when it turns out some of the cast and crew are already infected

The "Twinkle Toes Ballroom Academy, Texas" are in rehearsal when the Zombie Apocalypse hits. Armed only with their second amendment rights and hips that won't quit, they decide to fight their way to the regional dance finals. To do this they must cross two-hundred miles of zombie infested desert.

By changing the central characters, we get different stories. The thing to remember is we are just playing with ideas. By playing we increase our ability to craft story ideas. The key to this is to have fun. We're not committing to a project. We're just playing. We can be as ridiculous as we like. In fact, I encourage that.

3. combine loglines

When we generate several stories from a single idea and theme it may be possible to combine some of them. Our mind will often throw out pieces of a big idea in small lumps. We may not get the whole story idea in one go. I don't know why our brains do this. I just know, it's part of the experience. We need to look for potential idea combinations. Let's try this with some of our versions of the Zombie Ballroom idea. Let's combine these three ideas.

Australia's champion ballroom dancer, Murray Kline, is infected by the zombie virus. As a zombie, he is banned from all human competition. He's not a quitter. He may be a zombie, but his heart still beats to the rhythm of the Samba. So, Murray organises the first ever zombie ballroom dancing competition

The TV show "Dancing with the Stars" goes into lockdown when the Zombie Apocalypse hits the city. The producer, Carly Smith, decides the show must go on regardless. But things get out of hand when it turns out some of the cast and crew are already infected

The "Twinkle Toes Ballroom Academy, Texas" are in rehearsal when the Zombie Apocalypse hits. Armed only with their second amendment rights and hips that won't quit, they decide to fight their way to the regional dance finals. To do this they must cross two-hundred miles of zombie infested desert.

What we're looking for here, are aspects that fascinate us and also that work together. Here's our combined compass logline

When the Zombie Apocalypse hits, Carly Smith, the organiser of the Texas regional dance competition decides the competition must go on. When the zombie dancer Murray Kline demands to enter, the competition soon finds itself at the centre of the world's first zombie rights protest. Can they ban the world champion just because he's a zombie? This situation is only made worse by the arrival of the blood-soaked members of the Twinkle Toes Ballroom Ballroom Academy. They've just fought their way across two-hundred miles of zombie infested desert... and they're here to dance.

Combining our play loglines gives us a story which follows three different narratives. The first is that of the dance competition organiser who wants to run a great competition. The second is the narrative of a zombie dancer who desperately wants to compete. And, our final narrative is the story of a gun-toting dance academy who fights its way across the desert. They arrive only to discover they'll be dancing against the monsters they killed to get there. This combined logline may not be the final idea we take forward. The benefit in playing with ideas is it presents us with opportunities we can explore or put to one side.

4. playing with the when and where

If we change characters, we change the story. The same is true of the fictional world of the story. This another element we can play with. We can generate alternative suggestions for the place and period our story is set. Let's try this with one of the zombie ideas.

The "Twinkle Toes Ballroom Academy, Texas" are in rehearsal when the Zombie Apocalypse hits. Armed only with their second amendment rights and hips that won't quit, they decide to fight their way to the regional dance finals. To do this they must cross two-hundred miles of zombie infested desert.

Place	Period
Tokyo	present
London	1960s
Alaska	1899
on a cruise ship	1980s
on the moon	the future

We can generate as many periods and locations as we like. I always try to create a mix of suggestions that seem outlandish or odd. Or, in other words we should have fun by throwing in some bad ideas. So, for instance, we may not want to set our story in Tokyo or during the Klondike Gold Rush of 1899. But, throwing those suggestions into the mix may lead us to either a different idea.

We are trying to open our minds to ideas outside of the normal range. The one that stands out for me in this list is the idea of setting the story on a cruise ship. So, let's rewrite our logline to work with this idea.

Carly Smith, organises the "Florida Regional Ballroom Dance Competition," on a cruise ship. A local TV company cover the whole event. Things go horribly wrong when it turns out one of the contestants has the zombie virus. With only a copy of the rule book and a generous heart, Carly tries to meet her contractual obligations. She has to provide five live TV shows, over five increasingly chaotic nights.

5. what if the antagonist is the protagonist?

One of the simplest ways to change our story is to swap our protagonist for our antagonist. Or, to put it another way, what if our villain was really the hero? As a writer who has spent a lifetime playing with ideas, this is the one I come back to more often than any other. It's one that resonates for me. To try this method, we need a story with a clear protagonist and antagonist.

156

When a serial killer kills seven priests, FBI profiler, Micky Jones is the only one who can find the killer.

To change an antagonist to a protagonist we need to understand their motivation. Protagonists are always driven by their central motivation. When the FBI profiler was the protagonist, we knew their motivation. It is to catch the killer. We didn't care about the killer's motivation, at this stage. To turn our killer into the protagonist, we need to find a motivation for the killings. A motive that will allow the audience to accept a serial killer as a protagonist. As with any other part of the process, this is about generating alternatives.

Revenge for childhood sexual abuse

Unreliable narrator - he believes he is hunting demons

Revenge for the death of his sister, she was denied an abortion by their pro-life lobbying

The killer was an ex-nun who wanted to become a priest

Unreliable narrator - believes himself to be part of the inquisition

We can create as many alternatives as we want. The more work we put into it more ideas will flow.

When Sister Agnes escapes from hospital she is unable to return to the church. Depraved demons posing as priests prevent her. Determined to save the holy church from the forces of evil, she tracks them down and kills them. Her problems really start when the demons send a hunter from hell, in the guise of FBI profiler, Kit Larson

or

When Donnie's sister kills herself, he knows who to blame, the five priests who molested her as a child. When he discovers these priests have been transferred to new parishes, he makes a promise. They'll never hurt another child. He'll stop them regardless of what he has to do.

It's a rewarding exercise for a writer. Turning antagonists into protagonists.

Our writing improves when we learn how to see the world from the perspective of our characters. This is the start of a bigger process. It's how we start to understand our characters.

CHAPTER 21
Step 4. The Fictional World

Step four is a constant part of the writing process. That's because the goal of step four is to understand the world of our story. It is, in fact, the creation of this fictional world from research and imagination.

Sometimes this research comes from our life experience. This is called the write what you know approach. Although I always draw on my life experiences, I'm not a fan of using this idea to limit what I write. I advocate the write what you are passionate about approach. Regardless of which approach we decide to take, all screenwriting involves research. Googling terminology is research. So are face-to-face interviews. The need to gather information relevant to the script can occur at any time in the process. Even when we do extensive development research, we'll still need to check details as we write scenes. The creation of a fictional world is always about finding the right details. We strive to create a world which will draw in and fascinate our audience.

Compelling fictional worlds are the foundation of great scripts. That's because film scripts feed on detail, authenticity and a cinematic vision. Our personal experiences often aren't interesting enough to be source material. As writers, we have to invest time and energy into research. The creation of a compelling fictional world takes effort and dedication.

messy writing

For some writers the creation of a fictional world is what we do on-the-page. To them, being a writer is that experience. This is the messy writing approach to creating fictional worlds. This is OK. We can decide to write a draft to discover the fictional world. As long as we understand it is nothing more than exploratory. We will have to rewrite.

There are advantages to instinctive, on-the-page storytelling but there are also dangers. Without planning we will build inevitable and horrific flaws into our narrative. In drama, every new scene builds on the foundation of what we have already written. If we create a narrative problem in the first act, it ripples through the rest of the story. When we write cold, without any preparation, we are at our most ignorant in act one. We are definitely going to make narrative errors. This means a lot of script analysis, notes and rewriting. We get to the end result, a good story, by the sheer number of times we're prepared to rewrite.

The process of trial and error can be productive. But, it is an approach which takes a lot of time and discipline. Intuitive writing works best for writers who know how to rewrite. And by this, I mean, we start from scratch with a blank page. We can't unpick intuitive, first draft problems by copying and pasting scenes from one script to another. Messy drafts always need a second, blank page, rewrite. Emotional attachments to a messy first draft is one of the biggest problems in screenwriting. Nothing makes a script editor's life more miserable than a writer who can't gut an intuitive first draft.

Despite the dangers, there are a lot of advantages to the messy writing approach. We create our fictional world by chasing our fascination. One of the most interesting ways for a writer to chase their fascination is on the page. When we work without prior research, we discover the limits of our imagination. Knowing what we don't know is often the best starting place.

The thing is, intuitive writers do research, but they tend to do it as they write.

Steve is writing a historical crime drama. It's about the investigation of a murder in a coal mine, set in a 1960s pit village. Steve knows his central character is the vicar's wife. It's a good choice. Her position puts her at the heart of the community, but at the same time, it also makes her an outsider. Steve grew up in the North East, so he knows how tight-knit pit village communities were. He's an intuitive writer. So, he goes into an exploratory draft without doing any specific research. When he sits down to write his first scene he runs into a problem. It's set in the lift which goes down to the coal face. Before he can write the scene, he has to be able to visualise it. He does a quick Google search and finds an image. He also discovers the lift is called, the cage. This is a useful detail. However, the scene has to be populated with characters. Steve has some vague ideas about the main characters, but he's not sure how they speak to each other. He can't write the dialogue. So, he searches out some documentaries from that period. Watching them gives him a sense of the syntax and vocabulary. He now feels able to write his first scene.

This process, finding the limits of our knowledge/imagination is important. This style of research will be familiar to most writers. This is what creating a world on-the-page is like. We constantly crash into the limits of our ability to visualise the world we're creating. This visualisation is more than what a scene looks like, or how people dress. Our visualisation must extend to how people behave and how they speak.

There are definitely advantages to a messy writing approach. As we write, we discover the specific gaps in our understanding and we then fill those blanks. It's also the approach that feels the most natural to many writers. The eventual creation of our fictional world always happens on-the-page. The only question is how prepared we are for it. It's understandable for us to gravitate towards the fun, creative part of the process. However, rushing to figure things out on the page isn't without its downsides.

The disadvantage of messy writing is our ignorance gets in the way of the writing. If we research every little detail as we write, the writing is constantly interrupted. Our ability to get words onto the pages constantly runs into the limits of our visualisation. This is especially true at the start of the script. The attraction of this workflow is it feels creative. The to-and-fro between getting a couple of sentences on the page, followed by half an hour of research. It may feel productive because we're immersed in the creative process. In truth, it's a very inefficient way to write.

the most valuable thing about writing I was ever taught

My first professional job was writing radio commercials. My first boss ran one of the most successful writing teams in the industry. He trained more award-winning writers than anyone else I've ever met. His job was to train and mentor me into the industry. Most of what he taught me could be condensed down to a page of A4. He was an advocate of the axiom less is more. He taught me the most valuable lesson about writing I ever learned. It's a simple idea.

Don't write and edit at the same time.

This is the most profound lesson any writer can learn. Our natural inclination is to perfect each sentence as we write. But when we do that, we're doing two things at the same time. We're creating and we're editing. These are processes that don't mix. Creating requires us to be open to new ideas and inspiration, it is about being open to everything. Editing is about making decisions between the good and the bad. It's a selective process. It's about applying filters. One of the things we learned earlier is the way bad ideas can be the gateway to good ideas. The same is true of writing. Bad writing is the gateway to good writing. Or, in other words, writing has two steps, a creative step, where we write and then a selective process, when we edit.

The practice of separating writing and editing has a remarkable effect on the act of writing. We can train ourselves to focus on getting words on the page. We tune into the part of being a writer where the ideas and words flow. Writers often refer to this as being in-the-flow. It's an interesting experience. It's a productive way to write. This has implications for messy writing approaches to the world of story. Writing and researching at the same time also interrupts the flow of the writing. This is the main reason writers should invest time in separate research and preparation. When we write, all we should do is write. I'd like to amend my mentor's idea. This is my golden rule.

Write as much as you can, for as long as you can, without interrupting your flow.

My strongest criticism of most on-the-page, intuitive writers is that they combine writing with research. They interrupt the flow of writing too often.

the ordinary world

Anyone familiar with traditional structure will know the phrase, the ordinary world. In structural approaches, the ordinary world is the world of the protagonist before entering the adventure. So, if the protagonist is a postman, their ordinary world is delivering letters. If they then find themselves in the world of international spies, the world they enter is the world of the story. This distinction, between the protagonist's normal life and the adventure, works for some stories. Implicit in this model are ideas about calls to action and the hero entering new worlds. Personally, I don't make a distinction between the ordinary world and any other part of the story. The entire script takes place within a fictional world. It doesn't matter where the characters start, where they travel, or where they end up. It all takes place in the world of the story. For me the ordinary world is the fictional world of the story. Let's use a clear example to show how this works.

In the C.S. Lewis story, The Lion, The Witch and The Wardrobe, the central characters go to stay at a relative's house. In the house, they discover a wardrobe with an entrance to a magical land. They then have an adventure in that land.

From a structural point of view the ordinary world is the part of the story where the children go to the house. It ends when they enter the wardrobe. I see this story in a different way. The ordinary world of this story is one where a portal to a magical land exists within the house the children visit. Even though the children travel from one place to another, it's all the same, single, fictional world of story. For me, the ordinary world is the complete world of our story. Seeing as a coherent entity has advantages. Advantages that will become clearer as we get deeper into the process.

The world of story is always fictional. But what if we want to create a story that is as close as possible to real-life. There is an approach to writing theatre based on real events called verbatim theatre. The writer records interviews with people who experienced the actual event. They tell the story in their own words. All of the dialogue and the narrative of the play are taken verbatim from the recordings. The writer creates no new dialogue. This is as close as drama can get to recreating real life. But even when we mirror reality to this extent, the world created will always be fictional. When a writer decides what parts of the story to include, and what parts to exclude, we shape the narrative. It is no longer reality.

Screenwriters can learn a lot from the idea of verbatim theatre. Let's imagine we want to create a script based on a true-life event. The incident we're basing our story on happened on a housing estate. It involves a clash between a local youth-club and the police. The good news is, we have permission to go anywhere and interview anyone. We're planning to shoot the film in the locations it happened. So, what kind of research do we need to undertake? Let's see if we can draw up a list.

Visit all the locations and take photographs

Get a map of the area

Get inside all the buildings where things happened and take photos

Record interviews with the people from the youth club

Record interviews with the police officers

Record interviews with local people

Get any press reports of the events

Find any video or photographs of the events

This is the kind of planning you might do if you were making a documentary. Which is, actually, a useful way to think about researching and creating a fictional world. When we create a fictional world, we need to understand how that world works. We do this in the same way a documentary explores a story.

places

We need to gain an understanding of the physicality of the world in which our story is set. What does it look like? Where are the places in our fictional world that things happen? We have a choice to make. Are we setting our story in a fictional version of the world as it is or in a fantasy landscape? Let's look at some examples to clarify this idea.

real world locations		entirely fictional locations	
Alnwick Castle, UK	a real castle	Hogwarts School (Harry Potter)	a fictional school/castle
Mount Sunday, New Zealand	a real mountain	Edoras (Lord of the Rings)	a fictional mountain
Englefield House, Berkshire, UK	a real stately home	Xavier School for Gifted Children (X-Men)	a fictional school
The Millennium Bridge, London	a real bridge	The Planet Xandar (Guardians of the Galaxy)	a fictional planet

If we plan to use locations as they are in the real world, we need to research them. We need to know what they look like and how they work geographically. It would be reasonable for us to set stories in Alnwick Castle, on Mount Sunday, at Englefield House, or on the Millennium Bridge in London. To do this we would need to find out what these locations offer. We could look at photos and maps or even visit them. This is the kind of research we do when we set our story in the world as it is. But what happens when the place we want to write about doesn't exist?

When we create a fantasy world like Hogwarts or The Planet Xandar, we have to start with what we know. We draw our inspiration from the real world, art and other movies. We ask, how is Hogwarts like other castles? We could look at photos of castles and decide what kind of place it is like, what kind of landscape it occupies? We could use a real castle, like Alnwick, as inspiration. Our fictional, sci-fi planet might be inspired by a real-world, modern building. We're not trying to decide on actual locations. We're creating the world of story in our mind. We need to be able to visualise the places we are writing about. This is true whether it exists in the real world or not.

Even when we write about real locations, we distort and alter them. They are still fictional. There is a lot more crossover between real world locations and fantasy landscapes than you might imagine. Let's say we decide to use the exterior of Alnwick Castle for our story. But we want there to be a high-tech weapons laboratory under it. In the real world there isn't one. However, in the world of story, we are free to warp reality in any way we please. Alnwick Castle has a real-world geography. One we can't change in the real world. In our fictional version, we can change the geography. A character goes through a door in Alnwick Castle. In the real world it goes to the gift shop. In our fictional world it goes to New Zealand, or a pub, or the moon. We decide the geography of our fictional world.

The world of story is always entirely fictional

Our goal is always to visualise an entirely fictional landscape. This is true, even when we write about real-world locations.

visualisation

Films are a combination of drama, visual images, sound and music. So, when we come to write our script, we use most of these elements to tell our story. One aspect of both step four (the fictional world) and step five (character development) is the way they help us to visualise our story.
Step four visualisation questions

Where does this scene take place?

What does it look like?

What do the inhabitants of this fictional world look like?

How do they dress?

What kind of things exist in this place?

How do people behave?

What are the morality and rules of this place?

How do people speak?

What kind of vocabulary do they have?

What kind of syntax do they use?

Step five visualisation questions

What does this character do in this situation?

What does this character say in this situation?

Our visualisation is split into two issues. The physicality of the fictional world (questions 1-5 in step four). The second issue is about characters and the way they behave. The second issue exists in both steps four and five. We'll come back to characters, later. For the moment, let's concentrate on the physicality of the fictional world.

One way to think about the fictional world is to think of it as a simulation. It is like a video game. We are creating an environment. If we look at the first five questions in step four, they are all questions about the environment. This is the way our fictional world would appear if none of the characters existed. The world we imagine has an immediate effect on how the story is told.
Let's try an experiment. Goldilocks walks through the wilderness until she gets to the bear's house… what does the house look like?

What happens if we create three very different visualisations of the bear's house. The first one set in American, it's run down and abandoned. The second one looks old fashioned and European. The last one is set in winter and has a cabin-in-the-woods feel to it. It matters which of these three houses Goldilocks arrives at. Each offers a very different visualisation of the story.

EXT. BEAR'S HOUSE. DUSK

At the end of the dust track, a rundown shack. It's
constructed from the rotting remnants of a Union Pacific
railroad car. Where there once were windows, ragged, sack
curtains. They move in the wind.

Goldilocks drags her blistered feet and sunburned body
towards it.

The sun starts to dip below the ridge above the shack. As
the shadow hits the shack, Goldilocks freezes in her tracks.
The shack isn't abandoned, there's a faint light coming from
inside.

EXT. BEAR'S HOUSE. DUSK

Goldilocks skips over the neatly trimmed lawn towards the
neat and friendly cottage. A small wisp of smoke comes from
the chimney and there's a lamp in the window.

Goldilocks steps up to the front door, straightens her dress
and tidies her hair. She knocks on the door and slaps a warm
smile onto her face. There's no answer, so she knocks again.

```
EXT. BEAR'S HOUSE. DUSK

The light is fading. The last shaft of light skitters off
ice crystals on tree branches. Goldilocks drags her frozen
and aching legs through the snow. She leans against a tree,
the bitter wind throws sharp needles of ice into her face.
She throws her arm across her eyes to protect them.

As her vision returns, Goldilocks sees a faint light in the
clearing ahead. The light of a lamp and smoke from a fire.
Hidden, almost buried in the snow, a log cabin.

Goldilocks summons the last of her strength. She drags
herself towards shelter, light and warmth.
```

The way we visualise the location impacts on the story. It's not enough to write INT. BEAR'S HOUSE and then leave the rest to the director and location manager. To write the scene, we have to visualize the environment and the way our characters interact with it.

The way in which we build our visualization is up to us. Some of us may be able to conjure a complete environment in our minds. Our ability to do this is determined genetically. There is a neurological spectrum between hyperphantasia, the ability to strongly visualize and aphantasia, a complete lack of inner visualization. A writer with aphantasia may always need photos in front of them. Most of us are close to the midpoint on this scale. We'll need photographs and videos to help us build our visualization. We may also need to keep visual prompts close to hand when we write.

Creating a clear visualisation of the landscape is probably the easiest part of creating a fictional world. Despite this, failure to get that world onto-the-page is a common failing in early-career screenwriters. Scripts without a clear vision are really difficult to read. I suspect, this kind of failure happens when writers forget cinema is a visual medium. Far too many screenwriters become too wrapped up in the story and the dialogue. They forget the physicality of the world and how central it is to telling a cinematic story.

visualisation, culture and character

Our visualisation is more than an idea of the environments in which our story is set. The second half of this step is about the culture of the world of story. Or, in other words, it's about the way people behave and speak. This can be confusing. It seems like this is the work we should do when we move into step five (character development). However, there is a difference between these two pieces of work. Let's look back at the questions we created to understand what we need to visualize.

Step four

Where does this scene take place?

What does it look like?

What do the inhabitants of this world look like?

How do they dress?

What kind of things exist in this place?

How do people behave?

What are the morality and rules of this place?

How do people speak.

What kind of vocabulary do they have?

What kind of syntax do they use?

Step five

What does this character do in this situation?

What does this character say in this situation?

Although we are looking at how characters behave in steps four and five there is a difference. In step five, we will look at the way a specific character would behave and the things they would say. That is an exploration of the psychology and human traits of a specific character. In step four, we aren't looking at specific characters, we are looking at the culture they live in. Again, let's look at some photos to clarify this as an idea.

Here we have three very different environments and cultures. One is street musicians in Cuba. One is a street market in 1890s New York. The final image is a floating market in present day Bangkok. Let's look at our culture questions.

How do people behave?

What are the morality and rules of this place?

How do people speak?

What kind of vocabulary do they have?

What kind of syntax do they use?

When we look at these photos what do we know or imagine about the lives of the people who inhabit them? Do we believe the answers will be the same for each culture? Any truthful answer is likely to be a combination of yes and no. There are universal human experiences. We could pick out any person from any of these photos and assume that they will experience love. Their experiences of hardship, success, failure and family will also have universal qualities. But we would expect there to be differences in the rules, behaviour and morality. New York in 1890 will be different from present day Bangkok. The real question is this. Do we understand the culture we are writing about well enough to portray it?

A culture is formed by the ideas, customs and behaviours of a particular civilisation or people

The physical environment affects the behaviour of our characters. The same is true of their culture. We are creating fictional cultures. We can choose to take the audience into a culture based on real life. Or we can create something imaginary. Regardless of which we choose, the issues will always be the same. What do the people in this culture believe? How do they behave? What are their morals and customs?

The way we research and create the culture of our story will depend on the way we write and the kind of person we are. My background is in philosophy. I tend to focus on ideas, beliefs and values. My fascination is with the way people's beliefs drive their behaviour. My fascination drives the kind of research I do. We each have our fascinations. My main suggestion to writers is they cultivate their unique perspective on life.

Ultimately, creating the culture of our story is as much about imagination as it is about facts. In the same way we visualise a fictional geography, we also need to imagine the culture.

seed scenes and the power of prose

At the start of this chapter, we looked at a messy writing approach to creating a fictional world. To do that we write a first draft just to explore our fictional world. Some people call this a vomit draft. We just get our ideas onto the page without worrying about how bad the script is. I'm not a fan of messy first drafts. But, create it on-the-page writing can be a useful tool as part of the process.

We don't have to write the whole script to use messy writing to our advantage. There are two techniques worth exploring. The first of these is the seed scene method. A seed scene is what a writer does when we want to explore the world of our story without working on the actual story. We write a scene or sequence that allows us to play with the fictional world. We're not trying to write a scene that will be in the actual film. We are playing in the world our story is set. We're trying to get a feel for the culture.

Let's imagine we want to write a story about a Belfast punk band, set in 1977. It's a story about music. But, the troubles between Catholics, Protestants and the British Army are a constant backdrop. How might we write a scene to get a feel for that time and place? Remember, this is just us playing with the fictional world. We can just relax and write whatever comes to mind. It doesn't have to be good cinema or good drama. It's just an exploration.

```
EXT. THE FALLS ROAD. BELFAST. 1977. DAY

It's mayhem! A full riot is in progress with a Hundred
Protestors. These are young men, throwing rocks at Soldiers
huddled behind an armoured Land Rover.

A second Army Land Rover appears and hurtles towards the
Protestors. They scatter.

BEHIND A WALL:

Bobby lights a wad of cloth stuck in a milk bottle full of
petrol. He leaps out from behind the wall and lobs it
straight onto the windscreen of the vehicle. It covers the
vehicle in flames. A massive cheer goes up from the
Protestors. They pelt the burning vehicle with rocks.

AT THE CORNER:

Jimmy pokes his head around the corner. Soldiers pour out of
the back of the Land Rover. The crowd scatters as a canister
of tear gas is shot into the middle of them.

                    JIMMY
          Fuck!

He ducks back and turns to Nev, who leans casually against
the wall smoking a cigarette.

                    NEV
          Is it bad?

                    JIMMY
          Front page of The Daily Mail, News
          at Ten, horror on the Falls Road
          bad!
```

Seed scenes give us the opportunity to find the limits of our imagination and knowledge. I wouldn't expect this scene to end up in the final script. It's written as a springboard for research into Belfast circa 1977. It shows the limitations of our knowledge of the troubles and punk rock in the city.

For writers who like to work things out on-the-page seed scenes are a good technique. There is a lot to be said for writing scenes that aren't part of a larger story. Writing scenes purely as practice is beneficial. It's not a method that works for everyone. I don't like to write scenes when I'm not fully prepared. I prefer a different approach. I like to write prose to develop my fictional worlds.

A short story has advantages some useful over a film script. It allows us to get inside the heads of the characters. It allows us to write outside of the action and dialogue. For anyone wanting to understand the culture of a time and place, prose is a better tool than a seed scene. So, let's have a look at how a prose approach might work with our 1977, Belfast, punk rock idea.

> *Nev's suggestion they wander over to the Falls Road seemed particular idiotic. This was already a day stuffed to the bollocks with stupid ideas and bad decisions. You could hear the riots from streets away. Angry, feral voices, smashing glass, sirens, screams and gunshots. Jimmy's terror, as they dodged through back streets, felt equal parts sane and cowardly. In contrast, Nev's demeanour was relaxed. Nev, chain-smoking cigarettes and nodding his head along to the noise. It was as though the carnage was nothing but a fresh drum beat for him to throw chords over. And maybe Nev was right. Maybe the blood, rage and violence were a distraction from the serious business of getting their single played on John Peel's radio show. As they approached the Falls Road, Jimmy imagined telling this story on the TV. "Oh, during the riots of 1977, when the petrol bombs and rubber bullets were flying, me and Nev got caught right in the middle of it. We were desperate to get tickets to see The Clash from my idiot cousin. You might recognise him. He was the lad featured on News at Ten, throwing half-bricks from the roof of the newsagents.*

Seed scenes offer an opportunity to road test our visualisation. A prose approach is often much better at capturing what we know about a time and a place. It is possible to do things in prose we can't in a script. We can get into the heads of the characters. We get a sense of what's happening and how they feel about it. It's the cultural dynamics of this time and this place that matter. Writing short sections of prose can be a very rich and rewarding technique. It is also a way to bring intuitive, messy writing back into the development process. There is another advantage of writing prose. With prose there's no temptation to copy and paste our messy writing into the actual script. With seed scenes there will always be that temptation.

getting to grips with syntax, dialect, terminology and jargon

Our story happens in a specific time and a specific place. It happens in a subculture. This is true even if that subculture is mainstream. That means we need to be aware that language is going to be an issue. When people speak in real-life, we get an instant sense of who they are, what they stand for and where they come from. It's not just what people say that's important. It's also the way they say it. Let's look at a couple of examples.

"That's a canny wee dog!"

"That dog's a jolly fine specimen. Is it trained to the gun?"

"Hey! Mate! Nice mutt!"

The content of each of these pieces of dialogue is the same. The words used and the syntax is different for each of them. The way a character delivers a line tells us a lot about them. Capturing the syntax and vocabulary of characters is difficult. But it's not possible to write a great script if we don't nail this. We have to get the syntax and the vocabulary right. And, it is the one part of screenwriting that is always very difficult. Nothing will destroy the illusion of our fictional world faster than bad dialogue.

The problem of language isn't confined to regional and subcultural use of words and syntax. We run into the same problem when our story is set in a profession which uses specific terminology. To a screenwriter, the Police, IT consultants and Reiki healers are no different from any other cultural group. If they have their own distinct jargon and way of talking about the world our writing needs to reflect that.

Getting the language right is about two factors, having an ear for syntax, and research. Someone with a natural grasp (ear) for syntax may need to do less research to be able to reproduce it on the page. Writers with very strong training in correct English often struggle with alternative syntax. We have to listen and practice. We have to immerse ourselves in the spoken word.

Our ability to hear linguistic patterns is a skill that gets better with practice. The more we do it, the better we become. Early-career screenwriters tend to write characters with identical syntax. They all speak the same way. This is usually the speech pattern of the writer. We overcome this by immersing ourselves in the spoken word of the people we write about. We must learn how to listen to people. It doesn't matter whether we do that in the world, or whether we collect and listen to recordings. The important thing is to listen and to practice reproducing the language we hear.

However, there is another problem. Our audience is likely to be from outside of the subculture, profession or region that our story is set in. We can't expect an audience to be able to tune into a true representation of a dialect or a jargon laden profession. So, our job is to be authentic whilst keeping the dialogue accessible. Or, in other words, the job isn't to copy the reality of speech patterns, jargon or dialect. Our job is often to give the audience access to a world where they are outsiders. Let's look at an example.

> *I've nante jarry, nante latty and what's worse, nante doss. I'm living off the national handbag*

The sentence above is written in Polari. This is British, gay slang, common before homosexuality was decriminalised in 1967. This is an authentic use of language, syntax and vocabulary from that time and place. But, it's not accessible to many people. Here's the translation.

> *I haven't any food, anywhere to live or even a bed. I'm living on welfare.*

Neither of those two examples work as dialogue. The first because it's impossible to understand without prior knowledge. The second, plain English version lacks authenticity. Our job is to get a feel for the language rather than reproducing it. Deciding how far to go with the language is always a creative decision. There will always be projects where authenticity is more important than clarity. One of the ways we can cope with obscure language is to use a character as a surrogate for the audience. So, imagine we introduce a young gay man, new to the London gay scene of 1958. He doesn't understand Polari, so he can't make sense of half of the conversations. Someone befriends him and introduces him to the language. This also serves as an education for the audience.

what is the fictional world and how do we get to grips with it?

The most challenging aspect of screenwriting is creating the world of story. The fictional world is a complex visualisation of the environment, habits, behaviour, customs and language. It is the things about this time and this place that are special and interesting.

We aim to know what our world looks like. We want to understand the landscape. We try to understand the people of our world. We develop our understanding until it is as if we can step into this world in our imagination.

This step is about research and imagination. And, as mentioned before, we do this by chasing our fascination for the world we are creating. This is a focused process because we know the things we need to understand. They are...

Where does this story take place?

What does it look like?

What do the inhabitants of this world look like?

How do they dress?

What kind of things exist in this place?

How do people behave?

What are the customs, morality and rules of this place?

How do people speak?

What kind of vocabulary do they have?

What kind of syntax do they use?

The way we develop our visualisation will depend on the kind of writer we are. It is as much about exploring our visualisation on-the-page as it is about looking at photos. It is both research and imagination.

Our research will inevitably generate a collection of photographs, videos and audio recordings. This is because a great deal of our job is to understand what things look or sound like. But we also need to understand how our world of story works culturally. The kind of research that comes from biographies, diaries and first-hand accounts.

The one thing that guides our creation of the fictional world is the search for authenticity. We aren't interested in reality. That's something different. The world of our story is always a fictional world. Our visualisation of the fictional world informs every single aspect of the writing. Our success as screenwriters depends on the fictional world we create. Is it compelling? Is it fascinating? Is it authentic? If the answer to all three is, yes, we have done our job.

CHAPTER 22
Step 4. Practical Tools

1. collect photographs of specific location

The eventual script will be a series of scenes. Each scene will be set in a location. The fictional world is really a series of locations. We need to be able to visualise them. The best way to build that visualisation is to collate a massive collection of photos. The purpose of the photos is to inspire our visualisation. We can write to the locations we find, or we can use aspects of them to create a fictional geography. Basically, we're creating a sort of mood board.

2. find documentaries set in the culture which inspires us

Our visualisation is what allows us to write scenes. The more fascinating and authentic our world is the more we'll draw the audience into our story. The fastest way for us to get into a culture, sub-culture or lifestyle is to find a good documentary set in that world. This is often the best way to create the foundations of a fictional world. If we want to tell a story about war correspondents, there are a lot of good documentaries. There are also plenty of interviews. That is a world we can find our way into with very little effort. The same is true for most cultures. We have to be careful not to steal content from documentaries. We can't lift other people's stories and drop them into our fictional world. We use source material to create a brand new, imaginary and completely fictional world.

3. write some exploratory prose or seed scenes

We can explore the world of our story by writing a short section of prose. This is an effective way to combine messy, intuitive writing with research. It gives us a chance to find out what we know about our ordinary world and to do some focussed research. A seed scene is also an opportunity to explore the world of story. We use them to find the limitations of our understanding. The only thing that's important is that we use this writing as exploratory. We're not writing part of the movie. We're exploring events that happen outside of the narrative but in the same world.

4. research and nail the language

We've got to find ways to nail the way people speak in our world. Videos, podcasts, audio recordings and face-to-face interviews are all useful. There are lots of online resources for terminology and slang. Eventually we need to turn all the listening into writing. Seed scenes are really useful for practicing speech patterns and language. This is the one area where they are better than prose.

5. get a deeper understanding by reading

Our visualisation must include the behaviour, customs and morals of the culture. What we need for this kind of research are first-hand accounts.

Biographies are good, so are diaries and interviews. Good journalism is also worth digging out. Journalists tend to go to the places and talk to the people where good stories live. Again, when we use journalism as a source of our research, we can't lift stories from it and turn them into fiction. What we are trying to get a sense of that world. We can't use other people's intellectual property like it's an all-you-can-eat buffet!

CHAPTER 23
Step 5. Character Development

what is character development?

A story is what happens when a specific group of characters are forced to face a series of challenging circumstances

Without characters there is no story. We now know how important it is to make our fictional world fascinating and compelling. A world that must be both authentic and accessible. A story is the exploration of a fictional world. This means characters are our emotional connection to that world. Audiences invest effort and emotion to connect with and understand their favourite characters.

It ought to go without saying that characters and character development are important. But, what do we mean when we talk about character development? Character development is the job of creating and understanding a specific character. It is how we decide what a character will do or say when presented with a challenging circumstance. Character development is the way writers understand people's behaviour and motivations. As such, there are about four different approaches to this, each with its merits.

Intuitive – in the mind	The writer has complete faith in their internal visualisation	No development before writing
Intuitive – on the page	The write has faith they will uncover their chracters as they write	No development before writing
Exploratory	The writer explores characters in writing separate from the script	Developmental prose/seed scenes
Focussed	The writer has a systematic way to research and create their characters	A coherent planning document is created

intuitive character development

All characters are the products of the writer's imagination. This is true even if we are writing about a real person. The fictional character we create is still a product of our opinions and beliefs. They are the products of what we know about people and what we believe is possible. For this reason, it makes sense to approach character development intuitively. This is true, if we have a clear visualisation of our characters. It's also true if we intend to discover them on the page. By far the most common form of character development is done intuitively, on-the-page.

There's not a lot to say about this approach. If it works for you, go for it. But, in all honesty, I have yet to meet a writer who was capable of visualising fully formed characters without development work. Writers who claim they can often rely on cliched characters. They don't understand what character development work is. A generic maverick cop isn't a character unless that character is properly developed. This is a problem that tends to plague structural screenwriters. Their focus on the plot turns characters into mechanical devices. Devices that exist only to service the action. This in turn robs their script and any movie of its dramatic potential.

There is definitely a place for messy, intuitive character development. There are writers who excel at this. Truly intuitive writers play with and discover their characters on-the-page. They discover by writing and rewriting. Bad writers try to pass off clichés as characters. They claim their understanding is intuitive, but they don't really understand characters or how to develop them.

exploratory

Exploratory character development is a technique that works really well for intuitive writers. The kind who like to discover their characters on-the-page. Writers who know they need to do some development work before they start the actual script, but who don't like more focused techniques.

We can explore our characters by writing seed scenes or prose. These are the same techniques we used to play with our fictional world. Remember, we aren't writing a scene for the script. We are playing with our characters on-the-page. The writing is meant to be intuitive, messy and playful. Or, in other words, we try to have fun.

```
EXT. THE JETTY. LAKE COMO. ITALY. DUSK

This side of the lake is quiet. The other side of the lake
is awash with tourists, boats and seaplanes. The city of
Como looks like another country, far away and disconnected
from here.

The shadow of a giant rabbit appears on the jetty. Malcolm,
dressed in a tattered and dirty rabbit costume, trudges to
the end of the jetty. He stares out across the lake.

                    BETTY (OOS)
                (hollers in a New York
                    accent)
          Hey! Bunny Foo-Foo, are you going
          to be long?

Malcolm ignores her. He makes a couple of tiny steps closer
to the edge, so his fluffy feet are hanging over the jetty.

                    BETTY (OOS)
          Come on! Chop, chop!

Malcolm turns around and trudges back down the jetty. We
hear a clanking and groan.

                    BETTY (OOS)
          Really! This bullshit again?

Malcolm struggles down the jetty. This time he carries a
rusty, old anchor and a chain, which trails behind him. He
almost trips on it. Betty giggles. The bunny head turns and
looks daggers down the jetty.

At the jetty edge, Malcolm padlocks the chain around his
foot. He bends over and hoists the anchor up, he pauses.
```

Seed scenes are a pretty good way for intuitive writers to create characters. The above scene, about Malcolm and Betty, was inspired by a photograph. At the start of the writing I had no idea about either the person in the bunny suit (Malcolm) or any other characters. It took me about ten minutes to write this scene. At the end of writing, I can see the embryonic form of two interesting characters. Those characters have emerged instinctively from the writing. They aren't fully developed, yet. They are like rough sketches. The writer's version of a stickman drawing.

Again, it's important to point out that this kind of exploration happens before we start a first draft. These aren't scenes written to go into the script. This is an intuitive way for a writer to find our characters on-the-page. To really get to grips with Malcolm and Betty we'd need to write other scenes. We can write scenes from their childhoods or the first time they got their hearts broken. At this stage, I don't know what scenes we need to write because I don't know enough about them. It is exploratory and experimental writing.

The other exploratory/intuitive approach is to write prose. So, let's do that. Let's look at Malcolm and Betty in prose form.

Malcolm slid the bookmark into the book and closed it. He knew he'd never finish it. It was another book he started with good intentions but which, like life, bored him rigid. It was one hell of a realisation to come to at sixty-four years old. I am, he thought, still someone who wants to appear well read but who can't be bothered to make the effort. Yet more evidence of his feckless and irrelevant nature to add to his growing list of character defects. Not so much a man, more like the illusion of a man. In the shade of this tedious and mediocre tree he looked out over the clichéd lake. He tortured himself with the worst and most shameful moments of his life. All the moments he could gather as evidence of his petty, lazy and corrupt nature. All the lies he'd told others and himself. The broken women he seduced for the pleasure of rejecting them. The incident with the duck! The depravity of his masturbatory life. His shallow pursuit of praise from any source. The lovers he'd manipulated and

abused. The jobs he'd talked his way into only to immediately feel were beneath his glorious and shining talent. Whatever that was. There was scant little evidence of it anywhere. Yes, there was the book, the book that paid for the house and his self-indulgent-semi-retirement. He knew all too well, anyone can write a book that preys on people's natural self-loathing. One which offers a cheap and easy redemption. Perhaps, he reflected, that was the greatest of all his sins. Not the drunken, self-pity, porn depravity or temper tantrums. Ultimately, he was the man who persuaded thousands of people that a positive attitude was the answer to life's problems. Self-belief would manifest their dreams. That, he suspected, would be carved on his tombstone. Here lies the snivelling shit who sold us the lie, anything is possible! As usual, his self-loathing transformed into thoughts of suicide. But even these were tainted by his worthlessness. Deep down he recognised his plans to die were nothing more than cheap drama. Petty revenge and a childish cry for attention. What an utterly useless piece of shit!

Prose gives us the freedom to explore the inner-life and motivations of our characters. The section above doesn't work as a film because all the action takes place in Malcolm's mind. Yet, it is exactly that inner-life which will determine what he does and says. It is that we are striving to understand.

Prose and seed scenes are excellent ways for writers to create interesting characters. Characters whose actions are informed by their inner lives. However, it's not the only way. There is a focused approach. The rest of this chapter is about that approach.

focused character development

One question we could ask about character development is what are we trying to achieve? What kind of understanding are we trying to develop? We know the goal is for the writer to explore what it means to be human. We also know we need to predict what a character will do next and what they will say?

Screenwriting is the act of placing a character in a challenging situation. We then decide how they will react to it. There are some writers who seem to believe their characters can do anything the writer demands. This seems logical because the characters are fictional. It would seem sensible to believe if we can imagine a character doing it, we can write it. But, is that true? Let's test it out by taking some well-known characters and testing the limits of what they can do?

Batman robs a bank with a machine gun, killing many civilians. He spends the money on hookers and cocaine

Father Christmas destroys all the toys in the world, with a hammer, and wakes the children to make them watch

Darth Vader gives up his work for the Empire and becomes a beekeeper

Hannibal Lecter goes onto a reality TV singing show, only to be eliminated in the final round. He cries at the news.

Although we can imagine each of these scenarios, they leave us with one burning question. Why is this character behaving so out-of-character? Any story that does this must explain why these characters are behaving so weirdly. If it does the audience will accept it. But, if they don't learn why or don't believe the explanation, they will hate us for perverting the characters. For audiences, understanding why a character behaves the way they do is as important as what they do. It's not enough for Batman to rob a bank, the audience needs to know why he's doing it.

> *Character development. Our understanding of why characters do the things they do and say the things they say.*

Character development is always about understanding our characters. Characters are always representations of humanity. We aim to understand why human beings behave the way they do. If creating a fictional world is like anthropology, character development is psychology. We create fictional cultures. Then we create fictional people.

one-dimensional characters and clichés

Script editors and producers often talk about one-dimensional characters. As writers, we need to understand this concept, to avoid it. A one-dimensional character is someone in the story who is inauthentic. They don't seem human. Or, in other words, the character is a puppet of the plot. Let's see if we can create an example.

> *Brad is a bank-robber. He dresses like a bank robber and in the film he goes into a bank and robs the bank. The police arrive, so he has a gun battle with them. He escapes. The next day he robs another bank.*

In this story, Brad is our protagonist. He is a bank robber. We know that he robs banks. This is all we know. We don't know why he robs banks or how he feels about his life. We don't know if he has any ambitions, relationships or family. Brad is a one-dimensional bank robber. Let's see what happens if we fill him out a little bit.

> *Brad is a veteran with PTSD. He can't survive in normal jobs, surrounded by normal people. He can't relate to people. People find him threatening. He only feels OK when he's in action. No one will touch him for military work because of his PTSD. So, he robs a bank and gives the money away. He doesn't care about the money. He just wants to feel normal, and to feel normal he needs adrenaline, fire-fights and danger.*

When screenwriters write action films, they often make the same mistake. They believe the action is the most important thing in the scene. The action isn't important. What's important are the reasons why the action is happening.

It's not about pulling the trigger. The gun is irrelevant. It is about her ethical dilemma and emotional cost she has to pay for her decision.

One-dimensional characters are characters stripped of motivation and humanity. Or, in other words, a one-dimensional character is a woman who shoots a gun. She acts, but we don't understand why she's doing it. We don't know the potential cost to her. We don't understand the things that have driven her to this choice.

Producers, script editors, actors and audiences hate one-dimensional characters. This is because one-dimensional characters fail to create good drama.

One-dimensional characters = poor story

It the writer's job to have a deeper understanding of our character's needs, desires and motivations. We need this information because this is where stories come from. Our end goal is to create great, rounded characters. But we don't need to reject one-dimensional character ideas. Instead, we use one-dimensional characters as the starting point of our development process. Bad ideas lead to good ones if we work at it. Bad characters become good ones if we work at them. This is how the process works.

creating characters by creating character profiles

Our job is to find, research and create a method to create character profiles. It doesn't matter how we do it, it just needs to get done. In this section of the book, I am going to show how I develop character profiles. I'm doing it this way because I know my method works. Feel free to adapt, change or ignore any of this. As writers we each have to find our own path.

Dogma is the enemy of creativity

We need to understand why people behave the way they do. One approach for us might be to create a list of topics we'd want to know more about. This is my list.

Name
Who are they (a one-dimensional description)
Skills
Flaws
Insecurities
Strengths
Motivation
What do they want, need and desire?
Odd behaviour
Appearance
Dilemmas
Secrets
Theme
Sub-theme
Backstory
Potential seed scenes

This list works for me. It is how I understand human beings. A writer with a different understanding would create a different list. Regardless of the details there are four things every writer must address. They are name, skills, flaws and backstory.

Our story is the way our characters deal with the plot (challenging circumstances). We need to know how a character will solve problems (skills). We need to know what kinds of problems will be particularly challenging to them (flaws). And we need to know why they behave the way they do (backstory).

This approach is often appealing to intuitive writers who like to create characters on-the-page. The heavy work of understanding our characters comes from their backstory. Writing backstories is definitely a messy writing task. When we remove backstory, our characters become one-dimensional. A character with only skills and flaws doesn't generate drama. It can only react to plot-points mechanically.

simple character development

So, how can we use a basic, four-element approach to character development? Let's apply this approach to Malcolm, our suicidal self-help guru.

name	Malcolm Zinski
skills	intelligent, really articulate, a great public speaker, charismatic in public, really good at selling ideas and getting people to believe in him
flaws	alcoholism, depression, anxiety, shallow, full of self-pity, selfish, manipulative, misogynist, full of self-loathing, suicidal, narcissist
backstory	Malcolm grows up in a blue collar family in Bradford. He is a bright kid, but lazy with it. He manages to skate his way through school without ever really having to try. This gives him an overly inflated sense of his abilities. Something he soon discovers when he gets a first job in the textile factory. The same factory his father works in. He loathes and resented the job and sees it as a waste of his, as yet, undefined talents. As soon as he has a wage he creates a fake version of himself. He gets a train over to Leeds and passes himself off as a middle-class, Oxford student. A stunt he uses to pull girls and get credit. It's only a matter of time until he can't stand the factory anymore. So, he runs away to London, reinventing himself in the process. What he soon discovers is his ability to sell people on ideas is valuable. However, he doesn't find real success until he stumbles across the self-help industry. His creation, the Eight-Pillars of Success, rapidly goes from self-help book to self-help empire. The book itself is nothing more than a collage of other people's ideas and some jargon. Malcolm can barely believe how naive and gullible his readers are. However, his personal life is a disaster. Five marriages, affairs, drunkenness and history of depravity eventually lead to a coup in his business. He is put out to pasture. Now, he lives with his personal assistant, Betty, in a remote house on the shore of Lake Como. He's a recluse and for the first time in his life he is forced to look at who he is and how he's lived his life.

The backstory is what happened in Malcolm's life before the start of our story. This is not the plot for the film, nor is there any need for this to become part of the script. The backstory isn't written as a plan for flashbacks or exposition. What are creating is a fictional past for our fictional character. A past that lets us predict what they will do when presented with a challenging circumstance. So, does our understanding of Malcolm help us do that? Well, it certainly paints a picture. Here we have a character who has skated through life by presenting a false image of himself. We know he's rejected his past and reinvented himself. We also know he's written a self-help book to make money. He did this with zero intentions of actually helping anyone. He is a conman who finds the entire world ready to buy any nonsense he creates. At the same time, he's a man completely out of control in his personal life. He is a genuine mess. Now we know him a bit better, we can better predict his behaviour. So, let's write a new seed scene. One where he's approached by a journalist who might expose his hypocrisy.

EXT. THE JETTY. LAKE COMO. DAY

Malcolm sprawls, drunkenly on a ancient, wooden sun-lounger on the jetty. The sun creeps over the edge of the massive umbrella which is shading him. He bolts upright from his stupor, like he's been hit with a taser.

> MALCOLM
>> Mummy!

His mind finally catches up with his body. He glances round to see if anyone heard him. No one is there. He squints up at the sun and down at the lounger. He grapples with the umbrella, but it's too heavy and his frustration soon turns to rage. He beats the concrete base with his paperback book.

> MALCOLM
>> Bastard!

Using every ounce of his scrawny bodyweight he drags the lounger into the shade. He collapses onto it. He reaches for his cocktail, but now it's too far away. He leans further, supporting himself on one bony elbow. But, before he gets to it a woman's hand picks it up. He looks up.

DARLA (37), who looks like she ought to present a prime-time cable news show. She hands him the drink.

> DARLA
>> Mr Zinski? Your assistant told me
>> I'd find you out here.

Malcolm takes his drink, sips it and refuses to make eye-contact.

> MALCOLM
>> Divorce lawyer or a hooker?

```
She extends a business card, which he refuses to take, so
she puts it back into her purse.

                    DARLA
          Neither, I'm a writer, like you.

Malcolm snorts derisively.

                    MALCOLM
          Really? My sincere and deepest
          fucking regrets to you and your
          family.
```

Although this scene was easier to write than the first one, it still doesn't work as drama. It still feels like a seed scene. That's because knowing the skills, flaws and backstory of one character isn't enough to create drama. As writers, we need total access to Malcolm's inner life. The audience don't need this kind of access. The audience will create their own explanations about who Malcolm is and why he behaves the way he does. They do this based on their observations. This is one of the reasons reverse-engineering successful scripts is a flawed method to understand screenwriting. What makes it onto the page, or the screen, isn't the same as the process the writer used to get it on the page. It's like an iceberg. What you can see on the page is a fraction of the work that went into writing it.

Writers need to create characters whose behaviour is authentic and consistent. It's easy to spot an authentic character when we see one on the screen. Authentic characters take us by surprise without breaking the illusion. The audience believes this is a real person. Character authenticity is all about believability. The other thing audiences need from characters is consistency. The audience won't forgive a hero who is cruel or a genius detective who overlooks an obvious clue. Consistency comes from the quality of our understanding. Plot-driven writers often create characters who seem far-fetched or are inconsistent. If the only thing motivating a character is the plot, the character has no integrity. They'll do anything we write! A plot driven character can do anything at all. They'll do it regardless of how little sense it makes to the audience.

A lot of writers get away with basic character development. If the story is fairly simple, the character's skills, flaws and backstory may be enough. To do anything more sophisticated, we need to deepen our understanding.

Most plot problems are underlying character problems

complex character development

To create greater complexity in our characters we have to look at them in greater depth. One way to do this is to treat them as if there are real people. We can analyse a character in the same way we would a human being. This is a strong approach and one that suits some writers. I am always nervous of it because all characters are fictional and are definitely not people. But there is another way. A way to look at characters without seeing them as real people. We can treat characters as drama engines. A drama engine is any fictional character who has massive amounts of dramatic potential. Great characters tend to be good drama engines. They have the kind of fascinating character traits that add to any story in which they appear. To create a character who works as a drama engine, we need to create real depth. We develop them with the kind of character traits which will add to the drama. And, one way to do this is to add new categories into the mix. Let's see if we can transform our Malcolm character into a drama engine.

Focused character development is often about working from one category to another. We have an idea about a character's flaws. This flaw may also suggest part of their backstory. We create a few secrets. This reveals things about their motivations and desires. As always, we are playing with ideas. We use this part of the process to experiment. It's also important to remember, at this stage, we're not committed to a particular role in our story for Malcolm. He doesn't have to be our protagonist! He might be an antagonist, a mentor or a supporting character. We can create room for instinctive, messy writing in this very focused approach. By jotting down ideas for seed scenes we create space for us to play with characters on-the-page. It's all part of the development process.

name	Malcolm Zinkler	Betty McMartin
who are they?	misanthropic drunk	a failed writer
skills	he is a natural salesman and charismatic when he's sober. He's actually a pretty good writer.	she's diplomatic, organised and manipulative. She's also highly skilled at writing in other people's style or voice.
flaws	he's a dreadful drunk, he hates everyone, is rude and ill mannered, he's a petty narcissist, his self-loathing is a bottomless pit, he's a misanthrope and rejects everyone he meets	she's lazy, jealous and resentful.
insecurities	he feels like he's a fraud and fears anyone finding that out, He is particular vulnerable about his background. No one really knows about his working class background	she is really vulnerable about her writing and keeps her manuscripts hidden from everyone
strengths	he has no illusions about himself, he knows he's garbage but because of this there is a level on which he really understands accepts and forgives other people's frailty	she is really good at getting the lifestyle she thinks she deserves even when she has no way of affording it
motivation	he's deeply motivated to not feel anything but his deeper drive is to find a way to escape himself	to appears successful and to have an easy life

what do they want, need and desire?	what he wants more than anything else is to be genuinely seen and loved	she wants to have Malcolm's life and money - she is also desperate to be recognised as a successful writer
odd behaviour	he has developed the habit of going out in public dressed in animal costumes, he claims it's a thing about anonymity, everyone who knows him suspects it's a sex thing	she drugs Malcolm when she wants to write without dealing with his bullshit or just when she wants the house to herself
appearance	like a someone kicked a drunk potato farmer through the casual clothing section of the Armani store	she looks like a woman who is trying too hard to be effortlessly casual
dilemmas	whether to kill himself, whether to move permanently into the rabbit suit, whether to face the world as he is	whether to give her story to the journalist or not
secrets	1. that he genuinely and profoundly loved every single one of his wives and each divorce smashed him into tiny little pieces 2. that Betty wrote his last two books	1. she's written a memoir about her life with Malcolm that she intends to publish when he's dead 2. she wrote Malcolm's last two self-help books without his input
theme	an exploration of the personal and emotional cost of unearned success	the cost of unearned success
sub-theme	an exploration of the personal and emotional cost of crippling self-loathing	the cost of jealously and failure

| backstory | Malcolm grows up in a blue collar family in Bradford. He is a bright kid, but lazy. He manages to skate his way through school without ever trying. His mother and father are both salt-of-the-Earth, no nonsense, working class people who don't understand the strange boy they are raising. A boy who'd rather listen to music and read than play football. His academic success gives him an overly inflated sense of his abilities. Something his father tries to beat out of him by getting Malcolm his first job in the textile factory. The same factory his father works in. He loathes and resented the job and sees it as a waste of his, as yet, undefined talents. As soon as he has a wage he creates a fake version of himself. He gets a train over to Leeds every Saturday and passes himself off as a middle-class, Oxford student. A stunt he uses to pull girls and gatecrash his way into swanky events.
It's only a matter of time until he can't stand the factory anymore. So, he runs away to London, reinventing himself in the process. What he soon discovers is his ability to sell people on ideas is valuable. However, he doesn't find real success until he stumbles across the self-help industry. His creation, the Eight-Pillars of Success, rapidly goes from self-help book to self-help empire. The book itself is nothing more than a collage of other people's ideas and some jargon. Malcolm can barely believe how naïve and gullible his readers are. He loathes his fans and has taken to wearing a bunny suit to hide from them when he's in public.
His personal life is a disaster. Five marriages, affairs, drunkenness and history of depravity eventually lead to a coup in his business. He is put out to pasture. Now, he lives with his personal assistant, Betty, in a remote house on the shore of Lake Como. He's a recluse and for the first time in his life he is forced to look at who he is and how he's lived his life.
In the last year, his life has taken a turn into new areas of weirdness. He now refuses to go out in public unless he is wearing a bunny outfit. He's got a wardrobe full of them. And, he's also playing with the idea of suicide. His last thread of connection to humanity is his long-suffering personal assistant, Betty and the Zardoc the gardener / handyman, who is a deaf-mute. | Betty grew up in a middle-class bohemian family where everyone was either an artists or a writer. Both of her parents we're hugely successful. Her mother was an abstract painter and her father a novelist. Betty and her two sisters were educated in Montessori schools, moving to private schools which specialised in the arts as they got older. It was assumed that the girls would all go into the arts. Betty's two sisters have more than fulfilled their parent's ambitions for them. One of them is a gallery owner and the other is an internationally renowned performance artist. Betty's attempts to follow in her father's footsteps have been marked by one failure after another. Her first novel was so unsuccessful both her agent and her publisher dropped her. Her reputation was so badly wrecked by this first book she's struggled to get anyone to look at her second book. The moment which broke her heart was when her father refused to help her with the second novel and offered to get her jobs as a ghostwriter on celebrity autobiographies. This is how she has made a living for years. It's also how she met Malcolm. His company wanted an almost entirely fictional autobiography written to bolster sales of his self-help books and courses. She went over to his house on Lake Como to write the book and just never moved out. It's not clear whether Malcolm remembers that he never officially hired her as a live-in assistant. |

The table above shows the categories that I use to understand characters.

Writers are free to create their own categories. It is up to each of us to figure out what we need to know. We just need to understand the motivation and behaviour of our characters. My categories are largely influenced by people like Konstantin Stanislavski. He wrote *An Actor Prepares*. His ideas about the way actors create roles has had a huge effect on the way I create characters. We are writing characters for actors. It makes sense to use the same approaches in the writing as they do in their preparation. So, let's have a look at the categories and see what they offer us.

name

Names in movies matter. The second we give a character a name, we also give them whatever traits we associate with that name. Harold Minkie is a very different character from Brad Michaels. Betty McMartin is a different sort of character from Trixie La Roue. Character names almost always come with baggage. As human beings, we each have a complex set of prejudices and ideas about people. Prejudices we use to predict what kind of people they will be. One of the ways we judge people is by their names. Or, in other words, giving a character a name is definitely part of the creative process. It's also often the first thing we do. There is something almost magical that happens when we name a character. It is almost as if the act of naming them calls them into existence. I don't want to get too weird or wacky about this, but my experience is naming a character is a profound step in the creative process.

who are they?

When writers talk about clichés and tropes it is almost always with contempt. A character who makes it into the script as a cliché is always an indication of the writer's failure to do their job. But clichés and tropes are important to screenwriting. They can also work as archetypes. An archetype is a typical example of a certain person, thing or character. Audiences have an immediate and deep understanding of an archetype. Say, for instance, our character is a maverick cop. This is a mainstay of the film and tv industry. This is both a cliché and an archetype. It's a cliché if the writer serves up a poor imitation of previous versions of the character. It becomes an archetype if it conforms to the trope but has something new, fresh and fascinating to say.

Dirty Harry is an archetypal maverick cop, but so is Columbo. They could not be more different and yet, at their core they are both from the same archetype.

When we ask, "who is this character?" what we are asking is "is this character an archetype?" In most cases the answer is going to be yes, they are. The recognition that our character is a new version of a trope is important. If we don't see it and write it down, we run the risk of trotting out a cliched version of the archetype. If we do see it, own it and write it down, we have the opportunity to look at it with fresh eyes.

skills

All stories are driven by the skills of the character. If the skills are different, the story changes. Let's create an example. Our story is about our protagonist's struggle to recover a stolen book.

> *Elle is a detective. She is good at getting people to open up. She can get people to tell her things no other detective can. She recovers the stolen book by interviewing people. She goes from one confession to the next until it leads to the book.*

> *Horace is a con man. He uses his underworld contacts to discover the location of the book. He then plans a sophisticated and elegant con to get it back.*

> *Damien is a computer genius. He tracks the book on the dark-web by the data trail it creates. He then hacks security systems to find out who is behind it. He then uses a combination of blackmail and malware to force the original thief to return it.*

In each of these scenarios the central problem is the same. They could even have the same antagonists. Despite this, the story is different. It's determined by the skills of the central characters.

flaws

When we looked at drama, we realised it is as much about vulnerability and failure as it is about success. We need to understand where our characters are weak. Most movie scripts are simple stories. In most films the severity of the challenge increases as we approach the end. We answer the question, what price is this character willing to pay? In other words, we force our central character to face their worst nightmare to win. If they are afraid of heights, they'll end up hanging from a window ledge. If they are afraid of intimacy, we force them to open up to someone. When we create a list of a character's flaws, we are also creating the beats of a simple plot. This is because it's exactly these flaws our character will need to overcome to win in the end.

In more complicated stories character flaws are central to the writing process. In traditional tragedies a heroic character is often destroyed by their character flaws. There is also a massive connection between character flaws and their vulnerability. To expose a character's vulnerability, we force them to face their flaws. It's not necessary for them to heroically overcome them. Failure is as much a part of the human experience as success. It is possible to write great stories about failure.

insecurities

Imagine we create a male character who is silent whenever there is an attractive woman in the room. We, the audience, know he is insecure about forming relationships. He is shy with the opposite sex. What if we have a character who grows his hair long at the back he can comb it over his bald head? His insecurity is about his self-image and his age. His neurotic need to hide his baldness points to a deep-seated insecurity about how the world sees him. A character's insecurities force them to behave irrationally. That irrational behaviour tells the audience about the character's inner life. We can show the audience the difference between how a character is in public and how they are in private. It is often the contrast between these two that reveals a character's insecurities. There is an obvious connection between insecurity and plot-points. A dramatic moment is often when we give a character the choice between two paths. If one of the paths forces a character to face their insecurity it can drive them to failure or victory. But that failure may be exactly the experience they need to grow and develop.

strengths

Strengths are not the same as skills. A character can have huge amounts of determination but no real skills. Determination is this character's strength. Honesty can be a strength, as can kindness or empathy.

In simple stories a character's strengths are often the counterweight to their flaws. So, a character may be afraid of spiders, but their sense of duty is what forces them to face that fear at the vital moment. A character may be given the opportunity to win everything by telling one simple lie. But their honesty prevents them from cheating. This drives the story on to how they deal with the price of that decision.

In complicated stories a character's strengths are often the things that humanise them. Malcolm, the character in the table above is a good example of this. His behaviour is dreadful. Yet, he is someone who is able to understand and accept other people's frailties and failures. It is possible this could be the trait which redeems him. It would be possible to write a redemption story on that premise.

Although it looks like we're developing characters, we're really creating plot-points. And this is what it means to create a character to be a drama-engine. Each decision about a new character trait offers potential routes through the story. The stories flow out of the work we do on the characters.

motivation

A character's motivation is the thing that drives their behaviour. It is a cliché about actors that they'll ask a director what their motivation is for a scene. They need to know why their character reacts to this moment in this particular way. This suggests that a character's motivation may change from scene to scene. On one level this is true, a character may be driven by a short-term need or goal. Beneath that is the core motivation of the character. What is it that really drives them? A character can be driven by insecurities, ambition, lust, fear of failure, or a thousand other factors. A character's skills determine how a character solves problems. Their motivation explains why they are doing it.

what do they want or need?

A character may have short term wants or needs. A character may need to get through a door, or to prevent someone else getting through the door. That kind of need and desire is addressed at a scene level. So, it is like a character's motivation. In fact, the two are linked. A character needs to prevent someone coming through a door and their motivation to do this is to save their friend.

But there is a deeper level to character needs. A character may want to become a pop-star. This kind of need will drive a plot. This character's need to be famous begs another question, why does she want or need this? If the answer is because she's a narcissist that will determine the way she behaves. If she believes fame will cure her depression the story will travel a different path. Again, characters' needs and desires shape plots. A character with strong needs and desires is a powerful drama engine.

odd behaviour

Character development work is mainly about understanding the inner-life of the characters. This is problematic for screenwriters. Scripts don't offer immediate access to the inner-life of our characters. Yes, we can use voice-overs and exposition to do this, but both are really clunky methods. Most of the time, we ask the audience to figure out a character's inner-life by observing the character's behaviour and appearance.

A character's odd behaviour is a way to create a bridge between a character's inner-life and the audience. We ask ourselves, what is the most important idea we want the audience to get about this character? And, can we reveal this through their behaviour? If the character suffers from anxiety, how can we show this? If the character is motivated by the death of their mother, is there a way we can show that? Do they have a woman's locket in their pocket? Do they play with it when they make important decisions? How else might we indicate this to the audience?

appearance

We all understand the idea of creating a first impression. The first time we meet a new person we look at their appearance. We look at their clothes, their hair, their posture and we make an immediate judgement. That opinion may change over time, but that first impression is a powerful one. This means there is a huge connection between how a person appears and what kind of person they are. As screenwriters we depend on audiences making these kinds of judgements. A character's appearance is as much a window into their inner-life as their name is. When we get to the chapter on formatting, we'll go into detail on how a screenwriter introduces a new character. There are a lot of rules about this. It matters that we get it right. A character's appearance isn't their height, build and how sexy they are! A character's appearance needs to tell us the kind of person they are. Let's create some examples of character descriptions that tell us who the character is.

> *Gena Monroe. The kind science-geek who routinely trolls sci-fi writers for their failure to grasp string theory.*

> *Brad Petersen. If beige was a person, that person would find Brad tediously dull.*

> *Gillian Scott. What entitlement would look like, if you gave it a New York accent and a woolly hat.*

> *Norman Thewlis. A pair of battle-scarred, tattooed fists with the angry remnants of an alcoholic attached to them.*

In each case we can visualise the character from the description. Yet, very little of that description is about their physical appearance. The ability to evoke a character in one simple sentence is a core skill for screenwriters. As a reader, it's a pleasure to read any script where the writer knows how to evoke a character's appearance.

dilemmas

To get to a character's vulnerabilities we force them to make life-changing decisions. The dramatic impact of these decisions increases with the stakes. So, the more impact the decision has, the more dramatic the moment. At the same time, the more conflicted a choice is, the more powerful it becomes. The hero's journey structural model is very big on the idea of sacrifice and martyrdom in the final act. The hero has to choose to die in order save the world or whatever else is at stake. Writers use this idea so often it is at the tipping point between being an archetype and being a cliché. A dramatic dilemma doesn't have to be between personal sacrifice and the greater good. It's not the only way for a story to be powerful and dramatic. A dilemma can be between two impossible choices. This is often referred to as making *Sophie's Choice*. This phase comes from the book *Sophie's Choice*. In the book, the Nazis force Sophie to choose which of her two children will live and which will die. It is an impossible dilemma. Each choice is repugnant, but the consequences of not choosing are worse. Dilemmas don't have to be this brutal, but they do need to test our characters.

One of my personal beliefs about storytelling is that it is how a culture tests and spreads its moral code. Stories about heroes are always an exploration of what it means to be heroic. Stories about love are always about the morality of relationships. The moral choices we force on our characters are always about the morality of our culture as a whole. Does our character choose freedom or the rule of law? Does our character sacrifice a child to save a village or is all life sacred? The dilemmas we chose often go to the heart of our story's theme and meaning.

secrets

The hiding, protection and revelation of secrets is a very common dramatic device. The secrets a character wants to keep reveals a lot about them. If we want to create drama through conflict a character with a secret is a good drama engine. They will be in conflict and struggle with anyone trying to reveal it.

theme

In the chapter on theme we looked at how the theme guides every part of the storytelling. The theme tells us what our film is really about. The theme shows us which character traits increase a character's value to the story. It also tells us which ideas distract from the theme. It's useful, to keep a note of the main theme with our character development profiles. When create a character trait, we need to constantly ask, does this trait serve the theme of the story or not?

sub-theme

When we discussed theme, we also looked at the way sub-themes could create subplots. The sub-theme uncovers a different facet of the central theme. It defines a character's objectives. Let's look back at the example from the chapter on theme.

Character	Sub-Theme	Rough Overview
Kitty Bandit	Protecting her reputation	Bandit is the gang's up and coming enforcer. She's violent, ruthless and totally focused on making a name for herself
Queen Bee	Protecting her family	Queen Bee runs the gang. She's also the sister of the Duchess. She's all about protecting her family. However, what will she do when she has to choose between her blood kin and the gang?
Pistol	Revenge	Pistol is the gang's top enforcer. Everyone except Bandit is afraid of her. She believes every threat needs to be met with terrible and bloody revenge.
The Duchess	Escaping her family	The Duchess runs the legitimate front business which launders the gang's money. She desperately wants to escape gang life and her sister's influence.
Officer Monroe	Fighting for justice	Officer Monroe is the patrol officer in this block. She really wants justice for the ordinary people whose lives are ruined by the gang
Baby	Individual freedom	Baby is utterly unpredictable. She is part of the gang but doesn't follow orders and will not listen to anyone else. She commits crimes for the fun of it.

Sub-themes often reveal a supporting character's objectives and motivation. They are really useful for keeping characters on track when writing the script. They allows us to create subplots that complement our theme. We don't have to worry about a subplot distracting from our primary story because it's thematically linked. It's also a really useful technique when creating a show bible for a TV series. We can create a more rounded, dynamic cast if each character has a sub-theme.

backstory

A character's backstory is all the relevant moments in their life before the start of the story. It is about how their childhood formed the person they are today.

We look at their education and the choices they made. We figure out what turned them into the character they are at the start of the film. If we write a good backstory it makes sense of every other part of the character profile.

Malcolm is ashamed of his success. His backstory explains how that came about. He doesn't believe a word of the advice he gives to other people. He is alone and isolated. His history of drunken behaviour and broken relationships have led him to this point.

seed scenes

As we create a character it is inevitable that ideas for scenes will pop into our minds. We may find ourselves visualising moments of the film. This kind of spreadsheet character development is very focused, but it allows us to break away into messy writing. We note down any ideas for scene we have as they occur to us. We can then either write seed scenes or prose to get an instinctive feel for the character. If we learn anything new, we bring it back to the development profile. We are, in essence, practicing writing this character and learning as we write.

uncovering the real drama engines

It is possible to create a character who has so much dramatic potential they will carry an entire story. However, in most cases a character only starts to work as a drama engine in conjunction with other characters. The real power of focused character development happens when we develop a cast. A cast is more powerful than any individual character. Let's see how that might work.

name	Malcolm Zinkler	Betty McMartin
who are they?	misanthropic drunk	a failed writer
skills	he is a natural salesman and charismatic when he's sober. He's actually a pretty good writer.	she's diplomatic, organised and manipulative. She's also highly skilled at writing in other people's style or voice.
flaws	he's a dreadful drunk, he hates everyone, is rude and ill mannered, he's a petty narcissist, his self-loathing is a bottomless pit, he's a misanthrope and rejects everyone he meets	she's lazy, jealous and resentful.
insecurities	he feels like he's a fraud and fears anyone finding that out, He is particular vulnerable about his background. No one really knows about his working class background	she is really vulnerable about her writing and keeps her manuscripts hidden from everyone
strengths	he has no illusions about himself, he knows he's garbage but because of this there is a level on which he really understands accepts and forgives other people's frailty	she is really good at getting the lifestyle she thinks she deserves even when she has no way of affording it
motivation	he's deeply motivated to not feel anything but his deeper drive is to find a way to escape himself	to appears successful and to have an easy life

odd behaviour	he has developed the habit of going out in public dressed in animal costumes, he claims it's a thing about anonymity, everyone who knows him suspects it's a sex thing	she drugs Malcolm when she wants to write without dealing with his bullshit or just when she wants the house to herself
appearance	like a someone kicked a drunk potato farmer through the casual clothing section of the Armani store	she looks like a woman who is trying too hard to be effortlessly casual
dilemmas	whether to kill himself, whether to move permanently into the rabbit suit, whether to face the world as he is	whether to give her story to the journalist or not
secrets	that he genuinely and profoundly loved every single one of his wives and each divorce smashed him into tiny little pieces - that Betty wrote his last two books	she's written a memoir about her life with Malcolm that she intends to publish when he's dead - she wrote Malcolm's last two self-help books without his input
theme	an exploration of the personal and emotional cost of unearned success	the cost of unearned success
sub-theme	an exploration of the personal and emotional cost of crippling self-loathing	the cost of jealously and failure

backstory	Malcolm grows up in a blue collar family in Bradford. He is a bright kid, but lazy. He manages to skate his way through school without ever trying. His mother and father are both salt-of-the-Earth, no nonsense, working class people who don't understand the strange boy they are raising. A boy who'd rather listen to music and read than play football. His academic success gives him an overly inflated sense of his abilities. Something his father tries to beat out of him by getting Malcolm his first job in the textile factory. The same factory his father works in. He loathes and resented the job and sees it as a waste of his, as yet, undefined talents. As soon as he has a wage he creates a fake version of himself. He gets a train over to Leeds every Saturday and passes himself off as a middle-class, Oxford student. A stunt he uses to pull girls and gate-crash his way into swanky events. It's only a matter of time until he can't stand the factory anymore. So, he runs away to London, reinventing himself in the process. What he soon discovers is his ability to sell people on ideas is valuable. However, he doesn't find real success until he stumbles across the self-help industry. His creation, the Eight-Pillars of Success, rapidly goes from self-help book to self-help empire. The book itself is nothing more than a collage of other people's ideas and some jargon. Malcolm can barely believe how naive and gullible his readers are. He loathes his fans and has taken to wearing a bunny suit to hide from them when he's in public. His personal life is a disaster. Five marriages, affairs, drunkenness and history of depravity eventually lead to a coup in his business. He is put out to pasture. Now, he lives with his personal assistant, Betty, in a remote house on the shore of Lake Como. He's a recluse and for the first time in his life he is forced to look at who he is and how he's lived his life. In the last year, his life has taken a turn into new areas of weirdness. He now refuses to go out in public unless he is wearing a bunny outfit. He's got a wardrobe full of them. And, he's also playing with the idea of suicide. His last thread of connection to humanity is his long-suffering personal assistant, Betty and the Zardoc the gardener/handyman, who is a deaf-mute.	Betty grew up in a middle-class bohemian family where everyone was either an artists or a writer. Both of her parents we're hugely successful. Her mother was an abstract painter and her father a novelist. Betty and her two sisters were educated in Montessori schools, moving to private schools which specialised in the arts as they got older. It was assumed that the girls would all go into the arts. Betty's two sisters have more than fulfilled their parent's ambitions for them. One of them is a gallery owner and the other is an internationally renowned performance artist. Betty's attempts to follow in her father's footsteps have been marked by one failure after another. Her first novel was so unsuccessful both her agent and her publisher dropped her. Her reputation was so badly wrecked by this first book she's struggled to get anyone to look at her second book. The moment which broke her heart was when her father refused to help her with the second novel and offered to get her jobs as a ghost-writer on celebrity autobiographies. This is how she has made a living for years. It's also how she met Malcolm. His company wanted an almost entirely fictional autobiography written to bolster sales of his self-help books and courses. She went over to his house on Lake Como to write the book and just never moved out. It's not clear whether Malcolm remembers that he never officially hired her as a live-in assistant.
potential seed scenes	bunny suit at an AA Meeting -drunk bunny in Como - mute gardener in a bunny suit - Betty quits her job - Malcolm utterly abandoned by everyone - the bunny and the rabid Malcolm fan - bunny suicides - naked Malcolm on the jetty - Malcolm discovers Betty's manuscript - Malcolm hears about his dad's death and refuses to go to the funeral	Betty drugs Malcolm so she can pitch her tell-all biography to her publisher - Writing her book in the kitchen (the one room in the house Malcolm never visits) - Malcolm discovers Betty's manuscript - Betty hits Malcolm with a baseball bat

This is the point where developing our characters will create potential stories. The process creates stories out of the dramatic potential of two characters who have been put into the same fictional world. In this case, we're looking at Malcolm and Betty. Their character profiles are specifically designed to put them into conflict with each other. They are designed to expose each other's vulnerabilities. This is the opposite of creating a plot and then forcing characters to mechanically perform the plot. In this process, the plot is a natural development of creating these two characters and putting them into each other's lives. It doesn't matter whether they behave like real people, or whether they are likeable. All that matters are the tensions and traits we design into them. Their flawed personalities are the engine which drives the drama.

This is actually a two-part process. First, we create the tensions. Then we analyse the pros and cons of each character trait. This analysis tells us where to find the best story. This analysis is also how we train ourselves to analyse scripts. We can use the same analytical technique to take apart and understand the mechanisms of any story. Instead of judging it against a plot template, we decide whether the characters' dramatic potential is capable of carrying the story. We ask ourselves whether better character design would lead to a better story and a more dramatic script.

Let's think about how Malcolm and Betty as characters give us dramatic potential. What we're looking at is the relationship between our character's traits and potential plots

vulnerability

Pros. Betty's vulnerability comes from her sense of failure and her jealousy of Malcolm's success. Her rejection by her father is the wound she carries around with her. The story would need to lead her towards a visceral experience of this rejection. This could either come from either Malcolm as a surrogate father or from news of her father's death. Malcolm's vulnerability comes from his self-loathing and self-imposed isolation. The bunny suit looks very much like a metaphor for his retreat from the world. He requires a plot which forces him to form an emotional bond with another person. Or a plot which forces him back out into the public as himself rather than as the false image he has sold to the world. Given that Betty's tell-all biography achieves that, it may be this is central to the plot.

Cons. Both Betty and Malcolm are manipulative and selfish. Their primary character traits push them away from vulnerability rather than towards it. Their relationship seems to enable their worst features rather than exposing their vulnerabilities. Any plot would need to force them into challenges which expose their vulnerabilities.

It seems likely the story will need another character to expose their vulnerabilities. That character will need to be someone who is a threat to both of them in different ways. Malcolm's challenge is to form an emotional bond. Betty needs to keep control of Malcolm. This means a love interest for Malcolm would achieve both goals.

theme

Pros. Malcolm's relationship to the theme of unearned success is very direct. Betty's is more to do with a feeling that she is entitled to success despite her lacklustre career. She has moved in and taken over Malcolm's life because she wants it and feels she deserves it.

Cons. It's easy to see the way these characters' backstories relate to the theme. The challenge will be to create a plot that exposes that in the present. The danger would be to create a story that requires a lot of flashbacks and/or exposition.

overcoming problems

Pros. Malcolm has a litany of problems. Most of them are to do with his self-destructive nature. His alcoholism, his depression, his deep-seated feelings of self-loathing are primary challenges. When we start to look at how Betty adds to his problems, the big issue that pops out is her tell-all biography. If she tells the world about who he really is he'll be ruined. Betty's biggest challenge seems to be how she can keep control of Malcolm and also keep her biography a secret.

Cons. These two characters need some very challenging external circumstances to overcome. These can either come from plot points or the inclusion of another character to work as a stressor.

morality

Pros. Betty scores quite highly in this area because she is writing a tell-all biography. She will have to choose between caring for Malcolm and re-launching her career.

Cons. Malcolm is so utterly selfish he seems immune to moral dilemmas. This is an area that needs work. Malcolm would be stronger and more interesting if he had some redeeming features. These might lever him towards a difficult moral decision. Again, this indicates the story needs another character. Someone to draw Malcolm out and to challenge him to make moral decisions.

conflict

Pros. The primary area of conflict between Malcolm and Betty is Betty's tell-all biography. One way to craft a story would be to make that the central issue. But there are other areas of conflict. Both Malcolm and Betty are riddled with inner-conflict. Malcolm's primary conflict is between being a survivor and his self-destruction. Betty's inner-conflict is between protecting her lifestyle and redeeming herself as a writer.

Cons. These characters offer too many opportunities for comedic, surface conflict. The dramatic opportunities might get lost in the richness of their dysfunctional relationship. There is a very real danger of the script having too much character and not a lot of story.

Any screenwriter who has ever had feedback on their script will recognise the tone of the above analysis. That's because it sounds like the feedback a script-editor might give. This is a really important point. If we do focused character development and analyse it, it allows us to analyse a story before it's been written! I know, this is a radical idea, but it's also true. Good quality character development allows us to imagine the dramatic potential and risks of our story before we write. Pre-writing analysis allows us to add in new characters to solve problems before they arise. We can build on the aspects that appeal to us and to alter the traits of characters who don't work. And, remember, we are doing this before writing the first draft of our script. In fact, we haven't even nailed down our plot.

process, play and analysis

Character development is about a lot of different things. It is about authenticity and the understanding we need to write each character. On another level, character development is about our character's dramatic potential. The work we do forms the plot and determines the story. This is what it means when we talk about characters as drama engines.

The actual process is not a single writing task. We don't sit down, fill out the spreadsheet and work with what we've got. Instead, we take a first pass at our characters. Then, we write some seed scenes. After that, we go back and rework our character profiles. When story elements emerge from this work, we can analyse the pros and cons of the story we're creating. This analysis shows us the holes in the work we've done. Or it can even point out potential dangers. This work is exactly like the rest of the process. We play with ideas and try them out. We do this before we commit to writing the actual script.

Our story is created from the dynamics of our characters. Plot-points emerge from the dramatic potential of the characters. Characters drive the plot. Character development is how we create stories. It's also the source of all drama.

When we come to write scenes, it is the work we do now that will allow us to create powerful cinematic drama.

CHAPTER 24
Step 5. Practical Tools

character template

name	protagonist	antagonist	character 3	character 4
who are they?				
skills				
flaws				
insecurities				
strengths				
motivation				
what do they want, need and desire?				
odd behaviour				
appearance				
dilemmas				
secrets				
theme				
sub-theme				
backstory				
potential seed scenes				

Questions to help analyse our character profiles

Do our characters offer plot-points or dramatic potential? These questions help with that.

What the opportunities to expose these character's vulnerability?

What is preventing these characters from being vulnerable?

How do these characters explore the theme?

What aspects of these characters aren't related to the theme?

How do these characters pose problems for each other?

How do these characters force each other to face moral dilemmas?

How do these characters fail to challenge each other morally?

What are the conflicting objectives between these characters?

Where is there a lack of conflict between these characters?

What areas of human nature do these characters offer for us to explore?

get messy

Seed scenes and writing prose are great ways to use our instincts to discover characters. As we start to create drama-engines, we can test those engines in seed scenes. Playing with our characters on-the-page is as important as focused character development. The more we combine our instincts with focused planning the better our screenwriting will be.

CHAPTER 25
Step 6. Plotting

plot, sequences and structures

In the chapters on sequences and structure we looked at the ways writers think about stories. In particular, we looked at the most natural way to think about a story, which is as a list of sequences.

Goldilocks decides to go for a walk in the woods

She gets lost in the woods and struggles to find her way home

Realising she's lost, she searches for food, shelter and help

She finds a cabin in the woods and lets herself in

She's hungry so she helps herself to the porridge on the kitchen table

She wants a rest, so she tries out the furniture, breaking one chair

She's tired, so she goes upstairs, tries all of the beds and falls asleep

The bears come home discover their house has been invaded

They go to the kitchen and discover all the porridge has been spoiled

They find the wrecked furniture

They go upstairs and find Goldilocks asleep in the bed

Goldilocks wakes up, sees the bears, jumps out the window and runs away.

At first glance this appears to be the whole story, but it isn't. This is an overview of each key sequence. Each of these sequence descriptions will expand out into the writing of the story.

Sequence description = Goldilocks decides to go for a walk in the woods

```
INT. KITCHEN. GOLDILOCKS HOUSE. DAY

The kitchen sink is full to overflowing with dishes. Every
surface is covered with dust and the windows are so dirty
you can barely see out of them.

GOLDILOCKS (9) staggers down the stairs, rubs the sleep from
her eyes and surveys the mess. There are clothes and dishes
in heaps everywhere! She sticks out her tongue and blows a
raspberry at the neglected room.

Goldilocks throws open a cupboard door. She pours some
breakfast cereal into a cup and eats it with her fingers.
She heads for the front door.


EXT. GOLDILOCKS HOUSE. DAY

Goldilocks emerges into her overgrown garden. She finishes
her cup of cereal and rests the empty mug on top of a bird
table. She places it next to three others abandoned mugs,
each covered in cobwebs.

OVER THE FENCE:

MR BENSON (59) mows his immaculate garden. He scowls at
Goldilocks.

                    GOLDILOCKS
          Morning, Mr Benson! Nice day for
          it!

He turns his back and ignores her. She sticks her tongue out
at him.

She throws open the gate. In front of her a sign which reads
"TO THE WOODS" and another which reads "TO SCHOOL." She
steps out and, after a moment's hesitation, follows the path
towards the woods.
```

Our single line of plot only becomes the actual story when we turn it into cinematic narrative. Or, in other words, our plot is made up of the sequences we need to write. It's important to remember that a sequence will almost always turn into several scenes. So, creating a plot is nothing more than writing a list of the sequences that need writing. We put the sequences into the order that we want the audience to experience the story. By extension, this also means that the film's structure is a template for organising that list of sequences. Anyone confused by this should go back and read the chapters on sequence, story and structure?

As writers, it is our responsibility to decide what kind of structural approach we take. There isn't a shortage of screenwriting books about structure. We need to do our research and to figure out whether any of the existing ideas work for us. We can choose to be as structurally dogmatic or as experimental as we want.

This is our script and our story. What matters, at this point, is the process that we use to create our plot. So, let's look at some common approaches to plotting. Then I'll share mine, which may be new to a lot of screenwriters.

messy plotting

At this stage in the process, we know a lot about our story. Some of us will want to bypass the plotting step and to work out our story on-the-page. This will appeal to any writer who is suspicious of structural screenwriting. A writer who has a theme, compass logline, extensive research and character profiles has done a lot of work on their story. Messy writing now, isn't the same as someone who goes straight from their idea to writing the script. If our visualisation is vivid, we may want to set our characters free on-the-page immediately. If that's the case, then that's what we should do. We can afford to see where our characters and our storytelling instincts will take us. All we are risking, at this stage, is the need to do some more focused planning for our rewrite.

There are plenty of good reasons to take a messy writing approach to plotting. There are also a couple of caveats. A messy writing approach to plotting is a good idea if you have good instincts for crafting stories. It's a good idea if you are interested in exploring how stories are told cinematically. It's a good idea if you already know what your story is. However, it's a bad idea if you are writing to a tight deadline. It's not a good idea if you are writing for a producer who is averse to taking risks. If you're writing a spec script for producers you don't know that well, it might be better to do some planning. Messy writing of plots is great for exploration and innovation. It's a liability if your goal is to demonstrate your traditional skills

beat sheets

We already understand the beat sheet approach to plotting. It's what we did with the Goldilocks story above. Let's reproduce it, but this time let's lay it out like a beat sheet.

Act 1	1.	Goldilocks decides to go for a walk in the woods
	2.	she gets lost in the wood and struggles to find her way home
	3.	realising she's lost, she searches for food, shelter and help
Act 2	4.	she finds a cabin in the woods and lets herself in
	5.	she's hungry so she helps herself to the porridge on the kitchen table
	6.	she wants a rest so she tries out the furniture, breaking one chair in the process
	7.	she's tired, so she goes upstairs, tries out all of the beds and falls asleep
Mid Point	8.	the bears come home discover their house has been invaded
	9.	they go to the kitchen and discover all the porridge has been spoiled
	10.	they find the wrecked furniture
	11.	they go upstairs and find Goldilocks asleep in the bed
Act 3	12.	Goldilocks wakes up, sees the bears, jumps out the window and runs away

Pros. This kind of plotting is useful for structural writers. You can list the structure points you want to hit in one column and then create your plot in the column next to it. This works regardless of what your structural approach is. It's a simple, quick way to try ideas for plot. It's also an approach that stays focused on the eventual script. When we come to write, we will start at page one and end at the end. The story will flow from one sequence to the next. The beat sheet approach mirrors that linear process.

Cons. Beat sheets are good for organising your thoughts if you are telling a simple story. If you intend to follow the protagonist's journey through the story, a beat sheet makes sense. One of the most glaring flaws in the beat sheet for Goldilocks is the way the bears don't exist until they come home. That's fine if we're only interested in Goldilocks. But, it's not great cinematic storytelling.

Let's imagine we want to tell the story as experienced by all four primary characters. Not just Goldilocks' story arc, but also the arc of each of the bears. At this point, our beat sheet becomes more problematic. To create it we need to juggle four different narrative in our heads. We then need to assemble them into a linear story. This is tricky. One of the ways writers get past this problem is to use the file card method.

file cards

One of the ways screenwriters develop and plan more complicated plots is by using file cards. Instead of writing a linear list of sequences, we write each sequence on an individual file card.

Daddy Bear Arc (B) Plot

Daddy Bear is furious there isn't any honey for his porridge. He insists the whole family finds some before they can have breakfast

Goldilock Arc - (A) PLot

Goldilocks is desperate for water and shelter, she decides to go into the bears house so she can wait until help comes

Goldilocks Arc - (A) Plot

Goldilocks tries each of the chairs and is terrified when the smallest chair breaks. She gathers up the pieces and hides them in a cupboard

Daddy Bear (B) Plot

Daddy Bear finds a bee's nest in an old tree. He's too heavy to climb himself so he forces Baby Bear to climb right to the top. Mummy Bear is really scared... Baby Bear almost falls out of the tree.

Pros. The file card system lets us create multiple story arcs without having to commit to their final order. We can also play with the order of sequences without committing. Sequences can be taken out of the story, put to one side and brought back in at a later date. The eventual aim is to create a single, linear plot. But the biggest advantage of the file card method is the freedom it gives us to play with our plots before we commit.

Its other big advantage is the way we can create separate plots and subplots. Let's imagine we want to create the Daddy Bear story arc as a subplot.

Daddy Bear is furious there isn't any honey for his porridge. He insists the entire family go into the woods to get some for him.

Mommy Bear leads them through the woods to a place near the river where she saw a bee's nest

Daddy Bear gets up to the bee's nest, but the bees are long gone. There's no honey

Baby Bear is tired and hungry. Mommy Bear insists they have some berries before they hunt for honey. Daddy Bear wanders off by himself because he doesn't want berries.

Daddy Bear sees Goldilocks in the woods. She is throwing rocks at a bee's

nest in an old rotting, tree. She fails to get it down and has to run away from angry bees

Daddy Bear needs to calm the bees down, so he lights a fire to smoke them to sleep

Daddy Bear tries to climb the rotten tree, but it won't take his weight
Daddy Bear fetches Baby Bear and Mommy Bear.

Daddy Bear forces a scared Baby Bear to climb the tree. He does it and gets the honey

The Bears go back to their house

Daddy Bear discovers there has been an intruder

By putting each of these sequences in this sub-plot onto a separate file card. We don't have to worry about where each sequence will appear in the final plot. It is only when we decide on the final shape of our story, that we decide where in the story each sequence appears. To make this easier, we can even put each subplot on different coloured cards.

The final advantage of file card plotting is it allows is to tell stories out of order.

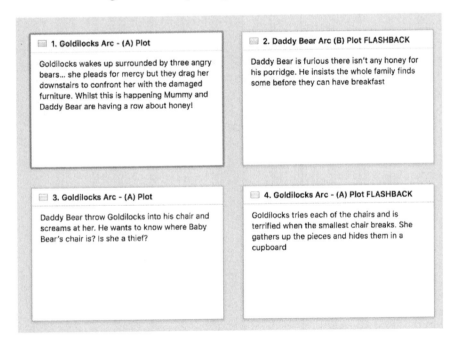

1. Goldilocks Arc - (A) Plot	2. Daddy Bear Arc (B) Plot FLASHBACK
Goldilocks wakes up surrounded by three angry bears... she pleads for mercy but they drag her downstairs to confront her with the damaged furniture. Whilst this is happening Mummy and Daddy Bear are having a row about honey!	Daddy Bear is furious there isn't any honey for his porridge. He insists the whole family finds some before they can have breakfast
3. Goldilocks Arc - (A) Plot	4. Goldilocks Arc - (A) Plot FLASHBACK
Daddy Bear throw Goldilocks into his chair and screams at her. He wants to know where Baby Bear's chair is? Is she a thief?	Goldilocks tries each of the chairs and is terrified when the smallest chair breaks. She gathers up the pieces and hides them in a cupboard

The advantage of file cards is they allow us to play with the order of the plot. We don't have to let the audience experience the story in real-time order. This is easy to do with file card plotting. We can put the cards in any order we want. The whole plot can consist of flashbacks and flash-forwards. With file cards we write the sequences in linear order. The order in which things happen for the character. However, we can they rearrange this order. We have complete control over what part of the story we reveal to the audience at any given moment. We know that playing with ideas is always productive. File cards give us a powerful tool to play with sequences and plotting.

Cons. The biggest disadvantage of file card plotting is its primary advantage, its flexibility. We can move a file card from first place in a stack to the midpoint, easily. But this doesn't mean any sequence can be put anywhere in the story. Stories have an internal logic. Every time we move a sequence, we alter its effect on the rest of the story. But that decision has a huge impact on the rest of the story. We can't just shuffle the remaining sequences without rewriting them.

The eventual goal is to get our plot into a linear sequence. File cards are limited by story-logic. We can't reorder the story without rewriting the sequences. Each sequence is affected by the sequence before it. Or, in other words, if we reorder our plot-points, we have to rewrite the plot! File card plotting is quite good for getting the broad strokes of our plot in place. But they're not great for nailing down the final plot.

treatments and plotting

A treatment is a prose document that tells the story as it is supposed to unfold for the audience. It's a really flexible piece of literature. Especially when we're writing it for ourselves rather than for a producer or any other reader. This is the story as we understand it and as we see it. And, because it is prose, we can write it in the way that best works for us. This is an entirely instinctive way to approach creating our story.

This is one of the techniques I use most often in my own process. For me, a script treatment often runs to between forty and fifty pages. That's about half the length of the script! Treatments are, by far, the most detailed way a writer can plot their movie script. Let's create a couple of paragraphs as an example.

> *On the edge of the woods sit two cottages, one is immaculate, the other is run down and overgrown. It is as though the forest is trying to reclaim this first building. Inside, it's not any better. There are piles of clothes and unwashed dishes everywhere. This is a place where spiders can create webs unmolested.*

Where a flurry of dust rises whenever anyone moves. This is the home of our heroine, Goldilocks. She is a scruffy nine-year old urchin who appears to live in the house by herself. Yet, rather than being terrified, she seems to be enjoying her feral existence. This is much to the annoyance of her neighbour. This morning, after foraging for breakfast, she faces the daily choice between school and playing in the woods. It's no surprise to anyone that she opts for a day spent playing in the woods.

Pros. Treatments offer huge advantages to any writer planning a script. Prose is a hugely valuable development tool. It takes us outside of the rules and conventions of screenwriting. Let's take an example from the paragraph above.

She is a scruffy nine-year old urchin who appears to live in the house by herself. Yet, rather than being terrified, she seems to be enjoying her almost feral existence. This is much to the annoyance of her neighbour

The idea of Goldilocks as a feral child, who likes her freedom, suggests the need for some set-up scenes. Scenes where we see her leading a wild, unfettered life, much to the annoyance of her neighbour. The opening of a script is where we introduce the central characters and the world, they live in. This kind of description does exactly that kind of job. And, because this is a new, rebooted version of Goldilocks, this introduction is really important. Although it's possible to get this kind of detail into a beat sheet, it's less likely. That's because beat sheets tend to be about nailing down plot-points. Unlike our treatment, which is used to evolve the story. By far the biggest advantage of a treatment is it is story-focused rather than plot focused. The entire goal of the process is to shift our attention to the elements which create our story. A treatment is often the moment when that work comes together. It is the perfect combination of instinctive writing and focused planning.

Cons. Writing a forty to fifty-page treatment is a time-consuming process. It could be argued that this time would be better spent exploring the story in the script, rather than as a treatment. There is merit to that idea. This is true for writers who have very strong instincts for story, drama and cinema. Some screenwriters struggle with prose. They feel less confident and more self-conscious when they write prose. If you are that kind of writer, then treatments aren't going to help your process. Treatments are a good tool for those writers, like me, who like to write prose and who find it liberating.

The other big downside of writing a treatment is the risk of literally losing the plot. Writing a treatment to create a plot is a messy writing approach. As we've discovered, messy writing approaches always come with the risk of losing focus. This is especially true when it comes to plotting. It's too easy to become engrossed in one idea and to lose track of the story arc in the process. Let me create an example to show how this can happen.

> *Goldilocks Cottage. It's run down, and uncared for. The garden is overgrown. Inside the house it's a mess, clothes and unwashed dishes everywhere. Goldilocks lives in this house, seemingly alone, like a feral child. She gets up eats and decides to go for a walk in the woods. Meanwhile, at the Bear's Cottage, it's another story. This is a well-kept, beautiful home. Daddy Bear is making the porridge, when Mummy Bear comes down carrying Baby Bear. She goes to the cupboard to get the honey out, but there's not enough left for everyone! She's furious, wasn't Daddy Bear supposed to get honey the night before! They have a massive row. She chases him around the house with a rolling pin, whilst Baby Bear laughs and throws things at him. Daddy Bear storms out of the cottage shouting "So, it's honey you want." Inside the house Baby Bear and Mummy Bear tidy the house and sit at the table waiting for the honey. Mummy Bear is still mad, so she calls her sister on the phone and they talk about Daddy Bear and what a loser he is. Baby Bear starts to repeat "Daddy is a loser! Daddy is a loser!"*

In the above paragraph, we can see an example of a writer getting lost in an idea. The story gets entangled in the writer's fascination with the details of the Bear's marital problems. The writer has forgotten about Goldilocks! This is a common problem when we use treatments as our primary form of plotting. The desire to dive into the details of our visualisation can destroy the value of a treatment. We need to avoid the pull towards a shot-by-shot description of the film.

The final disadvantage of using a treatment, is it isn't at all flexible. We can't take sections of a treatment out and replace them with different ideas. It's not as flexible as file cards or a beat sheet. If we make any changes in a treatment, everything after that point has to be rewritten. In terms of effort, this is very close to the effort of rewriting a script.

the spreadsheet method

The spreadsheet method is a way of plotting I developed and have been using for the last ten years. It is actually an extension of the way I develop characters. We do it on the same document. This method is useful if we want to juggle the story arcs of several characters. We can use it to create a structured script using any structural template we like. Or it can be used to create experimental structures. The spreadsheet method creates a beat-sheet for the arc of each major character. And we do this on the same document as their character profiles. It is focused plotting taken to its logical conclusion.

character name	Goldilocks	Daddy Bear	Mummy Bear
who are they?	An orphan and feral child	A father and husband	A mother and wife
skills	she's a survivor and curious about everything	he can find anyone or anything, he's a remarkable tracker	she's a brilliant dancer and a very good teacher
flaws	she won't ask people for help and doesn't trust people	he is overly protective of his family and has a tendency to overreact to criticism	she get easily irritated and lashes out without thinking
insecurities	she believes she has to fend for herself and never ask for help	since the death of his parents he is terrified of losing his family, to the extent he is over-protective	she's worried about how small her life has become since Daddy Bear started to become so controlling
strengths	very resilient	he's kind and hard working	she's kind and intelligent
motivation	to survive without ever asking anyone for help	he wants to feel valued and loved	she wants to feel valued as a person not just as a mother
what do they want, need and desire?	to be free	to look after his family the way a real bear should	to be more involved in the world
odd behaviour	she refuses to comb her hair	he beats his head on trees when he's frustrated	she puts her headphones on and dances whenever she gets a moment to herself
appearance	an unkempt urchin	a big bear	a middle-sized bear
dilemmas	whether to steal from the bears - whether to let the bears help her	what to do with Goldilocks, whether to assert his masculinity or whether to show compassion	whether to tell Daddy Bear about how his parents died
secrets	she believes she's been abandoned by her mother and father	his mother and father were killed in the incident that also killed Goldilocks' mum and dad	She knows that Daddy Bear's mother and father were killed in the incident that also killed Goldilocks' mum and dad

theme	the emotional and personal cost of losing your family	the emotional and personal cost of losing your family	the emotional and personal cost of losing your family
sub-theme	the emotional cost of rejecting help and support	the emotional cost of insecurity in your relationships	the personal and emotional cost of raising a child
backstory	Goldilocks used to live in a cottage by the edge of the woods with her parents. She was really happy and was doing well at school. Then, one day she came home from school and her parents weren't there. They hadn't come home from the market. She waited and waited. Hours, turned into days, turned into months. They've now been gone a whole year. Afraid to tell anyone in case they take her away, she has been doing her best to survive on her own.	Daddy Bear always wanted to be just like his own father. He was a kind, strong bear who protected and took care of his family. However, when his mother and father went missing a year ago he has changed from being a fun father and dad into an overly protective, controlling bear. His insecurities are starting to affect his marriage and this is just making them worst.	Mummy Bear was so happy to become a wife and a mother, she didn't even miss her former career as a dancer in the circus. However, for the last year, Daddy bear has started to make her feel trapped in her marriage. She longs for her former life in the circus. She also is carrying a massive secret... she saw the accident that killed Daddy Bear's mum and dad. They were in a tree that fell over a ravine, when it started to slip two humans trued to save them before it fell, but not soon enough and all four died together.

What we have here is our character development sheet. This is the same document we used to create our characters. To use this document for plotting all we have to do is extend each column and create the character arc for each of our main characters.

This is a very different and more flexible approach to plotting because it forces us to think away from the protagonist's journey. It forces us to think about how the story emerges from the interwoven journeys of our primary characters.

This method is really good at creating intelliegent drama, TV series show bibles and anything with an ensemble cast.

Let's look at how this works with the characters we developed for our reboot of Goldilocks. We follow the story arc of each character down the column.

Act One	Goldilocks' parents send her to school and set off through the woods to the market. They find two old bears stuck on a log over ravine, the log is starting to fall. They desperately try to save the bears, but the log breaks and they all fall to their deaths. That night Goldilocks comes home to an empty house. She waits for them to return but they never do	Daddy Bear meets a circus bear at his parents' funeral and falls in love with her. They get married	Mummy Bear is travelling with the circus, from her caravan she sees the two human rush to rescue the two old bears, only to fall to their deaths. She goes to the ravine and finds a photograph of the two humans and their daughter, Goldilocks
	THREE YEARS LATER: Goldilocks lives by herself in cottage by the edge of the woods, since her parents disappeared a year ago.	THREE YEARS LATER: Daddy Bear wakes up early because he hears a noise, he grabs his bat and creeps round the house looking for the intruder - he almost clobber BabyBear who gets up to see what his dad is doing	THREE YEARS LATER: Mummy Bear wakes up to a crash from downstairs. She discovers Daddy bear about to bash Baby Bear with a bat. She tells him off
	The school inspector calls around and she pretends everything is OK by putting on stilts and pretending to be her own mother	Daddy Bear makes the porridge	Mummy Bear listens to her music dances and remembers her time in the circus
	Goldilocks decides to ditch school agains and to have another search for her lost parents in the woods	The bear family sit down for breakfast only to discover there isn't enough honey for everyone	Mummy Bear is furious there isn't honey for everyone, wasn't Daddy Bear supposed to get honey last night!
	Goldilocks gets lost, she searches for food, shelter and help	Daddy Bear tries to explain that he couldn't get honey yesterday because of a little human girl in the woods	Mummy Bear refuses to go look for honey, she plays the martyr puts salt on hers, claims she doesn't even like honey

Act Two	Goldilocks finds a cabin in the woods and lets herself in	Daddy Bear loses his temper and forces the whole family to go into the woods to search for honey	Mummy Bear packs a bag, with rope, her Walkman and snacks for the Baby
	Goldilock is hungry so she helps herself to the porridge on the kitchen table	Daddy Bear leads the family through the woods to the bees' nest. But he discovers it's empty, the bees have moved	Mummy Bear sets up a picnic for her and Baby Bear. She dances whilst Daddy Bear is fussing about the bees nest
		Daddy Bear finds a single bee, he uses his tracking skills to follow its scent to the new nest in a rotten old tree. The tree won't support his weight.	Mummy Bear and Baby Bear have a little nap in the sunshine. Baby Bear hopes Daddy Bear is having a nice time. Mummy Bear doubts it
	she wants a rest so she tries out the furniture, breaking one chair in the process	Daddy Bear tries to build a tower to get him to the bees nest - it fails	Mummy Bear and Baby Beardance and Mummy Bear tells her son stories about the circus

MID-POINT	She's exhausted, so she goes upstairs, tries out all of the beds and falls asleep	Daddy Bear tries to swing to the bees nest from another tree branch, it snaps he fails	Mummy Bear teaches Baby Bear how to walk the tightrope by tying the rope between two trees
		Daddy Bear decides he needs help and goes to find Mummy Bear and Baby Bear	Mummy Bear and Baby Bear agree to help Daddy Bear
	Asleep - she dreams about her parents, she dreams they are falling and calling out her name	Daddy Bear works with Mummy Bear to get the honey. They let Baby Bear get the honey and use the rope to keep him safe. The bears are happy	Mummy Bear works with DaddyBear to get the honey. They let Baby Bear get the honey and use the rope to keep him safe. The bears are happy
	Asleep - she dreams she has a real family again	The Bears walk home happy they've got honey for breakfast	The Bears walk home happy they've got honey for breakfast
	Asleep - she dreams her teddy bear has become massive and is standing over her	Daddy Bear searches for Baby Bear's lost chair. He finds it in the cupboard broken into pieces… and then he hears movement upstairs	Mummy Bear comforts Baby Bear, who is really scared
	Asleep - she dreams her teddy bear has become massive and is standing over her	Daddy Bear searches for Baby Bear's lost chair. He finds it in the cupboard broken into pieces… and then he hears movement upstairs	Mummy Bear comforts Baby Bear, who is really scared

Act Three	Goldilocks wakes up to discover she is surrounded by angry bears - she runs away and leaps out of the window	Daddy Bear bellows at the sleeping girl who leaps out of the window he chases her	Mummy Bear see Goldilocks in the bed and recognises her from a photo she recovered at the time of Daddy Bear's parents accident
	Goldilocks runs through the woods chased by an angry bear	Daddy Bear chases Goldilocks, he's furious	Mummy Bear grabs Baby Bear and chases Daddy Bear trying to stop him
	Goldilocks climbs out onto a tree across a ravine	Daddy Bear corners her on the tree and starts to climb after her	Mummy Bear shouts at Daddy bear to stop. "This is how yourparents died!" She tells him "That little girl's parents died trying to save them"
	Goldilocks is rescued from the tree by baby bear, whilst Daddy Bear stops the tree from falling into the ravine	Daddy Bear uses all his strength to hold the tree in place whilst Baby Bear rescues Goldilocks	Mummy Bear ties a rope around Baby Bear to make sure he doesn't fall when he rescues Goldilocks
	Goldilocks learns the truth about her parent's deaths and is adopted by the bears. She is sent back to school and her hair is combed. Mummy Bear teaches her to dance.	Daddy Bear learns the truth about the death of his parents and that Goldilocks' lost her parents as a result of the accident. He suggests to Mummy Bear they should adopt her.	Mummy Bear reveals the truth about death of Daddy Bear's/Goldilocks parents. She realises she can be the bear she always was and still be a mother

At first glance, the spreadsheet method may seem complicated. It isn't. It's just an extension of what we've done already. The character profiles are the same as in the chapter on character development. All that's changed is we have added on a beat sheet for each of the primary characters. There are a couple of things worth understanding about this way of plotting.

solid (red) blocks

We can see there are a couple of blocks where there is nothing written. These blocks are coloured with a solid colour. I normally use red. This is because a character doesn't have to be active in every sequence of the story. There are going to be moments where we want to follow one story-arc rather than all of them. We don't need to be on Goldilocks all the time. At that point in the story the bears are about to come together and work as a family. This is an important foreshadowing of the way they eventually rescue Goldilocks.

interplay of story arcs

When we create arcs for several characters, it is important to thematically link them. It's almost impossible to plot this way if there isn't a common thread to hang everything together. The accident which kills their parents, is the link between Goldilocks and Daddy Bear. Mummy Bear is also connected to this event, as its only witness. Goldilocks is searching for her lost family. Daddy Bear mirrors this by fearing the loss of his family. Mummy Bear represents another form of loss of family. She's given up her life in the circus, her circus family, to start a new life with Daddy Bear.

structural flexibility

In this example, the left-hand column is very simple, act one, act two, midpoint, act three. However, this column can be as complicated as you like. You can put down the key points of your structure of choice. Let me give you an example using the hero's journey.

STRUCTURAL TEMPLATE	PROTAGONIST	ANTAGONIST	MENTOR
Act One - Ordinary World	stuff happens	bad stuff is done	
Inciting Incident	stuff happens	bad stuff is done	
Call to Action - Refuse the call	stuff happens	bad stuff is done	
Act Two	really bad stuff happens	really bad stuff is done	
Meet the Mentor	stuff happens		stuff is taught
Journey in the Wilderness	stuff happens		more stuff is taught

Entry to the Underworld	stuff happens	bad stuff is done	stuff is done
Defeat	really, really bad stuff	really, really bad stuff is done	I get murdered by the bad guy
Act Three	stuff happens	bad stuff happens	
Resolution	stuff happens	I fall off a building	
Returning Home	good stuff happens		

The strength of the spreadsheet method is the way it can be adapted to the needs and beliefs of any writer. We can put in as many story beats as we need. The story can be divided into as many acts as we like. We can use traditional structure or create our own. It can be as dogmatic or as experimental as we like. It is a tool to be adapted to our way of working rather than a dogmatic approach to writing.

what is plotting?

The answer to this question may depend on what we believe about structure.

For some of us, a plot will need to conform to a strict structural template. There is nothing wrong with this approach. That is providing that structure is supported by the other work needed to tell our story. There are a range of ideas about story structure out there. It's our job to find the ones that are useful for the stories we want to tell.

For less structural writers the plot is just a list which tells what us happens in each sequence. It is the order in which sequences are written.

The process of plotting can be achieved in many ways. Beat sheets are the simplest. File cards are useful for complex plots. Treatments allow us to explore the story before writing. The spreadsheet system is both focused and flexible. Ultimately, we may discover that we need more than one of these to get the job done.

My personal preference, when plotting, is to use the spreadsheet method first. Then I write a treatment. I like the mixture of both focused and messy plotting. I also tend to write stories where the conflict is driven by the character arcs.For that reason, the spreadsheet method plays to my strengths. Whatever plotting tools we use. The most important thing is that it plays to our strengths as a writer. It is also worth noting that different stories may need different approaches. That's why we call them tools. We select the right plotting tool for the right job.

CHAPTER 26
Step 7. Write!

at last!

So, at last, we are ready to write the script. If we have followed the steps in the process, we now have the following

An idea we are confident in because we have played with and tested it

A theme that expresses what the film is about

A compass logline that tells us when and where the story takes place. It gives us the primary characters and their main challenge

We have a complete visualisation of the world of our story and understand its culture

We have created a drama engine by developing characters with high-dramatic potential

We have a created a plot using our preferred structure (or lack of)

As a result of this work, we are ready to open our favourite screenwriting software and start writing.

Intuitive or structural screenwriters may start a new script without nailing the all of the elements in the list above. That's OK. We can sort those things about by rewriting. For messy and structural writers rewriting is the process!

Whether we are ultra-messy or ultra-focused writers the final step is always the same. The final chapters of this book are about the key aspects of writing our script. There are basic facts writers need to know about screenwriting. Let's start with them.

the basics

A script is three things. It is a cinematic-story, it's drama and it is the technical plan to assemble a film. This means a script needs to read like literature. It needs to work like a play. And, it must provide the information a production team needs to do their jobs. It is not enough to be good at one part of this, we need to do all three. To do this a screenwriter needs to develop three key skills

The ability to visualise
A simple, specific and evocative writing style
A strong sense of dramatic authenticity

visualisation

It doesn't matter whether we are about to write the first scene of our script or one smack bang in the middle. The job is always going to be the same. Our job is to visualise the scene we are writing. We imagine the world we want to show the audience. Then we answer the following questions

When and where are we?
Which characters are in this scene?
What do they do?
What do they say?

One of the most effective ways to do this is to visualise the scene before we write. Visualising a scene isn't the same thing as visualising the finished movie. It is more like putting our minds into the world of the story, so we can watch the drama unfold. This may sound like the same thing, but it isn't. Many early-career screenwriters don't understand this. They make the mistake of writing their script as if it was the movie. Let me give you an exaggerated example

```
INT. MONTY'S BAR. NEW YORK. NIGHT

CLOSE UP: WHISKEY POURED INTO A GLASS

WIDE SHOT: WE SEE THE ALL OF THE BAR FROM THE
POV OF THE ENTRANCE. IT IS FULL OF NEW YORK
DEADBEATS AND HOOKERS

MID-SHOT (REVERSE): THE DOOR OPENS AND BIG
JOHN MCKIRK WALKS IN AS THOUGH HE'S LOOKING
FOR TROUBLE

CLOSE UP: THE BARTENDER LOOKS TERRIFIED
```

Scenes in the final movie are edited together from a series of shots. The director and editor decide where to focus the audience's attention. This is the way we experience movies as consumers. A lot of early-career screenwriters make the mistake of thinking a script is a description of these shots. But that isn't what a script is. The visualisation we are aiming for isn't a shot-by-shot description of the final film. We treat our fictional world as though it was part of a simulation we have magically stepped into. Once we have stepped into the world our job is to describe what we see, what happens, who is there and what they do. So, let's try with that bar scene again. Only this time we're going to visualise it as if we were actually in the room as observers.

```
INT. MONTY'S BAR. NEW YORK. NIGHT

It's a dive, a flea-pit. DEADBEATS and SEMI-RETIRED HOOKERS
slouched on a motley collection of barely functional
barstools. Much of the furniture is held together with
gaffer tape. It's impossible to tell what colour the walls
were once because they are now the colour of old nicotine
stains. This is a bar for serious drinkers.

BEHIND THE BAR:

MORGAN (59), a rough, scrawny weasel of a man who looks like
he's spent half a lifetime in prison. He takes a cleanish
shot glass, slaps it down on the bar in front of a Deadbeat
and sloshes a generous shot into it.

AT THE DOOR:

BIG JOHN McKIRK (38), what you'd get if you stuffed nearly
six-foot-four of rage and resentment into an ancient Gold's
Gym hoodie and jeans. He slams open the door. He reaches
into his pocket and pulls out a photograph of Helen and
scans the room looking for her.

Only Morgan looks up. The Deadbeats and Hooker know better.
They bury themselves deeper in their drinks and
conversations.

                    MORGAN
                 (rasps)
          They're not here.
```

This kind of in-the-room description is what we are aiming for when we write a script. We visualise the scene as though it is a simulation we can step into as passive observers. As passive observers, we write what we see and hear. Of course, we're not seeing or hearing anything. It is all in our imagination. The thing that's important is we're imagining the world of the story rather than imagining a finished film. This may seem as though it's an unimportant distinction, but it isn't. Making a movie is a collaborative venture. There isn't a direct connection between the writer and the audience. Our job is the first step in a creative process. Others will use our writing as a springboard for their own creativity. Unless we direct and edit the movie ourselves, we will not determine how a scene is presented on the screen. We concentrate on the story and the drama of each scene. Or, in other words, we imagine a scene and write it in such a way other people can create their own version of that moment.

a simple, specific and evocative writing style

A screenplay isn't literature. But it is. But it isn't. A screenplay isn't literature because it has very particular rules about what you can write and what you can't. The most important one is

if we can't film it, we don't write it!

The most obvious example of this would be things like thoughts and feelings.

```
INT. MONTY'S BAR. NEW YORK. NIGHT

Morgan the barman wonders about the wasted lives he can see
around him in the bar. What has gone wrong in the life of
this Semi-Retired Hooker who is leaning over the bar towards
him.

                    SEMI-RETIRED HOOKER
              (with a sense of
               melancholy and
               desperation for
               attention)
          Can I get another, please?

She is too drunk for her flirtation to come across as
anything other than grotesque. Morgan mentally makes a note
to hit on her at closing time.
```

There is very little happening here that could be filmed. This is because all the action takes place inside people's heads. It might be useful for the actors to understand their thoughts and motivations. But it is a mistake to assume actors can translate this into something audiences will understand. How will the audience know Morgan is wondering about the wasted life of this hooker? If we want them to understand that, we'll need to find a way to show it explicitly.

The tools we use in literature to tell a story don't exist when we write a script. We are restricted to what we can see and what we hear. This is why writing from our visualisation is so important. Our restricted palette means our writing can't be literature. There are too many things we can't do on the page. For this reason alone, a script isn't literature and shouldn't be approached as though it is.

However, a script is literature. A script is designed for production teams and actors. But it doesn't become that until it has been sold. This means, in the first instance, we write a script to be read. Scripts need to be an easy and fun read. Screenwriting is competitive. Readers are brutal. So, a script needs to fight for the reader's attention on every single page. The writing of a script needs to be so compelling a reader is forced to turn the next page, and then the next page.

This battle for the reader's attention goes all the way to the last page. The ability to write in a way that inspires readers is the difference between having a career and not. The question is, how do we achieve that? Well, half of the battle is developing a writing style that is simple, specific and evocative. Let me demonstrate this in as simple a way as possible.

```
Martha walks to the door and leaves
```

The sentence "Martha walks to the door and leaves" may be all the information an actor or the director needs. But it tells us very little about what's going on. That's because verbs like "walk" and "leave" are generic and emotionally neutral. By being more specific and evocative we achieve a lot more with roughly the same number of words.

```
Martha stomps to the door and storms out

Martha glides to the door and slinks out of
the room

Martha staggers to the door and drunkenly
falls through it
```

We convey the emotional intent of the action by the way we describe it. Martha isn't just leaving the room. She's either storming out because she's furious or she's making a flirtatious and overtly sexual exit, or she's drunk. We are still describing our visualisation. It is what can be seen and heard. Only now, we're making specific and evocative descriptions.

Making specific and evocative observations of our character's behaviour is screenwriting. It is a skill many novelist's overlook. They give their reader's direct access to the thoughts and feelings of their characters. We can only do this by being really precise in our observations.

The idea of specific descriptions also applies to objects and things. Our descriptions of things and places needs to be equally specific. Again, let's see if I can create a simple example to explain this.

```
EXT. BRIDGE. NIGHT

TOURISTS wander over the bridge, pausing to
take selfies and to point at the sights of the
city.
```

So, the problem with the scene heading above is it is neither specific nor evocative. In fact, it raises more questions than it answers.

What kind of bridge is it, stone, steel, wooden, old, new, solid or derelict? Where is it, London, the Moon, over a stream, in a city, over the Grand Canyon?

Information-free-writing is a really common mistake in screenwriting. The writer may imagine a specific bridge. But what was in their mind didn't make it onto the page. By focusing on specific and evocative descriptions, we can do a better job for our readers.

```
EXT. ANCIENT STONE BRIDGE. PRAGUE. NIGHT

Even at 2am, the ancient, stone footbridge is
packed with good natured TOURIST COUPLES. They
take romantic selfies against the backdrop of
Prague's beauty.
```

By being specific and evocative we get a sense of what a place looks like and the mood of the moment. This is a mood we can do lots of things with, we can use it to introduce one of the couples. This works if our story is about their romance. We could use this mood to counterpoint the loneliness of our protagonist. Is she the only person on the bridge without a partner? Maybe we are creating a sense of warmth, safety and romance, so we can unleash an unspeakable act of violence. We use it to heighten the senseless brutality of the act. We have a mood to work with because our initial description has been specific and evocative.

So far, all our attention has been on the specific and evocative part of a screenwriter's style. Now let's look at the idea of a using a simple writing style.

As we have already seen, screenwriting isn't literature. One of the factors a screenwriter needs to take into account is the kind of people who will need to read the script. Most directors are fairly literate, as are a lot of creatives working on the production team. Producers, studio execs and investors are often less literary.

Producers and investors make big-money decisions when they turn a script into a film. Good producers rarely have extensive libraries of cutting-edge fiction.

A script needs to be simple, clear and devoid of words which present problems. It needs to be suitable for a reader of average education. So, for instance, I wouldn't be in a hurry to use the word "devoid."

Writers tend to pride ourselves on our vocabulary. We are proud of our ability to use the language in interesting ways. In screenwriting, it's best to emulate Hemingway. Use short sentences. Keep the sentences simple where possible. Use short paragraphs. Be evocative and muscular in the writing. Pack as much meaning into every sentence we can. I struggle with this discipline. It is one of the areas I still have to work on. One of the ways you can improve this skill is to use the Hemingway app online. It's an online tool that gives readability notes based on Hemingway's prose style. Using it can be a humbling experience. But it's worth the effort. Also, feel free to ignore this suggestion if it doesn't suit your natural writing style. Just be aware that our literary style doesn't define our voices in screenwriting. Our voice is defined by the way we handle drama and visualisation.

a strong sense of dramatic authenticity

A movie is an odd thing. Real people (actors) pretend to be fake people (characters). They deal with fake problems in a completely artificial world. We sit and watch it and although we know it is fake, we allow the illusion to become real. At least, we agree to treat it as though it was real.

The audience's acceptance that the illusion is real isn't given freely. The audience only suspends their disbelief if we do our jobs properly. If the drama seems authentic the audience will go with us. If it is inauthentic or false, they will hate us. Screenwriting is all about dramatic authenticity. If we don't give the actors and the director a firm foundation, they will struggle to create it on the screen. The firm foundation for a great performance is a great script.

To write authentic drama is a skill that takes a lifetime of practice. I don't believe there are any shortcuts or tricks. I do have a couple of suggestions of things to avoid.

> Being clever or showing off
> Being too meta
> Paying tribute to other films

The theatre director Yosida Oida wrote a book called *The Invisible Actor*. In this book, he suggests the actor's craft and skill should be invisible to the audience.

I completely agree. The moment we are forced to admire the skills of the actor, we have fallen out of the illusion. The actor's showing off has broken the dramatic authenticity. Writers can make the same mistake. We can egotistically draw the audience's attention to our own cleverness. It has exactly the same effect as a needy actor. Writers who want to be noticed are as bad as actors who need their craft to be the centre of attention.

We avoid being clever in our writing by paying attention to our own thoughts as we write. If we think "that's clever," it's worth taking a step back. We need to ask whether it serves the scene, the story or the drama... or whether we are just showing off?

There is a trend in modern films to be meta. An example of this would be breaking-the-fourth-wall. This is when a character looks directly into the camera and addresses the audience. This technique has been used brilliantly in films like *Deadpool*. Audiences like meta screenwriting precisely because it breaks the rule of dramatic authenticity. It appears to, but in truth it doesn't. Dramatic authenticity is always judged against the rules of the fictional world. If, within the world of story, a character is able to talk directly to the audience, their "meta" moment doesn't violate the authenticity of that fictional world. Let me try to give you a simple example of a writer's meta moment that always lands badly.

```
Martha grabs the bottle and smashes it down on
the counter. It doesn't break

                    MARTHA
                 (to herself)
        That always works in the movies!
```

When writers draw attention to the lack of reality in movies, it just draws attention to the fact that this is a movie! It's the worst kind of meta nonsense. It destroys the dramatic authenticity and draws attention to the writing.

Dramatic authenticity can also be destroyed by another form of in-joke writing. When we reference another film to create an in-joke, we run the risk of combining being clever and being meta. More often than not, this is another form of showing off. It rarely serves the dramatic authenticity of the script.

Again, there are very popular movies where there are exceptions. Edgar Wright and Simon Pegg built a career by putting film and TV references into their projects. As with *Deadpool,* these work because they were an established part of the fictional world. In *Spaced*, Simon and Edgar's TV show, the central character was a comic book nerd. His entire existence was defined by pop culture references. It wasn't them showing off, it was an integral part of the show. The same is true of the Marvel Universe. Marvel movies arrive at the screen with forty-plus years of backstory. They have fans who have followed that entire journey. When characters and stories have that kind of cultural baggage, it's mandatory to please the most devoted fans. Comic-book fans are pop-culture nerds. In this context, meta-in-jokes work.

There are almost no good reasons to bluntly reference other movies in most spec scripts. If we are writing an original piece of drama it won't have the cultural baggage of a Marvel movie. Our job is to create an authentic world. A world in which audiences can immerse themselves. Cultural references to other movies draw attention to the fact this is a movie. It's another example of writers being clever at the expense of the drama.

how do we write a script?

We write a script in scenes. To write a scene we must first visualise it. We imagine where we are, who is there, what they say and what happens? We then describe that visualisation in a simple, specific and evocative manner. We try to get as much information into each sentence as we can. All the time we try to keep the language simple enough for a twelve-year-old to understand. As we write, we resist the urge to show off. We don't want to draw attention to the writing. We also don't want to give the audience any reason to step out of the illusion that this is a real world. Our job is to write something so compelling readers must turn every page. They must discover what happens next. We strive to create the kind of fictional worlds where audiences can lose themselves.

CHAPTER 27
Step 7. Formatting

what is script formatting?

Script formatting is a catch-all term to cover the rules a screenwriter must follow. These rules cover the layout and presentation of our script.

Script formatting also dictates the elements used to write a script. The word element is a very important one in script formatting. The elements of a script are as follows

> Scene Headings
> Action
> Character
> Parenthetical
> Dialogue
> Transition

There is also a general text element, but I have never seen it used in a script and have no idea why anyone would use it. Each of these elements have their own position on the page, indent and or capitalisation. If you look at a page of script, you can tell one element from the others by how it looks.

scene headings look like this

```
INT. DESCRIPTION OF LOCATION. NIGHT

This is a description of the place. Someone enters. They do
things. Other people react to those things. Our attention is
drawn to a prop. Someone does something with that prop.
Another character fails to notice the change.

                    CHARACTER'S NAME
                (whispers in a Yorkshire
                 accent)
            But I am talking about this right
            now. These are the words I'm
            saying. Did you know I'm an actor!

                                    FADE OUT:
```

the action elements looks like this

```
INT. DESCRIPTION OF LOCATION. NIGHT

This is a description of the place. Someone enters. They do
things. Other people react to those things. Our attention is
drawn to a prop. Someone does something with that prop.
Another character fails to notice the change.

                        CHARACTER'S NAME
                   (whispers in a Yorkshire
                    accent)
              But I am talking about this right
              now. These are the words I'm
              saying. Did you know I'm an actor!

                                             FADE OUT:
```

the character element looks like this

```
INT. DESCRIPTION OF LOCATION. NIGHT

This is a description of the place. Someone enters. They do
things. Other people react to those things. Our attention is
drawn to a prop. Someone does something with that prop.
Another character fails to notice the change.

                        CHARACTER'S NAME
                   (whispers in a Yorkshire
                    accent)
              But I am talking about this right
              now. These are the words I'm
              saying. Did you know I'm an actor!

                                             FADE OUT:
```

the parentheical element looks like this

```
INT. DESCRIPTION OF LOCATION. NIGHT

This is a description of the place. Someone enters. They do
things. Other people react to those things. Our attention is
drawn to a prop. Someone does something with that prop.
Another character fails to notice the change.

                        CHARACTER'S NAME
                   (whispers in a Yorkshire
                    accent)
              But I am talking about this right
              now. These are the words I'm
              saying. Did you know I'm an actor!

                                             FADE OUT:
```

the the dialogue element looks like this

```
INT. DESCRIPTION OF LOCATION. NIGHT

This is a description of the place. Someone enters. They do
things. Other people react to those things. Our attention is
drawn to a prop. Someone does something with that prop.
Another character fails to notice the change.

                    CHARACTER'S NAME
                (whispers in a Yorkshire
                  accent)
            But I am talking about this right
            now. These are the words I'm
            saying. Did you know I'm an actor!


                                        FADE OUT:
```

the transition element looks like this

```
INT. DESCRIPTION OF LOCATION. NIGHT

This is a description of the place. Someone enters. They do
things. Other people react to those things. Our attention is
drawn to a prop. Someone does something with that prop.
Another character fails to notice the change.

                    CHARACTER'S NAME
                (whispers in a Yorkshire
                  accent)
            But I am talking about this right
            now. These are the words I'm
            saying. Did you know I'm an actor!


                                        FADE OUT:
```

Each has its own place on the page which makes it distinct from all the other elements. In every other area of screenwriting dogma is bad. The one area dogma is good is screenplay formatting. A screenplay MUST be formatted exactly to the rules. We don't get to choose which font, which size of font, the line spacing, or the amount of indentation for each element. There are only two kinds of script formatting, the right way and the wrong way. This is the reason screenwriters use screenwriting software. Screenwriting software allows us to switch quickly from one element to the next. We can do this without interrupting the flow of the writing. If we are going to write movie scripts, we need to use screenwriting software.

Screenwriting software automatically formats our scripts to industry standards. But that is not enough to correctly format a script. To correctly format a script, we need to understand quite a lot of different things. Here's the list!

What is each script element used for?

What is a scene?

What is an intercut?

What is a sub-slug?

How do we introduce a new character?

How do we use character's names?

How do we deal with flashbacks?

How do we deal with specific sound effects?

How do we deal with title cards or text?

What should my script look like?

what is each script element used for?

Each of the script elements is used for a very specific job and has its own rules. It's important that we understand these rules and we follow them.

scene headings

The Scene Heading element is used to introduce each new scene. There are a lot of rules that relate to this element and they're not negotiable. The first thing to understand is the formula we follow in a scene heading. It goes as follows:

```
INT OR EXT. DESCRIPTION OF LOCATION. CITY OR
YEAR. DAY OR NIGHT
```

We start our scene heading with one of three options INT, which means interior. EXT, which means exterior. Or, INT/EXT, which means a scene which cuts between the inside and outside of the location. The INT/EXT scene heading is most often used for scenes where the characters are driving in a car. A scene where the action cuts between what they're doing in the car and what's happening outside. We specify whether a scene takes place INT or EXT so the lighting team and camera crew know whether they're working inside or outside. We end this piece of information with a full stop or period.

The next part of a scene heading is a descriptive name of the location. This needs to be specific and evocative. We also need to be consistent in the way this name is used. Most locations are used many times in the same movie. If we introduce a location as HARRY'S DIVE BAR, we must use the same words every single time it appears in the script. Consistency is one of the most important factors in screenwriting. We end this piece of information with a full stop or period.

The next part of a scene heading is only used if we need to add in extra information. We might need to add in either the name of a specific region, city or period in history.

```
EXT. CAFE PICK ME UP. EAST VILLAGE, MANHATTAN.
1969. DAY
```

As we can see, in the above scene heading we give the location, Cafe Pick Me Up. We then go on to explain this is in the East Village of Manhattan and this scene is set in 1969. We aren't giving a precise address. All we are doing is making it possible for the production team to understand where and when this scene is set. We do exactly the same for a sci-fi movie

```
INT. SPACE COMMAND. CAMDEN LOCK, LONDON.
DISTANT FUTURE. DAY
```

If our story runs across several time periods, say the past and the present, we show which time zone this scene is in.

```
INT. JESSICA'S HOUSE. JESMOND, NEWCASTLE.
1880. NIGHT
```

```
EXT. JESSICA'S HOUSE. JESMOND. NEWCASTLE. THE
PRESENT. NIGHT
```

The final part of a scene heading tells us whether it is NIGHT or DAY. In very rare circumstances we can specify either DUSK or DAWN. There is no need to be any more specific than that. Again, this information is there for the lighting and camera teams. The reason we can be specific about either DUSK or DAWN is because the light at those times of day is distinctive. The light at DUSK is referred to in the film industry as the golden hour. That's because the light is beautiful at that time of day.

When we bring all those bits together, we get a scene heading. It should tell the production team whether it is inside or outside, night or day. It tells us where we are, and also what period the piece is set in. Our job is to write, specific, evocative and consistent scene headings.

```
INTERIOR - THE OLD BARN, 3PM
```

That's a bad scene heading. It doesn't give the information required in the correct format.

```
EXT. THE TOWER OF LONDON. 1945. NIGHT
```

This example is better. The information is presented in the right format. It tells the production team everything they need to know.

action

On one level, a script is what characters do and what they say. It is more complicated than that. But, it is a useful distinction for understanding formatting. If dialogue is what characters say, action must be what they do. That's a good starting point for understanding how the action element is used. A big part of the action element is a description of what our characters do. It's not an ideal description because it's used for more than this. A better description would be it's a description of what we see? Even this isn't a complete description of how the action element is used. It's actually used to do a lot of things.

Descriptions of what the characters do

Descriptions of action in the environment

Descriptions of locations

Introduction of key props

Introduction of new characters

Sound effects

Sub-slugs

Title cards info

The action element is it is used for everything in the script that isn't a scene heading, in dialogue or a transition. We use the action element more than any other.

The fact that we use the action element more than any other may come as a surprise to writers from a theatre background. In theatrical plays, the vast majority of the script is dialogue. The stage directions are sparse. In screenplays the opposite is true. Movie scripts are largely about the action and less dependent on dialogue. A common problem with many scripts is page after page of dialogue.

Let me create an example.

```
INT. MONTY'S BAR. NEW YORK. NIGHT

The bar is full of DEADBEATS and SEMI-RETIRED HOOKERS.

                    MORGAN
          What you having?

                    SEMI-RETIRED HOOKER
          The usual, no ice.

                    MORGAN
          Coming right up.

The door opens and BIG JOHN McKIRK enters

                    BIG JOHN MCKIRK
               (bellows)
          I'm lookin' for Mabel!

                    MORGAN
          No one of that name here, Mister.

                    BIG JOHN MCKIRK
          You haven't even looked at the
          picture.

                    SEMI-RETIRED HOOKER
          You heard him! No Mabel in here, so
          sling your hook!
```

Scripts that are all dialogue don't sell the writer's visualisation of the scene. I recommend writers to try this exercise, rewrite a dialogue heavy scene without any dialogue. The trick is to get across exactly the same meaning and drama by describing what happens. Let me show you how that might work by rewriting the scene above.

```
INT. MONTY'S BAR. NEW YORK. NIGHT
```

This must be the darkest, dirtiest bar in New York. Little pools of yellow, sickly light fall onto the customers. They are a rag-bag collection of broken old DEADBEATS and SEMI-RETIRED HOOKERS.

```
AT THE BAR:
```

MORGAN (78) the ancient barman, as dark and nicotine stained as the bar itself. He's a decaying weasel of man, pushes a dirty shot glass across the counter. The hand of the SEMI-RETIRED HOOKER who grabs it has broken nails. She has a fading prison tattoo and track scars from decades of heroin addiction. She bangs the glass on the counter. Morgan sloshes whiskey into it.

```
AT THE DOOR:
```

The door flies open. BIG JOHN McKIRK (38), what you'd get if you stuffed six-foot-four of rage and resentment into an ancient Gold's Gym hoodie and jeans. He steps in as if he owns the place.

Everyone except Morgan drops their head and slides back into the shadows. Morgan glances over, makes eye contact with Big John.

The big man strides up to the bar. Morgan bangs a glass down in front of Big John. He stares at it for a second and then pushes it to one side. In its place, he puts a photograph of Mabel. Big John watches the barman, hoping to spot a glimmer of recognition in his face. This isn't any, he doesn't even look at the photo.

Morgan picks up a glass and slaps it down on top the photo. He sloshes whiskey into it. Some of the booze spills over the rim and onto the photo. Morgan makes eye-contact with Big John as he pours and reaches under the bar. He grabs a sawn-off shot gun and places it on the counter. He rests his right hand on it.

Big John smiles. He knocks back the whisky. Wipes the photo on his shirt and puts it back in his pocket.

We force ourselves to tell the visual story. To do this, we have to be specific, evocative and more aware of the non-verbal communication. The characters tell the story by who they are and what they do. The visual details of the Semi-Retired Hooker's hands tell us lots about this bar. Her prison tattoo, the track marks, the broken nails reveal more than we'd get from a page of dialogue.

Screenwriting is a way to pass information from the writer to the reader. Visual storytelling is always rich in information in ways that dialogue isn't. And, the action element allows us to do visual storytelling.

The list we made of how action element is used starts with four things

Description of what the characters do

Descriptions of action in the environment

Descriptions of locations

Introduction of key props

If you combine those four things you get visual storytelling. It is what characters do, what happens in the environment, what the locations are like, and how props are used. If we remember to use the action element for visual storytelling we'll be on the right track.

introducing new characters and using character names

To create a budget for a film the line producer needs to know what actors appear in which scenes. Unlike playwrights, screenwriters do not create a list of characters at the start of the piece. We need to show the production team when a new character appears in a script. We also need to use the name consistently. Because this is vital information there are rules about how we do this. In the same way there is a formula for naming locations, the same is true of characters.

The formula is as follows

```
CHARACTER NAME (age), evocative description,
what they are doing
```

The first time we meet a character in the script we are told their name. They are introduced using the formula above. The character's name is in CAPS this first time. Every time after we write it in standard text.

```
DAVID SMITH (44), a twenty-five stone shambling mess of a
man, staggers into the bathroom and pukes in the sink.

David Smith takes a towel and runs it under the bath tap. He
wraps the wet towel over his face.
```

There is a certain amount of disagreement in the industry about name formatting. Some readers like the full name in caps first time it's introduced, DAVID SMITH. But after that they prefer a shortened name for the rest of the script, i.e. David. This is because it makes the script easier to read.

Production teams prefer exactly the same name to be used throughout the script. So, DAVID SMITH, the first time and, David Smith, for the rest of the script. Until very recently, I used full names throughout the script. But it can lead to some very awkward paragraphs.

```
Dr Martha Krawkowski perches on the edge of the desk. She
discretely kicks the folder over to her bag and throws her
coat over it. Detective Sgt Ruth Martin sticks her head
around the door. Dr Martha Krawkowski smiles at her.
```

Using the full names makes the read clunky. Regardless of whether we use the full name or a shortened version we need to be consistent. This isn't literature. There isn't any reason to use different versions. The following would be unacceptable.

```
Dr Krawkowski perches on the edge of the desk. She
discretely kicks the folder over to her bag and throws her
coat over it. Sgt Martin sticks her head around the door.
Martha smiles at her.
```

It's completely unacceptable to switch between Dr Krawkowski and Martha. It's too open to confusion. We have to pick a name and stick with it, even when it feels unnatural.

Once we give the character a name, we then put their age in brackets, (45). We do this for the casting director and to help the reader visualise the character. It makes a lot of difference. Let me give you some examples.

> Melody Weiss, (87)
> Melody Weiss, (24)
> Melody Weiss, (9)

When we read a name and an age, we visualise someone. The person we imagine when we know the woman is 87 years old is very different from our visualisation of a 9-year-old.

After we've established the name and age, we write our description of the character. Lots of writers get this wrong because they focus on a generic physical description. The following examples are typical but really bad.

> Gemma Monroe (23), a five-foot-three frumpy brunette.

Brad Petersen (36), a slim, blonde man of medium height

Gillian Scott (19), a perky blonde, sexier than she knows

Norman Thewlis (47), a muscular, six-foot-five Welshman

These are useless character descriptions. They don't tell us anything about who the characters are. They also narrow the casting choices in ways that aren't useful. When we describe characters, it isn't our physical visualisation of the character. It is about helping the reader to engage with the character. To do this we write descriptions that evoke the personality of the character. We try to do this without restricting the kind of actor who can be cast. This is how I would introduce the same characters.

Gemma Monroe (23), The kind science-geek who trolls sci-fi writers for their poor use of string theory.

Brad Petersen (36), If beige was a person, that person would find Brad tediously dull.

Gillian Scott (19), what entitlement would look like if you gave it a New York accent and a woolly hat.

Norman Thewlis (47), A pair of battle-scarred, tattooed fists with the angry remnants of an alcoholic attached to them.

These are very different descriptions. They have been written to evoke a character rather than describe them physically. These descriptions leave the reader free to create a unique visualisation. We are not trying to force our imagination of the character onto the reader. Instead, we aim to inspire the reader to find their own way of seeing the character. It's a much more powerful and engaging way to write.

The final part of introducing characters is to have the character do something. We are introducing them to the audience. It's an important moment. What this means, is the introduction of a new character often creates a small paragraph in the script.

```
Gillian Scott (19), what entitlement would look like if you
gave it a New York accent and a woolly hat. She strides down
the centre of the sidewalk, face buried in her iPhone. She
forces PEDESTRIANS to leap out of her path.
```

Introducing characters is a skill that takes practice. It's easy to learn the formula. It takes years to nail down the technique. Character introductions indicate to a reader the experience level of the writer. Poor character introductions usually mean it's a poor script. A writer who can't evoke a character in a couple of sentences is unlikely to excel at visual storytelling.

sub-slugs

A scene heading only tells us what the location is. The description that follows allows the reader to visualise the place as a whole. This works fine with simple locations. This is adequate for scenes where all the action takes place in one simple location. When things get more complicated, we need to find ways to help the reader follow the action. We do this in the action element by creating sub-slugs. A sub-slug is a short description to locate a specific part of a location. Let's have a look at a couple of examples.

```
AT THE DOOR:
AT THE DESK:
ON THE FLOOR BEHIND THE BAR:
```

We do this formatting manually. It's always done the same way, in CAPS. To understand how to use sub-slugs let's look at a scene that uses them.

```
INT. MONTY'S BAR. NEW YORK. DAY

The place is empty except for Morgan. He drags a mop full of
dirty water round the floor.

AT THE DOOR:

Big John staggers in. He's holding his shoulder, blood runs
through his fingers. He collapses on the floor. Tables and
chairs are smashed as he crashes through them.

Morgan drops the mop and runs over to Big John.

                    MORGAN
               (bellows)
          Mabel!
```

```
BEHIND THE BAR:

A trap door flies opens. Mabel clambers out. She drags
herself to her feet, sees Morgan putting compression onto
Big John wound.
```

The sub-slugs tell the reader where in a location action is happening. This is useful when we need to focus the reader's attention on one part of the location. It is also useful when two separate lines of action are happening in the same location. Let's see what that looks like.

```
INT. MONTY'S BAR. NEW YORK. NIGHT

Big John and Mabel hunker down the darkness of the corner
booth.

                    MABEL
          How's the shoulder?

Big John shrugs. He nurses his drink.

AT THE BAR:

Morgan watches them. The Semi-Retired Hooker bangs her glass
on the table to get his attention.

                    SEMI-RETIRED HOOKER
          Another!

Morgan pours it. He sees Big John slide a $20 bill across
the booth's table.

IN THE BOOTH:

Mabel picks up the $20. It's got a phone number scrawled on
it.
```

A sub-slug says to the reader, "look over here!" We move the reader's attention without dictating shots. We aren't doing the director's job for them. Sub-slugs make it easier for the reader to visualise what's happening.

title cards and sound effects

The action element is for visual storytelling. It is about what characters do and descriptions of the environment. There are two exceptions to this, title cards and sound effects.

Title cards are used when we need to put written text on the screen. We might use this to tell the audience we've shifted in time.

```
TITLE: THREE WEEKS EARLIER
```

We can also use title cards to tell the audience about a change of location.

```
TITLE: AMSTERDAM
```

The formatting for title cards is simple. We use the action element. It's written all in CAPS. We write TITLE and put a colon. We then write the text in CAPS.

```
TITLE: THE WORDS WE WANT ON THE SCREEN
```

It's simple. We always use the same format. We write this as a separate paragraph from other action. It's done this way because editors add the titles. They need to find them without any effort.

Another post-production job is Foley artist. A Foley artist adds in sound-effects. They need to know any sounds that are significant to the story. We treat them the same way as titles. The only difference is we put SFX rather than title.

```
SFX: BOOM! A GUNSHOT RINGS OUT
```

Sound effects are important because an unusual sound is often a cue for a character's response.

```
SFX: SMASH! THE SOUND OF A WINDOW BREAKING DOWNSTAIRS

IN THE BED:

Jodie sits bolt upright. She reaches for the baseball bat.
She listens, intently.
```

Even though we are dealing with sounds, they are still part of the visual storytelling. This is why they are written in the action element. And, just like titles, we write them as a separate paragraph.

The action element is the workhorse of screenwriting. It has many uses. The main purpose of the action element is visual storytelling. Cinematic-drama is visual storytelling. As such, we will use the action element more than any other. This will be true in most scripts. It's not a rule. It's just the way most scripts are written.

the character, parenthetical and dialogue elements

The character, parenthetical and dialogue elements are used together. These are the elements we use to write dialogue. The character element is only used to tell the reader who is speaking.

MORGAN

The character element tells the actor playing Morgan to say the line underneath. The line written underneath the character name is the dialogue element.

```
            MORGAN
    I've got a shotgun. It's aimed at
your guts.
```

A line of dialogue can be followed by either action or another character's line.

```
            MORGAN
    I've got a gun. It's aimed at your
guts.

Big John takes out a cigarette. He reaches for his matches
on the counter.

            BIG JOHN
    Have I got time for a last smoke?
```

When we look at a page of script, it is easy to tell the difference between the action and the dialogue. The action goes across the page like prose. The dialogue sits in a column in the centre, like the script for a play. The character element is always in CAPS. If we are writing in screenwriting software, the software does this for us. The dialogue is always in a column of regular text. Again, the screenwriting software does this for us.

There are times the actors/director may need additional information about a line. We may need to give significant information about how a line is said or where it is coming from. Early-career screenwriters can find this confusing. This is because some information is put in brackets in the character element. Some information is given using the parenthetical element.

When we need to indicate where the line is spoken, we put that information in the character element. And to make it more complicated, we use abbreviations.

```
            MORGAN (OOS)
    Get out!
```

The most common abbreviations used in the character line are OOS, which means Out of Shot. The other is VO, which means Voice Over. We use OOS when we want to indicate the character is there, at the location, but they can't be seen. We use VO when the script uses a narrator to tell part of the story. This is providing the narrator isn't seen.

```
                  THE GENERAL (VO)
            It was in the year of our Lord,
            seventeen-hundred and ninety-five,
            that my father first stepped onto
            American soil.
```

The parenthetical element is used to give instructions about accents or the emotional content of a line.

```
                        MORGAN
                  (broad Boston-Irish
                        Accent)
                  Drink?
```

            or

```
                        MORGAN
                  (Bellows)
            Get Out!
```

It's generally advised to keep acting directions to an absolute minimum. Actors don't like them and if they can't work out the delivery of the line from the context, the dialogue is probably wrong.

Writers also use the parenthetical element to show a change in who the line is directed at.

```
                  BIG JOHN
            I told you I'd be back.
                  (to Mabel)
            Wait by the door until I'm done.
                  (to Morgan)
            We need to talk.
```

Some writers use the parenthetical element to give minor action directions in mid-dialogue. I don't like it as a practice. It's always better to write the action in the action element.

transitions

A script always starts with FADE IN and ends with a FADE OUT. These two instructions are always written in the transition element. This element always sits on the right-hand side of the page.

It looks like this.

```
                                    FADE IN:
                                    FADE OUT:
```

There are very few occasions when writers need to use transitions in a script. So, for instance, it's a mistake to end every scene with CUT TO. Please don't do this! However, there are times when we need to use a specific transition to make the story work. An example of this is when a character is knocked-out. We may want to indicate this moment by taking the image to black.

```
Big John steps in and throws a right hook at Morgan. He
ducks but catches it full in the face.

                                    CRASH TO BLACK:

SFX: Distorted sounds of conversation.

                                    FADE IN:

Morgan's vision slowly comes back into focus.
```

A writer's ability to use the language of film editing to tell their story will vary from writer to writer. It depends on their understanding of editing techniques. For most writers, suggesting specific transitions isn't a good idea. It's only something a writer does when they are confident that a particular editing strategy is essential to convey the story.

using the elements

Once we understand how the elements work, we can slip between them to tell our story. Each scene starts with a scene heading. We then use a combination of visual storytelling in the action element and dialogue using the character, parenthetical and dialogue elements. When used properly these elements create a document that will be useful to the cast and crew. A process we must achieve whilst still making the script readable.

```
INT. RIVERSIDE WAREHOUSE OF RIDLEY & SONS: DAY

The warehouse is a huge barn, filled with crates. The back
of the warehouse is completely open to the river.

RUFFIANS enter. They scour the shadows.

A voice from the shadows, in the centre of the warehouse.
Handsome Jack sits cross-legged on the floor of the
warehouse, leaning against a crate. He is bleeding from a
minor flesh wound.

                    HANDSOME JACK
               You've ruined this jacket. Where
               should my tailor send the bill for
               its repair?

RUFFIAN WITH PISTOL steps towards Handsome Jack and raises
his pistol.

                    RUFFIAN WITH PISTOL
                 (strong Bristol accent)
               Have him send it to Newgate prison,
               your new address. Or he can send it
               to the gates of Hell itself, if you
               wish to spare yourself the rope.

Ruffian With Pistol cocks his gun.

SFX: BOOM! Gunshot.

                                        CRASH TO BLACK
```

As we can see, a script shifts constantly between the elements. This is the reason screenwriting software is an essential tool for the job.

If we get the formatting correct the cast and crew will follow our story easily.

Formatting is almost entirely for the production team and the actors. However, even if we understand how to format a script, we still don't know how to write our scenes. To do that, we need to look at how a scene works dramatically.

CHAPTER 28
Step 7. Writing Drama

The real challenge of screenwriting is to write drama. In this chapter we'll take all the work we did in our preparation and use it to write our script. Drama comes from a deep understanding of our characters and a fearless exploration of theme.

As we prepare to write we have our planning to guide us. This is a simple version of a document that is as complex or simple as we need it to be. The example below is the prep for a simple independent movie. It can be more detailed and complicated than this. Generally, it would also be about more than two characters.

title	The Long-Pig Cafe
raw idea	A performance artist is arrested for serving human-flesh to people as part of an exhibition
theme	The personal and emotional cost of challenging cultural taboos
compass logline	When the performance artist, Kim Steltz, reads a story about Victorian sailors who turn cannibal to survive being shipwrecked, she becomes obsessed with the taboo of cannibalism. As she prepares for her biggest show ever, at the New York Museum of Modern Art, rumours start to emerge that Steltz intends to cook and serve human flesh as part of her installation. When the museum comes under intense media and legal pressure, curator Pearl Grotlz is forced to deal with an artist who may be planning the unthinkable and a public outraged by the mere idea of cannibalism.

name	Kim Steltz	Pearl Grotlz
who are they?	Steltz is a famous artist known for her controversial exhibitions	curator of MOMA
skills	Steltz has a real talent for turning negative press into money and fame - her view of the world is utterly unique	she's organised, diplomatic and a political animal - she knows how to manipulate people into doing what she wants
flaws	Steltz craves negative attention, she believes she's a genius, she won't accept criticism or other people's ideas	she relentlessly ambitious, she believes she can control any situation by sheer force of will and manipulation
insecurities	that people will cease to be shocked by her	that one day she'll fail in a spectacular way
strengths	Steltz is fearless	she is relentless
motivation	to create art which changes the world and creates spectacle	to become the most important person in the world of modern art

what do they want, need and desire?	Steltz needs the hatred of the masses	she needs the adulation of the art world
odd behaviour	Steltz lives a media free life. her home is a single room with a futon, a shower and toilet. she goes days without speaking and makes notes with a fountain pen in tiny handwriting with incredibly detailed sketches. she always controls any communication with people. she ritualises everything. She also makes all of her own clothes.	her private life is a mystery - no one has ever been inside her apartment - her sexual relationships happen in hotel rooms - her private life is the subject of a lot of speculation in the art world.
appearance	Steltz is deeply androgynous. She always wears medical scrubs and is barefoot. She cuts her own hair. She tattoos herself after each show. Each tattoo is another hexagon with a symbol in it.	she is a person who oozes confidence — she only wears Vivienne Westwood suits for work. she looks like she's never worn a pair of jeans in her life - yet, despite this there is something deeply ordinary about her - it is as though her appearance is an entirely artificial creation - there's no hint of who the real person is under the facade
dilemmas	whether to murder her assistant when her deal for legal human flesh falls through.	whether to shut down the exhibition when she believes Steltz is planning a murder as part of the exhibition
secrets	Steltz is entirely asexual and lives a monastically bland existence - this isn't an aesthetic choice - she's not making an artistic statement by doing this - she finds the noise and emotional complexity of people baffling and distasteful	She collects paintings by outsider artists - when she found her mother's dead body, aged 14, she felt like she was looking at an art installation. she's deeply conflicted about this moment in her life - her apartment isn't stylish, it's ridiculously comfortable and homely.
theme	The personal and emotional cost of challenging cultural taboos	The personal and emotional cost of challenging cultural taboos
sub-theme	the cost of craving negative attention	the cost of ambition

		Pearl comes from a New York gallery owner family - She grew up surrounded by artists - her parents always took her to exhibitions - she has an encyclopaedic understanding of the New York art scene — her mother committed suicide when Pearl was fourteen. Pearl discovered her body. It was a bizarre experience for her. On one level it was a heart-breaking discovery. At the same time, part of her say it as though it was an installation — Pearl's ambition to be the most important person in the art world stems from her deep need for her to be the daughter of the gallery owner who killed herself.
backstory	Steltz grew up in the 1970's. Her low-level autism wasn't diagnosed. Instead, she was just "that weird kid." She was that kid who drew all day. No amount of discipline or punishment changed her. Art school chose her rather than the other way around. In art school her silence and insistence of wearing medical scrubs made her an object of attention, awe and ridicule. She loved the ridicule. Her first exhibition was a self-portrait created with used condoms she asked students to donate through-out the year.	
potential seed scenes	Steltz's monastic life in her simple apartment Steltz conversation with the German cannibal Steltz in the ham shop	Pearl and Steltz discuss her exhibition Pearl talks to Steltz about the death of her mother

Act One - Loner

Act One - Loner		
Ordinary World	Steltz sits cross legged in her spartan apartment. It is devoid of art. She sews a new set of scrubs. She showers, dresses. She collects her notebooks and pen. Her assistant and driver collect her. We discover she is a famous artist.	Pearl meets with her marketing team at MOMA. They discuss Steltz's upcoming exhibition. It's meant to be THE event of the season. They are nervous about the lack of communication for her about the content. Pearl and Steltz meet in the gallery space over a very formal tea. Steltz speaks through her assistant. Pearl is concerned that Steltz's plans for the exhibition aren't concrete. Her idea seems vague. She talks about sitting with members of the public and feeding them. Pearl is concerned it's too like Maria Abromovic's piece. Steltz leaves when Abromovic's name is mentioned.
Inciting Incident	Steltz receives an unexpected delivery. An old book. It is the tale of a Victorian murder trial. Two sailors who killed and eat a young boy to survive a shipwreck.	Pearl and an art critic friend meet for a meal. The critic says the public is too jaded to be shocked by modern art. They recount the days when a pile of bricks was enough to light the fire of public fury and indignation
	Steltz reads the book in a tiny shop that sells Serrano Ham. She nibbles a small piece and spends hours sketching. She writes notes in tiny little letters — she visits the Long Island zoo and demands a meeting with the pigs.	Steltz's assistant arrives with a sketch from Steltz. It's the build requirements for a restaurant installation.

253

Act Two - Wanderer	Steltz flies to Germany - she does a TV interview - they talk about her most controversial works - they ask her why she is in Germany - "research"	Pearl "accidentally" drops the title LONG PIG CAFE in a meeting with a journalist. When he mentions the connection between that phrase and cannibalism, she feigns ignorance. She tells him not to be stupid.
	Steltz goes to a German prison and meets with a prisoner. They share tea and talk.	The New York press discovers Steltz has met notorious cannibal Armin Mewes. They ask Pearl why? She refuses to answer. The press goes wild with speculation.
	Steltz calls a press conference and announces to the world she is going to serve human flesh to visitors at her exhibition	Pearl reassures the press that Steltz is being metaphorical. That the museum would never endorse cannibalism. She is keen to talk about the idea of taboos and breaking them, rather than the actual act of eating human flesh.
	Steltz visits a hospital. She talks to a surgeon. She talks to patients. Pearl demands a meeting.	Steltz informs Pearl she absolutely intends to run a cafe where she offers people slivers of human flesh.
	Steltz collects a parcel from the hospital. It's a human leg. She takes it home and salts it, just the way Serrano ham is prepared.	Pearl leaks a story to the press that Steltz is trying to buy amputated limbs
MID-POINT - Warrior	Steltz is arrested — the press goes crazy	Pearl is presented with video footage of Steltz preparing the human leg. It's meant to be for the exhibition — Pearl leaks it to a conservative cable TV channel.

	The Police raid Steltz's apartment and discover the leg — more press insanity several galleries worldwide contact her to cancel shows - one collector publicly burns one of Steltz's paintings.	There are massive public protests at the museum — Pearl is forced to defend her decision not to cancel the exhibition — she tells them they're on the front page of every paper worldwide. "Art is front page news again." She lists every major work of art that incited this level of engagement.
	Steltz's trial — the state argues cannibalism is against the law — Steltz's lawyers argue there is no evidence of cannibalism, only of preserving a human limb in salt — Steltz refuses speak in court	Pearl is forced to testify to testify at Steltz's trial — her dilemma — whether to maximise the publicity by keeping Steltz in jail or whether to get her released for the show — she intends to put the show back and only relents when she realises she might loses a Van Gogh retrospective if she does that.
	Steltz is released with no charge — she is cautioned if she ever serves human flesh at a public event, she will be arrested	Pearl and Steltz meet. Pearl wants to know if the exhibition is going to be cancelled — Steltz asks Pearl to arrange a prime TV appearance for her.
	Steltz appears on a TV show — she is asked about the installation — she confirms it will happen. — The district attorney tells the show her source of "meat" is illegal if she buys it for human consumption — she tells the world that the show will definitely open as planned in exactly one month.	Pearl watches the TV show — she takes a call from her marketing team — no one can believe the show is going ahead.

	Steltz retreats to her room. She sews five pairs of scrubs to match the colour scheme of the Long Pig Cafe — she lays them out next to ten colour coordinated nappy-pins	Pearl tries to arrange more press for Steltz but is refused — Steltz won't speak to anyone between now and the exhibition. — Pearl hires a man to find and follow Steltz's people.
Act Three - Martyr	Steltz is disguised and taken to an appointment at the hospital. The surgeon is worried about the press but is reassured by the promise of anonymity.	Pearl learns Steltz has been to the hospital again — she calls the DA and tells him — she tells the press Steltz is about to be arrested again
	Steltz disappears - her assistant tells Pearl she won't appear again until the installation opens — Steltz's assistant takes over the get in for the installation	Steltz's studio and apartment is raided. They find nothing — she has disappeared.
	The day of the installation - police arrive to arrest Steltz if she serves human food. There are protests outside, press and a massive queue of people wanting to see the show.	The press goes mental over Steltz's disappearance — Pearl does a lot of TV shows — she keeps on saying the exhibition is being built — she has no reason to doubt it is happening — Her man can't find Steltz. She's really disappeared.
	The installation opens — Steltz has two preserved human legs on a table — she carefully slices slivers as though it was ham — she feeds these slivers to a pig.	The day of the exhibition and Pearl is prevented from talking to Steltz — it's her team only — she tries to throw her weight about but is given a simple choice "We do it Steltz's way or not at all."
	The DA and the police want to arrest Steltz but are stopped by her lawyers — they drag them into a back room — They answer every legal point — but the real issue appears to be the purchase of surgical waste — the lawyers instruct the DA to look under the table — Steltz has no legs below the knee — she is feeding the pig her own legs	After the first day's exhibition Steltz's assistant hands the old book back to Pearl — Steltz and Pearl talk — Steltz tells Pearl that no person can make her do anything she doesn't want to or prevent her from doing what she thinks is right — Pearl doesn't deny sending the book, or manipulating the press — Steltz tells Pearl she's the exhibit, she was always the exhibit. Steltz shows Pearl page after page of notes that explain the whole process — Steltz was aware of every move and was the hidden hand behind everything

process-driven screenwriting - entering the fictional world

We are ready to open a new script document. We type FADE IN. We know roughly what will happen. We know who the characters are. We know the story. We are not staring into the void. We can invest all our efforts into writing drama because we have prepared. By making creative decisions before we write, we can now write cinematic-drama. We can concentrate on visual-storytelling and exploring our theme.

Let's look at how we do this by writing the first page of the script. As we write, we'll look at the purpose of each paragraph.

```
                                                    FADE IN:


EXT. MANHATTAN BRIDGE. NEW YORK. DAY

Morning traffic on the Manhattan Bridge is brutal but
moving.

Travelling towards Manhattan an old-fashioned short bus,
with tinted windows. We follow it across the bridge into
Manhattan.

A taxi cab blares its horn as the short bus pushes its nose
into the left-hand lane on Canal Street.

It's common to bring the audience physically into the world
of our story. This is why so many movies open with the
camera flying over water towards a city. It is the same as
saying "this is where our story is set." Our story takes
place in New York. We follow the short bus. More than that,
I have created a small incident to draw attention to that
single vehicle. This could all be reduced to; our story
takes place in modern day New York and this bus is important
to the story.


INT. STELTZ APARTMENT. SOHO. NEW YORK. DAY

The apartment is tiny. This room is barely 8-foot-wide and
12 feet long. It is also strangely empty and sterile. One
wall is white painted bricks. The wall opposite is all built
in storage units with sliding door panels. An entire section
of that wall is open. On the perfectly organised, spartan,
shelves are stacks of identical notebooks. On the left, new
ones. On the right, used ones. On the shelf below, a bolt of
charcoal grey cotton. Next to that, an old-fashioned, hand
powered sewing Singer machine. On the shelf below that a
Japanese tea pot, two small glass tea cups and a wooden box.
On the shelf below that, two open, empty wooden boxes.
```

It's common to bring the audience physically into the world of our story. This is why so many movies open with the camera flying over water towards a city. It is the same as saying "this is where our story is set." Our story takes place in New York. We follow the short bus. More than that, I have created a small incident to draw attention to that single vehicle. This could all be reduced to: our story takes place in modern day New York and this bus is important to the story.

```
INT. STELTZ APARTMENT. SOHO. NEW YORK. DAY

The apartment is tiny. This room is barely 8-foot-wide and
12 feet long. It is also strangely empty and sterile. One
wall is white painted bricks. The wall opposite is all built
in storage units with sliding door panels. An entire section
of that wall is open. On the perfectly organised, spartan,
shelves are stacks of identical notebooks. On the left, new
ones. On the right, used ones. On the shelf below, a bolt of
charcoal grey cotton. Next to that, an old-fashioned, hand
powered sewing Singer machine. On the shelf below that a
Japanese tea pot, two small glass tea cups and a wooden box.
On the shelf below that, two open, empty wooden boxes.
```

This paragraph has been written to do a couple of things.

We are introducing one of the story's central characters. We show the audience her apartment. We let them see the contents of her shelves. We want them to get a sense of her strangeness before they meet her. For what's written the audience know she is organised. They may suspect she has OCD. Her life is very different from their life.

The visual storytelling aspect of this paragraph is about contrast. The contrast between the still, monastic apartment and the bustle of New York. The difference is very stark. Again, this tells us that the inhabitant of this room is not ordinary. She has removed herself from the hustle of everyday life.

```
SFX: THE BUZZ OF A TATTOO MACHINE

Sat cross-legged on a simple futon, KIM STETLZ (48), a
deeply androgynous and alien person. She's dressed in plain,
grey cotton underwear. She tattoos a simple hexagon onto her
thigh. Both of her arms and one of her legs are covered in
these hexagons. All but this new one are healed. Each one
contains a different symbol. The new one is empty.

In front of her, a small medical kit and a roll of
clingfilm.
```

This paragraph introduces our primary character, Kim Steltz. Again, the visual storytelling operates on a couple of levels. A woman sat on a futon tattooing herself is odd. It is not everyday behaviour. The repetitive nature of the tattoos re-enforces the idea she has OCD tendencies. The whole scene is ritualistic. In our character development (we decided Steltz lives an almost monastic existence. These moments of ritual establish this fact about her. At the same time, we are showing something very simple and basic. Kim is a visual artist. The first thing we see her do is drawing on her own skin. She is also a conceptual artist. The first artistic thing we witness is her using herself as the canvas for her own art. This moment encapsulates the whole film. The body alteration. The artist making an image. The ritual, and the use of her own body as a canvas. This is what the film is about.

```
INT/EXT. SHORT BUS. CANAL STREET. NEW YORK DAY

The short bus slowly turns off Canal Street and towards
Soho.

IN THE SHORT BUS:

CARMEN (29), a woman who exudes intimidating confidence and
flawless taste, has her face buried in a smart-phone. She
thumb-types as the bus turns. She is the only passenger. The
DRIVER (60), a muscular female presence at the wheel sucks
her teeth as a taxi cuts them up.

SFX: TEXT SENT SOUND


INT. STELTZ APARTMENT. SOHO. NEW YORK. DAY

SFX: A PHONE CHIMES

Steltz wraps her tattoo in cling film. She leans over, takes
an ancient Blackberry Classic phone from on top of a small
pile of art book. She scans the text.

TEXT: ETA 9 MINUTES

Steltz places the phone precisely back onto the pile of
books, right in the centre.
```

This section of script introduces two new characters, Kim's assistant and her Driver. It also establishes the relationship between the short bus and our protagonist. The entire sequence, so far, is about establishing our fictional world. We introduce characters and places. We give the audience the opportunity to settle into the ordinary world of the story. So far, this is about a page of script. We are one minute into the film. In the next couple of paragraphs, we'll wrap up this sequence. Each sequence has a distinct beginning, middle and end. This is just like the film as a whole.

```
INT. STAIRS. STELTZ APARTMENT. SOHO. NEW YORK. DAY

Steltz's bare feet make a light slapping sound as she walks
down the stone stairs. Her movements are other-worldly and
odd. It is as if her upper body is motionless. She glides.

INT./EXT. SHORT BUS. WEST BROADWAY. SOHO. NEW YORK. DAY

The Driver pulls into a space in front of an old apartment
building over a Starbucks. She pulls the lever and the bus
door opens.

ON THE STREET:

The apartment door opens. Steltz steps out into the street,
bare-foot. She glides to the bus and steps in.

IN THE BUS:

The door closes behind Steltz. She goes to the back of the
bus and sits. Carmen nods at the Driver.

                    CARMEN
          The Museum of Modern Art. Rear
          Entrance.

ON THE STREET:

The short-bus pulls into traffic
```

In our final section of this sequence, we bring the two strands of our story together and send them off to the next plot-point. The script, at this point, represents two-and-a-half minutes of screen time (2.5 pages). There has only been one line of dialogue. This isn't unusual at the start of a script.

The opening of a script is different from the rest of it. It is about introducing characters and the fictional world. In drama, we always look for challenging circumstances and vulnerability. However, in the opening pages our focus is human behaviour and establishing our theme. Here, we have established a central character whose lifestyle is strange. She challenges cultural norms. This matches our theme of challenging taboos. We have also taken the audience into a new and unusual world. Very few members of the audience will be conceptual artists.

At this stage, the audience should have more questions than answers. Yes, they know we are in New York. They know Steltz is an odd woman. But why is she going to the museum and what is about to happen in her life? Will the audience care enough to want answers to those questions? Is she fascinating enough to hold their attention? It's difficult to tell at this point. As the writer, all I know is she fascinates me. All I can hope is the audience will share my fascination.

process-driven screenwriting - thematic writing and plot-points

A story is what happens when a specific group of characters are forced to face a series of challenging circumstances

To create a story, we need to give our characters challenges. The first challenge is called the inciting incident. It often happens in the first ten pages. We then expose our character's vulnerabilities by forcing them to face new challenges. Some of the challenges are environmental. They also come in the form of conflict with other people. Some of the challenges are thematic.

This is different from writing the opening pages. The emphasis is still on visual storytelling, but as we progress, we pay more attention to theme and drama. Not every scene needs to drive the plot, especially early in the script. But the one thing we need to do in every single scene is to explore the theme dramatically.

Creating example pages of mid-script scenes is difficult. That is because drama comes from accumulated knowledge. The audience learns more about the fictional world with each scene. The characters and the situation evolve. Each scene, therefore, sits on the shoulders of everything that's already happened. The best I can offer as examples are some seed scenes. Let's look at a scene in the first act that does a couple of different jobs. It hits a plot point and foreshadows the end of the film. It explores the theme and is a microcosm of the entire story.

```
EXT. LONG ISLAND ZOO. DAY

The zoo is quiet. A few TOURISTS and FAMILIES wander around.

Steltz leans on the rail of the pig enclosure. She holds her
notebook with one hand and draws a fine line image of a pig.
Next to it, a mass of tiny writing, too small to be easily
read.

A LITTLE GIRL (6) trots over to where Steltz is drawing. She
stares at Steltz's bare feet.

                    LITTLE GIRL
               (amazed)
          You don't have any shoes!

Steltz stops drawing. She looks at the girl as if she's an
exhibit.

                    LITTLE GIRL
          Why not?
```

```
Steltz squats down to her level. She makes eye-contact.

                    STELTZ
          Why should I?

The Little Girl thinks

                    LITTLE GIRL
          Everyone has to wear shoes.

                    STELTZ
          Do they?

Steltz leans in and whispers

                    STELTZ
          I don't like shoes.

                    LITTLE GIRL
              (whispers)
          Me neither.

Steltz points at the nearest pig.

                    STELTZ
          Do you like pigs?

                    LITTLE GIRL
          They're funny.

                    STELTZ
          They are very cute. Do you like
          bacon?

                    LITTLE GIRL
          I love bacon.

Steltz stands, she makes little notes in her notebook. The
Little Girl wanders away.
```

It's important to understand this scene in context. At this point in the story Steltz has read the book on cannibalism and visited the Serrano Ham deli. The audience knows her exhibition is called the *Long Pig Cafe*. They also know long pig refers to human flesh. They have learned the myth that human flesh tastes like pork. They also know Steltz wants to do an installation about food and feeding people. Her visit to the zoo to sketch pigs is a natural extension of her thought process. She's an artist. She's doing research. From this perspective, this scene hits a plot point. It furthers her story of an artist exploring ideas of food and taboos.

When we look at our theme, this scene works. Our theme is the personal and emotional cost of challenging cultural taboos. Her conversation with the Little Girl shows how her refusal to wear shoes is as much about disrupting social norms as it is about choice. Yes, she chooses not to wear shoes. But, one of her reasons is artistic. She wants to challenge normal thinking. Even if it's only a with a little girl.

The scene is also about foreshadowing. The audience won't understand the real significance of this scene until the end of the film. This scene foreshadows Steltz feeding her own leg to a pig, in the gallery. That is why her final conversation with the girl is important. We like pigs. They are cute. We also like bacon. There is something very weird and very human about those contradictions. Steltz's final art installation is about those ethical dilemmas. At the end of the film, the audience will understand why she visited the zoo. They don't understand at the time of the scene.

This scene is a microcosm of the whole film. The points we make are, Steltz is weird and provocative. Her life choices always have artistic intentions. She chooses to be weird and provocative for a reason. Part of her process is to see things as they actually are. There is no reason why people shouldn't walk around barefooted, but we don't. If we like pigs and we find them cute, we shouldn't eat them. But some of us do. If we eat an animal we love and find cute, why can't we eat humans? After all, we love them and find them cute. What, is the moral difference between eating a person and eating a pig? This is important on a few levels. Early in the book, I suggested that storytelling is always about morality. We could also say it's always about politics. It is definitely about what it means to be human. Our character, Steltz, allows us to ask questions of ourselves and the world. Sometimes it's enough to ask the questions and let the audience respond to them.

Screenwriting doesn't have to be simple. It can be as philosophical and intellectual as we want. We can use cinematic-drama to explore difficult ideas. However, it needs to work on many levels. This film is about difficult ideas. It's about food and what it means to eat meat. It is about art. It's about public outrage. It's about cannibalism. It's about ambition. It's also about what it means to live your life outside normal conventions and thinking. Despite this, this scene is accessible. That's important. It's possible to tackle difficult issues without being preachy or excluding people. Screenwriting is as diverse and flexible as any other art form.

Screenwriters are often taught that conflict happens between two individuals. The protagonist and the antagonist. This film and this scene seem to have neither. But, that's not strictly true. Having an actual person as the antagonist is a simple way to create drama. That's why it's often used in action movies. However, a character can battle many things. The environment might be one example. In disaster movies, the protagonists struggles against the volcano, tornado, tidal wave or fire. Nature becomes the antagonist. Concepts can also become the antagonist. In this film the antagonist is human hypocrisy. That is the thing Steltz sets herself against. The conflict in this scene is subtle. It appears in her conversation with the little girl about pigs and bacon. The girl likes pigs, she also loves bacon. Steltz can see the hypocrisy of these statements. She doesn't feel the need to lecture the little girl. She lets the truth hang there. A real, penny in the air... penny drops moment. The conflict here is hidden inside the little girl's understanding of the world. She lives in a world where everybody has to wear shoes. She knows pigs are cute. She knows she loves bacon. In this scene, Steltz's struggle is against these ideas.

This scene is early in the film, so at this point the struggle doesn't cost her anything. That's about to change. So, let's look at that. Let's look at a scene where characters are forced to pay the price for their struggle.

process-driven screenwriting - paying the cost

The idea that the drama builds as a film progresses seems sensible. The protagonist's struggle may have seemed simple at the start. As the story moves on, the challenges become more testing. One of the main ways this happens is the cost the characters have to pay. We use the phrase the personal and emotional cost of something to create a theme. We do this to remind ourselves about the cost of the struggle. The theme reminds us characters must pay for their struggle. So, let's create a seed scene/sequence that is about paying the price.

```
INT. COUNTY JAIL. BOOKING CENTRE. DAY

The PRISON OFFICER (29), a hard, no nonsense woman, roughly
manhandles Steltz to the booking desk. Behind it the BOOKING
OFFICER (55) taps away at her computer.

                    PRISON OFFICER
                    (to Steltz)
            Stand behind the line.

Steltz looks down. There is a line of well-worn paint about
three feet from the desk. Her feet are behind it. She slides
her left foot forward so her toes just cross the line.

Bang! He slams her head onto the desk. Boots kick her legs
from underneath her. The Prison Officer pins her hands down.
Another OFFICER steps in and pushes her face into the desk.

The Prison Officer roughly kicks Steltz's legs back and
apart. He pats her down, roughly.
```

>   PRISON OFFICER
>   (to the Booking Officer)
>   Kim Steltz. On remand pending
>   charges. Arrested for desecration
>   of human remains and the illegal
>   trafficking of medical waste.

The Booking Officer looks up, glances at Steltz.

>   BOOKING OFFICER
>   (to the Prison Officer)
>   Is she a biter?
>   (to Steltz)
>   Steltz says nothing.

>   BOOKING OFFICER
>   (to Prison Officer)
>   Get her up.

He yanks Steltz to her feet.

>   PRISON OFFICER
>   (to Steltz)
>   Stand! Properly! Behind the line!
>   Answer all the questions. Do you
>   understand?

Steltz looks down at her feet. She places them precisely
behind the line, her big toes grazing the edge of it. She
makes eye-contact with the Prison Officer. Without
hesitation, the Prison Officer pulls out her baton and slams
it down on Steltz toes.

>   PRISON OFFICER
>   I said, behind! Not past it! Not on
>   it! Behind!

Steltz screams. He slams her onto the desk again and
restrained. The Booking Officer turns back to her computer.

>   BOOKING OFFICER
>   Kim, have you taken any narcotics
>   today?

He waits. The Prison Officer increases the force of the
restraint.

>   STELTZ
>   I have not taken any narcotics or
>   other drugs.

I always judge a scene by its relationship to the theme. In this case, the theme is the personal and emotional cost of challenging cultural taboos. This scene happens just after the mid-point in the film. In traditional film structure this moment often features a reversal of fortune. I prefer to think of the midpoint as being when the costs really start to escalate. Our protagonist's loss of freedom is very real. She has been arrested. It could be that her career as an artist is over. She may be going to prison for a very long time. This is the plot-point the scene needs to hit.

This is where the difference between plot and drama becomes really stark. We can hit the plot-point "Kim is arrested" without writing a dramatic scene. We can simply have her arrested. She is still in the same jeopardy. She is still facing prison and loss of her career. The problem is, if we only hit the plot point, we're missing the opportunity to explore the theme. We miss the opportunity to write drama.

This scene is all about dramatising the cost Steltz is willing to pay. As an artist, when Steltz sees a rule, she breaks it. But normally she is rewarded for her behaviour. She is a famous artist because she behaves this way. Now, she is in an environment where failure to follow rules is dealt with harshly. She is dealing with a world she doesn't understand. The Prison Guards need absolute obedience from her. They need people to do what they are told without question. For the guards that is a matter of life and death. So, when Steltz puts a toe over the line it is seen as a physical threat. When she tests the boundaries a second time, she is going to get hurt. This goes directly to our theme. The question is what price is Steltz willing to pay to challenge cultural taboos? The answer is she's willing to be arrested and to be restrained. However, we also discover a limit. She does comply when the pain is increased

This scene is about the exercise of power. Steltz tries to retain power. It is taken away by the brutality of the system. The drama comes from Steltz's struggle with rules and the state's power to enforce them. When people say drama comes from conflict this is what they mean. Although it may appear the conflict is between Steltz and a brutal prison guard, it isn't. The conflict is Steltz's struggle with rules and the need for absolute obedience in prison.

When we write drama, we push our characters to their limits. We do this to reveal their vulnerability. That is where this scene takes us. By the end of the scene Steltz is compliant. She discovers the limits of her freedom. For me, the key moment is the one time in the movie someone calls her "Kim." She's not the artist, Steltz at that moment. She's Kim. She is transformed into just another prisoner.

process-driven screenwriting - the first draft

A lot of screenwriters refer to their first draft as a vomit draft. They are content for their first draft to be nothing more than an unstructured spewing of ideas. This is the ultimate expression of messy writing. In that draft, messy screenwriters try to do everything at the same time. They try to hone their ideas whilst creating a plot. They create characters whilst trying to visualise the world of their story. They pull characters out of thin air and then give them dialogue. All this, whilst trying to write cinematic-drama.

The expectations for a vomit draft are very low. They know they will have to rewrite. This kind of screenwriter believes it's impossible to write a good vomit draft. Many screenwriters believe it is impossible to write a decent first draft. They're wrong.

The whole point of process-driven screenwriting is to make first drafts readable. The first draft doesn't need to be an incoherent mess. It is possible for a screenwriter to have their script producer-ready in two drafts. We do this by using the process.

The scenes written above weren't pulled from an existing script. I have written them as I wrote the book. None of them took more than fifteen minutes to write. They are all first draft scenes. However, they are not vomit scenes. That's because I wrote each of them knowing the theme, who my characters are, the plot and the story. Knowing all those things, I could concentrate on the actual writing. I was able to think about visual storytelling and metaphor. I was able to explore the theme and drama. These are things you can't do when you write a vomit draft.

Process-driven screenwriting is simple. We make the job of screenwriting easier by breaking the task down into manageable steps. Proper preparation allows us to write a better script. Our first draft is going to be readable. We will still need to rewrite. We will always learn new things when we write a first draft. We will want to have at least one more go at getting the best story. We'll want to look for opportunities to get more drama from a scene. We'll want to rewrite. The only question we need to ask is how many rewrites do we want to commit to?

developing our own process

At the start of this book I stated

Dogma is the enemy of creativity

It is. The process isn't a set of rules. The process is the way we as unique and individual writers prepare to write our scripts. That process can be whatever works best for us. What I know is that my process, the one I have shared in this book works for me. I have absolute confidence in it. So do the producers I work with. Every producer I have ever shown the spreadsheet method for planning a movie demanded a copy. It's a really sensible way for writers and producers to talk about script development. It's also a good way to create show bibles.

Each writer is unique. Not everyone loves spreadsheets. I know! Go figure! That's why it is every writer's responsibility to understand and develop their own process. A real process-driven screenwriter is someone who understands how their creativity works. They know what they need to do to write. They create a workflow which plays to their strengths. They find ways to compensate for their weaknesses.

I want to finish this book with a question and a suggestion.

How many drafts does it take you to get from a raw idea to a producer-ready script?

If your answer is more than two or three there may be something wrong with your process. I hope this book has given you enough clues to find a better process. The process that will allow you to be the best writer you can be.

ABOUT THE AUTHOR

Clive Frayne is a screenwriter, script-editor, lecturer and author.

Alongside his work as a screenwriter and script-editor, Clive teaches process-driven screenwriting. A technique he developed during fifteen years of writing for independent film producers.

Clive started his professional writing career twenty-eight years ago. His first paid writing job was working in broadcast radio. He worked in one of the best writing teams in the industry. That experience taught him how to write for actors, and how to direct. His writing won industry awards, both in the UK and America. After proving he could be a successful writer, Clive moved into running writing teams. For years, he hired, managed and mentored award-winning writing teams.

Fifteen years ago, Clive decided to take on new writing challenges. He'd always dreamed of writing movie scripts. So, he wrote a script which was optioned by the first producer who read it. Since then he has written and directed several award-winning short films and features.

Clive currently writes scripts for independent producers, fixes script for clients and teaches screenwriting in colleges and universities in the UK and America. His specialist subjects are process-driven screenwriting and independent cinema.

Printed in Great Britain
by Amazon